The conduct of the Duke of Marlborough during the present war. With original papers.

Francis Hare

The conduct of the Duke of Marlborough during the present war. With original papers.
Hare, Francis
ESTCID: T031151
Reproduction from British Library
Anonymous. By Francis Hare.
London : printed in the year, 1712.
[2],329,[1]p. ; 8°

Eighteenth Century
Collections Online
Print Editions

Gale ECCO Print Editions

Relive history with *Eighteenth Century Collections Online*, now available in print for the independent historian and collector. This series includes the most significant English-language and foreign-language works printed in Great Britain during the eighteenth century, and is organized in seven different subject areas including literature and language; medicine, science, and technology; and religion and philosophy. The collection also includes thousands of important works from the Americas.

The eighteenth century has been called "The Age of Enlightenment." It was a period of rapid advance in print culture and publishing, in world exploration, and in the rapid growth of science and technology – all of which had a profound impact on the political and cultural landscape. At the end of the century the American Revolution, French Revolution and Industrial Revolution, perhaps three of the most significant events in modern history, set in motion developments that eventually dominated world political, economic, and social life.

In a groundbreaking effort, Gale initiated a revolution of its own: digitization of epic proportions to preserve these invaluable works in the largest online archive of its kind. Contributions from major world libraries constitute over 175,000 original printed works. Scanned images of the actual pages, rather than transcriptions, recreate the works ***as they first appeared.***

Now for the first time, these high-quality digital scans of original works are available via print-on-demand, making them readily accessible to libraries, students, independent scholars, and readers of all ages.

For our initial release we have created seven robust collections to form one the world's most comprehensive catalogs of 18th century works.

Initial Gale ECCO Print Editions collections include:

> ### *History and Geography*
> Rich in titles on English life and social history, this collection spans the world as it was known to eighteenth-century historians and explorers. Titles include a wealth of travel accounts and diaries, histories of nations from throughout the world, and maps and charts of a world that was still being discovered. Students of the War of American Independence will find fascinating accounts from the British side of conflict.

Social Science
Delve into what it was like to live during the eighteenth century by reading the first-hand accounts of everyday people, including city dwellers and farmers, businessmen and bankers, artisans and merchants, artists and their patrons, politicians and their constituents. Original texts make the American, French, and Industrial revolutions vividly contemporary.

Medicine, Science and Technology
Medical theory and practice of the 1700s developed rapidly, as is evidenced by the extensive collection, which includes descriptions of diseases, their conditions, and treatments. Books on science and technology, agriculture, military technology, natural philosophy, even cookbooks, are all contained here.

Literature and Language
Western literary study flows out of eighteenth-century works by Alexander Pope, Daniel Defoe, Henry Fielding, Frances Burney, Denis Diderot, Johann Gottfried Herder, Johann Wolfgang von Goethe, and others. Experience the birth of the modern novel, or compare the development of language using dictionaries and grammar discourses.

Religion and Philosophy
The Age of Enlightenment profoundly enriched religious and philosophical understanding and continues to influence present-day thinking. Works collected here include masterpieces by David Hume, Immanuel Kant, and Jean-Jacques Rousseau, as well as religious sermons and moral debates on the issues of the day, such as the slave trade. The Age of Reason saw conflict between Protestantism and Catholicism transformed into one between faith and logic -- a debate that continues in the twenty-first century.

Law and Reference
This collection reveals the history of English common law and Empire law in a vastly changing world of British expansion. Dominating the legal field is the *Commentaries of the Law of England* by Sir William Blackstone, which first appeared in 1765. Reference works such as almanacs and catalogues continue to educate us by revealing the day-to-day workings of society.

Fine Arts
The eighteenth-century fascination with Greek and Roman antiquity followed the systematic excavation of the ruins at Pompeii and Herculaneum in southern Italy; and after 1750 a neoclassical style dominated all artistic fields. The titles here trace developments in mostly English-language works on painting, sculpture, architecture, music, theater, and other disciplines. Instructional works on musical instruments, catalogs of art objects, comic operas, and more are also included.

The BiblioLife Network

This project was made possible in part by the BiblioLife Network (BLN), a project aimed at addressing some of the huge challenges facing book preservationists around the world. The BLN includes libraries, library networks, archives, subject matter experts, online communities and library service providers. We believe every book ever published should be available as a high-quality print reproduction; printed on-demand anywhere in the world. This insures the ongoing accessibility of the content and helps generate sustainable revenue for the libraries and organizations that work to preserve these important materials.

The following book is in the "public domain" and represents an authentic reproduction of the text as printed by the original publisher. While we have attempted to accurately maintain the integrity of the original work, there are sometimes problems with the original work or the micro-film from which the books were digitized. This can result in minor errors in reproduction. Possible imperfections include missing and blurred pages, poor pictures, markings and other reproduction issues beyond our control. Because this work is culturally important, we have made it available as part of our commitment to protecting, preserving, and promoting the world's literature.

GUIDE TO FOLD-OUTS MAPS and OVERSIZED IMAGES

The book you are reading was digitized from microfilm captured over the past thirty to forty years. Years after the creation of the original microfilm, the book was converted to digital files and made available in an online database.

In an online database, page images do not need to conform to the size restrictions found in a printed book. When converting these images back into a printed bound book, the page sizes are standardized in ways that maintain the detail of the original. For large images, such as fold-out maps, the original page image is split into two or more pages

Guidelines used to determine how to split the page image follows:

- Some images are split vertically; large images require vertical and horizontal splits.
- For horizontal splits, the content is split left to right.
- For vertical splits, the content is split from top to bottom.
- For both vertical and horizontal splits, the image is processed from top left to bottom right.

THE CONDUCT
Of the DUKE of MARLBOROUGH
During the Present WAR.
WITH ORIGINAL PAPERS.

By Dr. Hare.

---

*——Quid non efficient manus,
Quas & benigno numine Jupiter
Defendit, & curæ sagaces
Expediunt per acuta belli.*

Hor.

LONDON:
Printed in the Year M.DCC.XII.

AN ACCOUNT OF THE Duke of *Marlborough*'s Conduct IN THE PRESENT WAR.

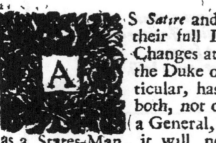S *Satire* and *Panegyrick* have had their full Loose since the late Changes at Court, and his Grace, the Duke of *Marlborough*, in particular, has been the Subject of both, not only in his Actions, as a General, but his Consultations, as a States-Man, it will not be amiss, at this Juncture, to take an *Impartial View* of what he has done, that it may more readily appear wherein he has been deficient. Such an honest Enquiry as this, cannot but be satisfactory to all Parties since his Enemies thereby will have it in their power

to

to point out what wrong Measures he has at any Time pursued, (if any such shall appear) and his Friends will be instructed how to go on with their just Praises of him, if he has taken no Steps but what have been right.

To do this, I am to have nothing but Matter of Fact in my View, and make use of a Fidelity, which is neither to give way to Fear of offending, nor be seduc'd by Hopes of being rewarded, that those who reproach him with *Attempts to be a General for Life, and with Designs of prolonging the War*, may see what Grounds they have for such Conjectures, and those who are incessant in his Commendations, and scarce allow him to be *Fallible*, may have wherewith to add Weight to their Opinions. Not that I am any ways inclin'd to encourage such Tempers as malign at true Merit, or declare my self in favour of those who are for applauding what is Fictitious, but would so carry my self between Two Extremes, that how partial so ever the *Reader* of these MEMOIRS may be, the *Writer* may stand acquitted of all manner of Tendency to any thing like it.

Pens that are taken into the Pay of this or that Party, are generally employ'd in detracting from what is Just and Honourable, and giving false Glosses to what is Blame-worthy, and of Evil-report. The Business which I have taken in Hand, is abhorrent of such Practices; and my *Reader* is to expect a *Narrative* from me, not a *Declamation*. In order to this, I shall inform him, That King *William*, some Time before his Death, had nominated the Earl of *Marlborough* General of the *English* Forces, and Plenipotentiary to the *States* of *Holland*, and was no sooner deceas'd, but Her Majesty confirm'd that Grant, making it One of the First Acts of Her Administration to dispatch him to *Holland*, with the last of these Characters; where, at his Audience, after having given in his

Royal

Royal Mistress's Letter, and his Credentials, he made the following SPEECH to the States General.

High and Mighty LORDS,   [1702.]

"IT having pleas'd God, in his Divine Providence, to take to himself his Majesty, King *William*, of Glorious Memory, to the great Loss of his Kingdoms, the States of your High and Mighty LORDSHIPS, and of all *Europe*; The QUEEN, my Mistress, as it has pleased the same Providence, doth succeed on the Throne of Her Ancestors, as your High and Mighty LORDSHIPS have been informed by Her Majesty's Letter, hath commanded me, at the same time, to express to your LORDSHIPS, Her Majesty's great Affliction upon this Subject, to make known to you the Interest Her Majesty takes in that which this great Misfortune occasions to your LORDSHIPS in particular.

"The First of Her Majesty's Cares was to let your High and Mighty LORDSHIPS understand Her sincere Desire and Inclination, to entertain with you the same Union, Friendship, and strict Correspondence, as hath subsisted during the Course of the preceding Reign, as being persuaded, that nothing in the World can be more Useful and Beneficial for the Good of both Nations, whose Interests are the same.

"Her Majesty has therefore commanded me to acquaint your High and Mighty LORDSHIPS, That She is firmly resolved to contribute all that lies in Her Power, towards the Advancing and Increasing the said Union, Friendship, and Correspondence, and to make that a constant Maxim of Her Government.

"He

(4)

"Her Majesty has further order'd me to assure your High and Mighty LORDSHIPS; That She will not only exactly and faithfully observe and execute the Treaties and Alliances made between the Kings, Her Predecessors, and your High and Mighty LORDSHIPS, but that She is likewise ready to Renew and Confirm them. As also to concur with you in all the Measures which have been taken by the late King of Glorious Memory, in pursuance of the said Alliances.

"Her Majesty is likewise disposed to enter into such other strict Alliances and Engagements, which shall most conduce to the Interests of both Nations, the Preservation of the Liberty of *Europe*, and reducing within just Bounds the exorbitant Power of *France*.

"In the mean Time, Her Majesty is ready, from this Moment, and without any Delay, to concur with your High and Mighty LORDSHIPS, and the other Allies, to this End, with all Her Forces, as well by Sea as Land.

"And Her Majesty, to shew Her Zeal the more, has been pleased to authorize me to concert with your High and Mighty LORDSHIPS, the necessary Operations

"These Motives obliged Her Majesty to order me to depart, with all diligence, in order to come hither, and give your High and Mighty LORDSHIPS all possible Assurances thereof without stopping at the ordinary Formalities.

"And I look upon it as an Extraordinary Happiness, that Her Majesty has done me the Honour to employ me in this Commission, since it gives me the Opportunity of expressing to your High and Mighty LORDSHIPS, the Zeal I have for your Service.

To this Speech Monsieur *Dyckvelt*, President of the Assembly, made Answer in the Name of the States, "That they could not but be affected to "the last Degree, for the Death of the late King; "that they heartily congratulated Her Majesty's "Succession to the Throne, and return'd their "most unfeigned Thanks for the Assurances of "Her Friendship; that they were readily resolved "to concur with Her Majesty, in a vigorous Prose- "cution of the Common Interest; and that, for his "Part, his Person was highly acceptable to them, "not only on account of his great Merits, and the "Choice the QUEEN had made of him upon "this Occasion, but that of King *William*, who "had invested him with that Character, before "his Decease. But as it was the Interest of *France* to disappoint his Endeavours in his Negotiations, so Monsieur *de Barre*, the *French* Resident, was not wanting, both in Promises and Threats, to amuse the *Dutch*, and draw them off from making good their Resolutions; however his Lordship made use of such Dexterity and Address, as to bring them entirely into his Measures; and he had the Happiness and Satisfaction, to return to his Royal Mistress, with the Articles of such an Alliance between Her, the States-General, and other Potentates, as enabled Her Majesty to make an open Declaration of War against *France*, on the 4th of *May* following.

Hereupon, the *French*, as usual, were the First in the Field, and tho' the Allies form'd the Siege of *Keyserswaert*, (according to the Earl's Proposal, before he left the *Hague*) and took it, had driven the *Dutch* Army, under the command of the Earl of *Athlone*, under the Cannon of *Nimeguen*, which put the States General into a mighty Consternation: When, upon the Arrival of the Earl of *Marlborough*, to make the Campagne, they sent Orders to all their General and other Officers, to obey his Commands, for which every body applauded their Prudence and Policy; for as no Person was better qualified for that supreme Dignity, than his Excellency, so nothing could endear the *Dutch* more to Her Majesty, than this additional Honour which they bestow'd on the General of Her Forces.

His Excellency having had several Conferences with the Deputies of the States, left the *Hague* on the 30th of *June*, (N. S.) and, on the 2d of *July*, arrived at *Nimeguen*, where the Earl of *Athlone*, and Lieutenant-General *Dopff* came to him the next Day to receive his Orders. At the same Time, 19 Battalions of the Troops employ'd in the Siege of *Keyserswaert*; the Troops of *Hesse* and *Lunenburgh*; the *English* Forces from *Breda*, under Major-General *Lumley*, and other Troops by his Excellency's Direction, hasten'd from all Parts, to form a Camp at *Duckemburgh*, where the Earl of *Marlborough* being come, on the 8th he called a Council of War, consisting of all the General-Officers, to concert the further Operations of the Campagne. On the 16th his Excellency marched the Army over the *Maese*, and pitch'd his Camp at *Over-Assely*, near *Grave*, within 2 Leagues and a half of the Enemy, who had entrench'd themselves between *Goch* and *Gennep*. On the 26th the Confederate Army re-pass'd the *Maese*, below *Grave*, and on the 28th encamped at *Geldorp*, upon which Motion the *French* went over the same River, about *Vanloe*. Two Days after, the Allies removed from *Geldorp* to *Gravenbroech*, where finding a *French* Garrison in the Castle, seated in a Morass, and surrounded with a double Ditch, and good Pallisadoes, they briskly attack'd it, and after some Resistance, forc'd it to surrender at Discretion. From hence they advanc'd on the 2d of *August*, (N. S.) to *Petit-Brugel*, following the Enemy

Enemy so close, that they were obliged to abandon the *Spanish-Guelderland*. Thus the *Hollanders* had the Pleasure to see the *French* fly in their Turn. And thus were the *United-Provinces* preserved by the Prudence and Vigilance of an *English* Leader; whilst the Duke of *Burgundy*, who was generally reported to have come to the Army to be taught how to Fight, learn'd nothing from Mareschal *Boufflers*, but how to avoid an Engagement.

His Excellency not being able to bring the *French* to a Battle upon equal Terms, and the Deputies of the States-General, who followed the Army, having represented to him, That it was much more for the Advantage of *Holland*, to dispossess the Enemy of the Places they held in the *Spanish-Guelderland*, whereby the free Navigation of the *Maeze* was interrupted, and the important Town of *Maestricht*, in a manner, block'd up; all Things were disposed for the Siege of *Venloe*. In the mean Time General *Schultz* was order'd to reduce the Town and Castle of *Wertz*, which capitulated after a short Resistance. And the Confederate Army march'd from *Everbeck* to *Helsteen*, in order to force the *French* to quit their Camp at *Bergtick*, or cut off their Convoys. When the former came to their Ground, the Enemy appear'd in order of Battle, behind several Morasses and Defiles; whereupon the Confederates advanced against them, but their Eagerness to fight was disappointed, by the badness of the Situation, which would not suffer them to come at the *French*, without apparent Danger, from a great Disadvantage, so that the Earl of *Marlborough* decamped from thence, and march'd to *Asch*. The same Day, (the 29th of *August*) the Town of *Venloe* was invested, when the Duke of *Burgundy* return'd to *Paris*, to avoid being witness of the taking of that Place.

On

On the 7th of *September*, the Trenches were opened on both Sides the *Maeze*, and the Town surrender'd on the 25th of the same Month, after Fort St. *Michael* had been Storm'd and Taken by the *English*, under the command of the Lord *Cutts*, who, with several other Officers of the same Nation, show'd an incredible Bravery, on that hazardous Occasion.

His Excellency proceeded hence with the Army under his command, to sit down before *Ruremond*, the Second City of *Guelders*, standing upon the *Maeze*, at the Confluence of that River and the *Roer*, which, after a very vigorous Siege, beat a Parley on the 6th of *October* following, was given into his Hands upon Articles. At the same Time *Stevenswaert*, a fortified Place, seated on the *Maeze*, about 5 Miles from *Ruremond*, to the South, also capitulated, upon which Successes of the Confederates, Mareschal *Boufflers* thought it high Time to provide for the Security of *Liege*, which he justly apprehended to be in no small danger. Therefore, being accompanied by the Duke of *Maine*, and taking with him some Engineers, he went to view the Fortifications of the Citadel, and, after that, the most considerable Posts between that City and *Maestricht*, as if he had intended to encamp there, but finding it impracticable, by the approach of the Confederates, that were marching towards *Liege*, he retreated to *Tongeren*, with great Precipitation, and went towards *Brabant*, to defend such Places as, at that Time, were not intended to be attack'd.

When the Confederate Army came before *Liege*, they found the Suburb of St *Walburgh* set on Fire by the *French* Garrison, who, after that, retired, one Part into the Citadel, and the other into the *Chartreuse*; after which, the City was deliver'd up to the Besiegers, by a Treaty betwixt his Excellency, the Deputies of the States General, and Commissioners

oners from the Chapter and Magistracy, on the 14th of *October*. Six Days after the Trenches were open'd against the great Citadel, which was likewise taken by Storm, through the Invincible Courage of the *English*, on the 23d of the same Month, notwithstanding Monsieur *Violaine*, the Governor, five Days before, upon a Summons to surrender, sent the Earl of *Marlborough* Word, that *it would be Time enough to think of that six Weeks hence*. The Assailants having behav'd themselves to admiration, and put most of the Garrison to the Sword; got a considerable Booty, besides Honour, for in the Cash of Treasure alone, there were 300000 *Florins* in Gold and Silver, and Notes for 120000 *Florins*, upon substantial Merchants at *Liege*, which were all accepted and turn'd into ready Money.

So soon as the Confederates were thus become Masters of the City and Citadel of *Liege*, his Excellency thought the Reduction of them important enough to acquaint the States-General with it, in the following Letter.

High and Mighty LORDS,

" I Write this to congratulate your High and
" Mightinesses, upon the happy Successes of
" the Arms of the Allies, who, notwithstanding
" the great number of the Soldiers in Garrison,
" have taken the Citadel this Evening, by As-
" sault, with the greatest Gallantry imaginable,
" and made the Governour, and those who re-
" mained Prisoners at Discretion. Monsieur *de*
" *Coehorn* is going, this Moment, to give Orders
" to attack the *Chartreuse*, and make use of this
" good Weather, while it lasts. I cannot yet
" give your High Mightinesses the Particulars of
" this glorious Action, being not willing to stay
" the *Courier*, who is going to you with this
" News

"News, longer than only to assure you, that I
"am, with the greatest Respect,

High and Mighty LORDS,

Your most Humble, and most Obedient Servant,

At the Camp before
Liege, Oct. 23 1702.

MARLBOROUGH.

Answer of the States-General.

My LORD,

"WE believe it would be superfluous to tell
"your Excellency, that the good News
"which you have been pleas'd to send us in
"your Letter of the 23d Instant, was agreeable
"to us, since an Action, so well Laid so vigo-
"rously Executed, and attended with that good
"and glorious Success, cannot but be so in the
"highest Degree. We likewise, on our Part, con-
"gratulate with you, since this great Action adds
"no less to the Glory of your Excellency, and
"to the Reputation of the Arms of the Allies,
"under your prudent Conduct than it is advan-
"tagious to the common Cause, and to our State
"in particular. We wish your Excellency the
"same good Success before the *Chartreuse*, and in
"all your Enterprizes; and we desire you will
"believe that we are truly,

Your EXCELLENCY's,

Most Affectionate to serve You,

At the Hag e,
Oct. 25 1702.

The STATES GENERAL *of the*
United-Provinces *of the* Low-Countries.

The

The foregoing Victory, at the Taking of the Citadel, was soon after compleated by the surrender of the *Chartreuse*, which the Confederates would have attack'd 2 Days sooner, had not the Stormy Weather, on the 26th and 27th disorder'd their Bridge of Boats: For on the 29th, the Day that his Excellency receiv'd their High Mightinesses Congratulatory Letter, about 10 in the Morning the Mortars began to play, which having set most part of the Buildings in flames, and about 2 in the Afternoon the Besiegers Cannon beginning to batter the Place, the Garrison presently desired to capitulate, whereupon it was agreed that the Garrison should march out on the 31st in the Evening, with their Arms, Colours flying, Drums beating, and be conducted by *Tongeres*, *Vogelsanck*, and *Herental* to *Antwerp*.

Thus ended the Campagne in 1702, when the Confederate Army being separated, on the 3d of *November*, the Earl of *Marlborough* went the same Day from *Liege* to *Maestricht*, where he embark'd that Evening, on the *Maeze*, for *Holland*, in company with Monsieur *Geldermalsen*, one of the Deputies of the States, and Monsieur *d'Obdam*, General of Horse, taking on board with them 25 Soldiers, under the Command of a Lieutenant, to serve as a Convoy. The next Morning their Excellencies came to *Ruremond*, where they join'd Monsieur *Coehorne*, and having din'd with the Prince of *Holstein-Beck*, Commander of that Garrison, continued their Voyage together, having order'd a Party of 50 Horse, (besides 60 Men that were in Monsieur *Coehorn*'s Boat) for their further Security, against any of the Enemies Parties. About 7 that Evening their Excellencies came to *Venloe*, where the Party of Horse being reliev'd by a like number of that Garrison: They pursued their Voyage, but the Boats being separated in the Night, and the Horse at some distance from the River side, a

Party

Party of 15 of the Garrison of *Guelder*, who lay skulking on the Banks, near 3 Leagues on this side *Venloe*, having by surprize seiz'd the Rope with which the Boat was drawn, and hawl'd it on shore, they immediately made a discharge of their small Arms into it; and then threw in several Grenadoes, with which some of their Excellencies Retinue being wounded, the Party enter'd and having examin'd the several Passports, whereof the Earl of *Marlborough* had one formerly belonging to his Brother, General *Churchill*, who was out of Date, but shewn with a particular presence of Mind, they not knowing his Lordship, dismiss'd him with the other Generals, having first rifled the Trunks and Baggage, taking what Plate, &c. which they found there, and made their Excellencies Guard Prisoners.

I mention this, because his Excellency was afterwards requir'd to surrender himself Prisoner in *France*, by that Court, on account of the Invallidity of his Passport, tho' he did not think fit to comply with it, and the *Party Man* was hang'd for his Negligence, in not making a timely Discovery.

The Governor of *Venloe* having soon notice of the Surprizal of the Boat, concluded their Excellencies to be taken, and marched out with his whole Garrison, by break of Day, to invest *Guelder*, after he had sent an Express to the States, which reaching them on the 6th at Night, they assembled upon it the next Morning, and all the People at the *Hague* were in the greatest Consternation imaginable, till the Arrival of his Excellency that Evening. Hereupon the Streets were so crouded, that it was with much difficulty that his Excellency pass'd to his House, and all possible Demonstrations were shewn, by all Ranks of People, for his Excellency's Escape, and safe Arrival.

Thus,

Thus, having receiv'd the Compliments of all the Foreign Ministers, and Persons of Quality, upon his glorious Campagne this Summer, and concerted Measures for that which was to ensue, his Excellency embark'd for *England*, and came to *London* on the 28th of *November*, and receiv'd the Thanks of the House of Commons then sitting, by Sir *Edward Seymour*, Comptroller of the Queen's Houshold, who reported that his Lordship expressed himself thus.

"Nothing can add to the Satisfaction I take
" in the Queen's most Gracious Accep-
" tance of my hearty and sincere Endeavours for
" the Public Service, but the obliging and favou-
" rable Sense, which the House of Commons is
" pleased to express of them: of which Honour
" no Man can be more truly sensible than my self.
" Our Success is chiefly to be imputed to God's
" Blessing upon Her Majesty's happy Conduct,
" and the great Bravery of Her own Troops, and
" those of Her Allies.

His Lordship having mention'd the Queen's Gracious Acceptance of his hearty and sincere Endeavours, it is altogether to the purpose, to close the Account of the Proceedings that relate to him, in the Year 1702, with Her Majesty's Declaration to a Committee of Council, on the 2d of *December*, and Her Majesty's Message, on the 10th of the same Month, to the House of Commons, in his Favour. — The First contain'd, in substance,
" That She was so satisfied of the Eminent Ser-
" vices of my Lord *Marlborough* to the Public,
" both in the Command of the Army, and the
" entire Confidence he had settled between Her
" and the States General, that She intended to
" make him a Duke. The last was in these Words.

ANNE

ANNE R.

"THE Earl of *Marlborough*'s Services to Her
"Majesty, and the Public, have been so
"eminent, both in his Command of the Army,
"and in his having established an entire Confi-
"dence between Her Majesty, and the States
"General, that She has thought fit to grant the
"Title of a Duke of this Kingdom to him, and
"the Heirs Male of his Body, and also a Pension
"of 5000 Pounds *per Annum*, upon the Revenue
"of the Post-Office, for the support of this Ho-
"nour, during Her Majesty's Natural Life. If
"it had been in Her Majesty's Power, She would
"have granted the same Term in the Pension, as
"in the Honour; and She hopes you will think
"it so reasonable, in this Case, as to find some
"proper Methods of doing it.

It is to be confess'd, that this Message had not
its desired Effect, for the Commons excus'd themselves from complying with it, on Account of their
Unwillingness to make a Precedent for Alienations
of the Crown Revenues, but they testified, in their
Address upon that Subject their entire Satisfaction in his Grace's Conduct, by saying, " He had
" retriev'd the Ancient Honour and Glory of the
" *English* Nation, and that they were infinitely
" pleas'd to observe, by Her Majesty's Gracious
" Acceptance of the Duke of *Marlborough*'s Servi-
" ces, that the only way to obtain Her Majesty's
" Favour, was to deserve well from the Public.

His Grace being return'd to the *Hague*, where he
concerted the Operations of the following Campagne with the States General, and resolv'd to
open it with the Siege of *Bon*, drew the Army together for that purpose, and caus'd that Place to
be

be invested on the 24th of *April*, 1703, which after some Consultation amongst the Generals, was order'd to have Three Attacks form'd against it. The First was against the Fort, on the other side of the *Rhine*, and the other Two against the City, and the Out-works that secur'd it, each of which had Twelve Regiments to carry them on, and open'd their Trenches, on the 3d of *May*, with very inconsiderable Loss, through the great Care of the Generals, and Engineers. On the 8th of the same Month they began to fire upon the Town, from their Batteries, with such Success, that on the Day following a practicable Breach was made in the Fort, whereupon his Grace order'd Preparations for Storming it; but the *French* not thinking themselves safe there, set fire to the Cazarns, and retreated into the Ravelins, in order to get into the Town in Boats, which Design was prevented by the Besiegers Diligence and Valour, so that the Commander, and 30 of his Men were made Prisoners, the rest being either killed or drowned. His Grace having sent a Detachment to take possession of the Fort issued out his Commands for a great Battery to be raised upon it, which began to play on the 12th to the number of 70 Pieces of heavy Cannon, and 18 Mortars, and made a Breaches, upon which all Things being in a readiness to assault the Counterscarp, and Cover'd-Way; the Besiegers seconded by the continued Fire, both from the Cannon and Mortars of several Attacks, forced their Way forwards, drove the Enemy from their Works, and lodg'd themselves upon them. In which brisk Action, General *Tettau* was wounded, with about 10 Officers, and a 150 Soldiers killed, together with the Engineer that had the Direction of the Batteries. So much Bravery in the Besiegers, and such an amazing Tempest of Artificial Thunder and Lightning, astonished the Besieged to that degree, that fearing a second Assault, fault, the next Day they beat a Parley, and on the 14th of *May*, surrender'd the Place upon honourable Terms, which were signed by the Duke of *Marlborough*, and Monsieur *Allegre*, the *French* Governour. So that this strong Town was taken in 11 Days after opening the Trenches.

During the foregoing Siege, the Marshals, *Villeroy* and *Boufflers*, thinking to surprize the Forces that lay dispersed about *Maestricht*, under the command of Monsieur *Overkirk*, and to have bombarded the Town it self, after which, they designed to have fallen upon *Liege*, advanced into the Neighbourhood of *Tongeren*, which they made themselves Masters of, and 2 Battalions of Foot, one *English* and one *Dutch*, who defended themselves with extraordinary Bravery for 28 Hours, and gave the Confederate Army an Opportunity of posting themselves advantagiously. Which the *French* perceiving, quitted their Attempt against *Maestricht*, and continued encamped in the Neighbourhood of *Tongeren*, wherefore, after *Bon* was taken, the Duke of *Marlborough* joined the Troops near *Maestricht*, and set forward toward *Liege*, as well to secure that Place, as to force the Enemy to decamp from thence. To which purpose his Grace having pass'd the River *Jecker*, advanc'd to *Hautm.*, where the *French* intended to have forraged that Morning, but upon Notice of the Confederates approach, remov'd to some further distance, where they continued under their Arms that Night, though, upon his Grace's advancing to *Nieudorp*, they march'd, with great Precipitation to *Bockworn*, not daring to stand the hazard of a Battle. They also quitted *Tongeren*, after having dismantled it, and blown up the Tower. The Duke followed them, and came up within half a League of their Camp, but the *Jecker* parted the Two Armies, and the Enemy had secured all the Bridges and Passes of the River. Nevertheless they thought themselves not safe in

to

so doing, but retreated to *Hannuye*, after they had drawn up in order of Battle, as if they intended to have fought. But their Courage fail'd them, and they return'd into their Lines.

His Grace finding it impossible to bring the *French* to the Decision of a Battle, took a Resolution to force them in their Entrenchments, which General *Coehorn*, and Baron *Spaar* perform'd with Success in the County of *Waes*, by making themselves Masters of St. *Anthony's-Hoek*, and the *Pearl-Fort*, and defeating 8 Battalions of regular Forces, and 6000 Militia.

On the other Hand, the *French* were not wanting to catch at all Opportunities that offer'd, and Marshal *Boufflers*, and the Prince *Serclaes de Tilly* came out of their Lines, with a great Detachment, and attack'd the Forces that were sent on the same Errand as the former, under Monsieur *Opdam*, who being defeated, was forc'd to fly to *Breda*, with great precipitation. The Battle was fought at *Eckeren*, with great Bravery, on the side of the Confederates, who, forced to give way to Numbers, left 3000 dead upon the Field of Action, and the loss of it was imputed by General *Slangenbergh*, who signaliz'd himself wonderfully in it, to want of Conduct in the Duke of *Marlborough*, who having Notice of the Enemies March, did not send them Re-inforcements: But whosoever was in the Fault, the States General sought to cover their Disgrace with Rewards and Thanks to the Officers and Soldiers that surviv'd; and by reason of a Misunderstanding that arose from hence, between His Grace, and the aforesaid General, dismiss'd the latter some Time after from his Attendance in the Camp.

All this while the Duke of *Marlborough* held daily Consultations, and used all possible Stratagems to bring the *French* to an Engagement. But failing in his Design, His Grace, attended with several General-

General Officers, and a Guard of Four thousand Horse and Dragoons, went to view the Enemies Lines: Lieutenant *Benson*, of the *English* Royal-Regiment of Dragoons, with about Thirty *English*, being detach'd, fell in with One of the Enemies Out Guards, of Forty Horse, who, after one Discharge, retired, and were chased, by the *English*, to the very Barrier of their Entrenchments, which gave the Confederate-Generals an Opportunity to view them within Musket-shot, and from that, prompted His Grace to lay Schemes for Forcing them; tho' the Execution of that Project was industriously put off from Time to Time, by the Deputies of the States-General.

Hereupon His Grace, that could not lie still without Action, sent a Detachment, under the command of Count *Noyelles*, to besiege *Huy*, upon whose approach the Governour broke down the Bridge between the Two Towns, and retired, with his Garrison, into the Castle, and the Fort St. *Joseph*, Fort *Picard*, and Fort *Rouge*, all which the Besiegers were Masters of after the Trenches had been open'd 8 Days, with the Soldiers that defended them, who, after having desired an Honourable Capitulation were disarmed, and made Prisoners of War, to the number of Nine hundred Men, commanded by Two Brigadier Generals.

Three Days before a Grand-Council of War was held at the Confederate-Camp, at *Val Nostra-Dame*, wherein were present His Grace, the Deputies of the States-General, Monsieur *d'Auverquerque*, Monsieur *Slangenburgh*, the Lieutenant-Generals, and several Major-Generals. The Question in debate was, *What Undertaking should be gone upon, after* Huy *was taken?* And the Siege of *Limburgh* being propos'd by the *Dutch* Deputies, the Generals, whose Names are subscribed, gave the following Opinion, rather for attacking the Enemies Lines, between the *Mehaigne* and *Leuwe*, as an Enterprize

that

that would contribute much more to the Glory and Advantage of the Arms of the High Allies: Being also of Opinion, That *Limburgh* might be attack'd by a Detachment, when the Season was more advanced,

I. "THE Enemies having great Magazines at
" *Namure*, for the Subsistence of their Army, and
" we being, by our Superiority in Number, in a
" Condition to give them Umbrage on that Side,
" they will be obliged, after we are possess'd of
" *Huy*, to put a great Garrison into that Place,
" for the Security of their Magazines, our Supe-
" riority will then be so much the greater, and
" they will be less able to oppose our Efforts.

II. "WE having here a Level Ground before
" us, of above 2 Leagues and a half in extent,
" where the Enemies Lines are weakest, it seems
" to be the only Place where we should chuse to
" attack them; and seeing our whole Army may
" act, it is to be believ'd, if the Enemy should
" stand us, it would be impossible for them to de-
" fend such an Extent

III. "IN Case they should venture an Engage-
" ment with us, seeing 'tis what we have been
" seeking all this Campagne, we are of Opinion,
" we ought gladly to embrace the Occasion, be-
" cause we have a greater Superiority at this Time
" than ever.

IV. "IF we do not attack the Enemy in this
" Place, with the finest Troops that can be seen,
" and such a Superiority as we cannot expect to
" have next Year, it will be evident, not only
" to our Allies, (to their great Disparagement)
" but the Enemy may, with reason, boast, that
" these Lines, which they will make stronger
' every

" every Day, are an Invincible Barrier againſt the
" Troops of the Allies.

V. " IN Caſe we do not attack the Lines,
" there is no other Courſe to be taken, than ei-
" ther to retire to the other Side of the *Maeze*,
" or to march away to the Right, to be nearer to
" the *Mayory* of *Bolduc*, there being no Forrage
" left in theſe Parts The Firſt would be diſho-
" nourable to the Allies, for their getting the Ri-
" ver between them and the Enemy, would look
" as they durſt not ſtand them, and the Latter
" might be very dangerous to the States ; and, be-
" ſides, the Enemy, by means of their Magazines,
" would be in a Condition to undertake any
" Thing. Whereas, if we attempt their Lines,
" ſhould they pretend to defend them, we may,
" with the Aſſiſtance of the Almighty, hope to
" gain a compleat Victory, the Conſequence of
" which may be of more Importance than can be
" foreſeen ; and ſhould they think beſt to retire,
" there is Ground to hope, we might puſh forward
" very ſucceſsfully, and draw mighty Advantages
" from it.

VI. " WE conſider likewiſe, that the Enemy
" being ſuperior in *Italy*, and in the Empire, and
" being out-numbred no where but here, the Eyes
" of all the Allies are fix'd upon Us, and they
" will have Cauſe juſtly to blame our Conduct,
" if we do not all that is poſſible to relieve them,
" by obliging the Enemy to call back Succours,
" into theſe Parts, which is not to be done, but
" by puſhing boldly.

Signed,

MARLBOUROUGH.

Generals

Generals of the *English* { *Charles Churchill*, *Cutts*, *H. Lumley*.

Generals of the *Danes*. { *Charles Rudolph*, Duke of *Wirtembergh*, *J. Scholten*.

Generals of the *Lunenburghers*. { *C. Somerfelt*, *M. Bulow*, *Earnest Augustus*, Duke of *Brunswick*, *Count de Noyelles*.

Generals of the *Hessians*. { *Frederick*, Prince of *Hesse*, *Spiegel de Diesenbergh*, *A. Van Tettau*.

These Reasons were oppos'd by the Deputies of the States, and the *Dutch* Generals, who would not consent to hazard their Troops, in an Action, which, they said, was at best very dubious, and if attended with success, would yield no further Advantage, than to find the Enemy retired into their Fortified Towns; whereas, on the contrary, should the *French* get the Victory, the *United Provinces* would remain exposed to their Incursions. Thereupon the very useful Project, of attacking their Lines, was laid aside, and the Resolution taken to besiege *Limburgh*, which was accordingly invested, by Lieutenant-General *Bulow*, with 24 Squadrons of Horse and Dragoons, on the 10th of *September*. His Grace following them with the heavy Artillery, and a further Detachment of 15 Squadrons, and 24 Battalions, on the 21st of the same Month. By which Time the Besiegers had taken possession of the lower Town, without any Resistance, and the Batteries being finished on the 25th they play'd

Night

Night and Day from thence on the upper Town. By the 27th, the Breach was wide enough for an Assault, which the *French* seeing the Confederates prepared to give, beat a Parley: But all the Conditions they could obtain, were, "That the Garrison should remain Prisoners of War: That the Officers and Soldiers might keep what was their own; and that the Officers should be allowed 12 Waggons, to carry away their Baggage, provided they delivered up one of their Gates within half an Hour after this Agreement This being submitted to, the Besieged, consisting of One thousand four hundred Men, having laid down their Arms, march'd out, leaving the possession of the Place to the Allies. This Conquest put an End to the Campagne, which must be acknowledg'd to be very Glorious, since, besides the taking of Three Important Places, *Bon*, *Huy*, and *Limburgh*, the Duke of *Marlborough* did all that lay in the power of the most able Commander, to draw the Enemy to a decisive Battle. But, it seems, the *French* were contented to stand upon the Defensive in *Flanders*, where they were indeed inferior, while their superiority on the *Rhine*, and in the Empire, gave them signal Advantages.

What remain'd for His Excellency to do on this Side of the Water, was after his paying his Respects in the Name of his Royal Mistress, to the King of *Spain*, at *Dusseldorp*, who, at his taking leave of him, presented him with a Sword set with Diamonds, expressing himself with a lively Air, to this purpose, *My Lord, I need not be ashamed to say I am a poor Prince. I have only my Cloak and Sword; the latter will be a useful Present to your Excellency; I hope you will not think it worse for my wearing it to Day*, to set out for the *Hague*, whence having negotiated Affairs belonging to his Character, he went for *England*, but whether from the Disagreement between the Two Houses of Parliament, or the

the Opinion they had, that his Services this Campaign did come up to what he had done in that, which Preceeded it, neither of those *August* Bodies presented him with theirs, which was look'd upon by his Friends, as Derogatory to his Merit, while others that were more Impartial esteem'd, the Conquest he had then made, not Important enough to be Rewarded with such Marks of Distinction.

Some time after the Dukes Arrival, a Memorial was sent to Her Majesty by Count *Wratislaw*, the Emperors Envoy Extraordinary: "Represent-
" ing the pressing Necessities of the Empire, by
" the breaking in a considerable Number of *French*
" into *Bavaria*, and the Defection of the Prince
" of that Country to the Enemy, and requesting
" that Her Majesty out of the same Zeal, for pre-
" serving the Liberties of *Europe*; for which She
" was so much Fam'd among the Potentates in Al-
" liance with Her, would be pleased to order his
" Grace the Duke of *Marlborough* Her Captain Ge-
" neral, seriously to Consult with the States of
" *Holland*, of the speediest Method of Assisting
" the Empire; by Conducting at least, some Part
" of the Troops in Her Majesty's Pay, to preserve
" *Germany* from a Total Subversion.

But either the foregoing Memorial was but matter of Form, or the Emperor's Envoy was then unacquainted with the Project his Grace had already form'd to Deliver the Empire; and which 'tis said, he had Communicated to Three Persons in *England*, viz. the Queen, Prince, and Lord Treasurer, and not to above two Persons more in *Holland*, the Grand *Penshionary*, and Monsieur *Geldermansen*, and not to any of the Imperial Court, before he was ready to put it in Execution. In order to which, his Grace Embark'd at *Harwich*, towards the middle of *April* 1704, and two Days after, safely Arrived at *Marsland-Sluys*, and came the same Evening to the *Hague*. The 23d of *April N. S.*

N. S. He was attended by a Deputation of the States General, with whom he had a Preliminary Conference about the Measures he thought most proper for the ensuing Campaign; and sent Orders for the Troops that had been cantoon'd in the Neighbourhood of *Leige* and *Maistrich*, with part of the Garrisons of those Places, to Assemble on the rising Ground of *Leen*, and Encamp'd at the Village of *Harcourt*. On the 2d of *May* his Grace had another long Conference with the Deputies of the States General, wherein he declar'd to them the Schemes he had laid long before, and of which, he had only given some Hints to those whom he could most Confide in; declaring that he thought his March into *Germany* would most conduce to the Advantage of the Confederacy. The States spent a whole Day upon the Dukes Proposals, which yet, nevertheless many of their Assembly were very backward in giving their Assent to. The next Day his Excellency, had a Conference with the States General themselves, and the Council of State to whom he made a very lively Representation of the great Danger that threatned the whole Empire, and indeed all *Europe*, if a speedy check were not given to the Progress of the *French* and *Bavarians* in *Germany*; adding, that being now entire Masters of the *Maese*, and all *Spanish Guelderland* (by the Reduction of *Gelder* which Surrender'd to a Blockade during the Winter) a small Number of Forces were able to secure their Frontiers. These Reasons supported by the Reputation of him that deliver'd them, and back'd by the Imperial Ministers and those of other *German* Princes, made so great an Impression on that Wise Body of Men, that all Affairs relating to the Operation of the Campaigns, were in this one Conference happily adjusted. After which, the Duke took his Leave of their Highmightynesses, and Arriv'd at *Ruremond*, on the 8th of *May*, giving Orders for the *English* Troops, and

other

other Troops posted thereabouts, to join and March toward *Coblentz*, and a Bridge to be Built, over which, as it was Industriously reported, the Forces were to March to the *Moselle*. Two Days after his Grace went to *Maeßricht*, and reviewed the *Dutch* Army, part of which, with five Squadrons, and Eleven pieces of Cannon were order'd to March after the *English*, led by General *Goor* and Brigadier *Ferguson*.

The *French* in *Flanders* during these Preparations, imagin'd his Grace design'd no less than to open the Campaign with the Siege of *Traerbach*, and endeavour to penetrate into *France* along the *Moselle*, upon which Supposition, they Detached Eight Battalions, and Sixteen Squadrons towards that River, and gave out, that they would Besiege *Huy*, thinking by this Report to stop his Progress; but his Grace slighting this Amusement, as well knowing the Forces he had left in *Flanders* were sufficient to frustrate any Attempt he could make on that side, continued his March and Advanced towards *Germany*; making Visits to, and having Interviews with the chief Princes of it, as the Electors of *Mentz* and *Triers*, and other Potentates during the course of it.

The Dukes bending his March towards the *Danube*, was a great surprize to the *French*, who after the first Disappointment in their Conjectures, that his Grace would Act on the *Moselle*, had entertained a Jealousy, that he would Advance to the *Upper-Rhine*, and had a Design upon *Landau*, both from his Graces March to *Mayence*, and from the Governour of *Phillipsburgh*'s, making a Bridge over the *Rhine*. Upon this suspicion, Mareschal *Tallard* Repass'd the *Rhine* at *Altenheim*, in order, either to join the Mareschal *de Villeroy*, or to Oppose his Grace's Passage of that River. But the Mareschal was mistaken in his Measures, and his Grace joined Prince *Lewis* of *Baden* near *Launsheim*, on the 23d of *Jine*, who at his Arrival amongst other Expressions of Civility that pass'd between them, was pleased to say, *That his Grace was come to Save the Empire, and give him an Opportunity to vindicate his Honour, which he was sensible, was in some Measure at the last Stake.* Prince *Eugene* at the Review of the Forces under his Graces Command, likewise Complimented him with saying, My LORD, *I never saw better Horses, better Cloaths, finer Belts and Accoutrements: Yet all these may be had for Money, but there is a Spirit in the Looks of your Men, which I never saw in my Life.* To which his Grace made Reply, Sir, *If it be as you say, that Spirit is inspired to them by your Presence.*

On the 29th All the Forces of the several Nations which the Army was compos'd of, being joined at the Camp between *Hubressing* and *Gingen*, on the River *Brentz*. The Duke and the Prince of *Baden*, who were to have the Supreme Command alternately, held a Council of War, wherein it was resolved to draw near *Donawaert*: Whereupon, the Confederate Army Decamp'd, and March'd in sight of the Elector of *Bavaria*'s Army at *Dillingen*; who rightly judging their Intentions, sent a considerable Detachment of his best Troops to join Count *d'Arco*, who was Posted at *Schellembergh*, a rising Ground near that Place, where he had already cast up strong Intrenchments, and employ'd some Thousands of Pioneers for several Days. But notwithstanding that great Advantage, the Duke resolved to drive the Enemy from that Important Post. Accordingly the necessary Orders were given, and His Grace advanced the next Day at Three in the Morning with a Detachment of Six Thousand Foot, and Thirty Squadrons of *English* and *Dutch* Horse, besides Three Battalions of Imperial Grenadiers; the rest of the Army under Prince *Lewis*, following with all possible Diligence. But the Way being very bad and long,

the

the Detachment led by his Grace, could not come to the River *Werniz*, which runs by *Donawert* till about Noon, after which, it was Three of the Clock, before they could get over that River with the Artillery. The Duke having pass'd the same at the Head of the Cavalry, view'd the Entrenchments, and made the necessary Dispositions for the Attack: In the mean, the *English* and *Dutch* Cannon began to Thunder against the Enemy, who answer'd them briskly from their Batteries, and made it judg'd by their Dispositions, that the Action would be very hot.

These Preparations being over, the *English* and *Dutch*, Commanded by Lieutenant General *Gour*, and Brigadier *Ferguson*, began the Attack with unparallel'd Valour and Intrepedity, before the Imperialists could come up, and met with such a Resistance, that they were twice Repulsed: But after an Engagement of near an Hour and a Half, the Imperialists being at that time advanc'd to the Attack, the Entrenchments were forced, and the Confederates made a terrible Slaughter, pursuing the Enemy to the very *Danube*, where a great part of them follow'd the Example of the Count *de Arco*, and other General Officers, who saved themselves by Swimming over that River. The Victors took Fifteen Pieces of Cannon, with all the Runaways Ammunition, Tents and Baggage, and Thirteen Colours, besides Count *de Arco*'s Plate, which, with other Rich Booty, was distributed among the Soldiers for their future Encouragement.

All the Confederate Troops that engag'd, behav'd themselves with incredible Bravery and Resolution, and the Horse and Dragoons shar'd the Glory of the Day with the Infantry. But the Attack being begun by a Battalion of the *English* Guards, and the Regiments of *Orkney* and *Ingoldsby*, they suffer'd more than any others. The Forces of the Enemy confifted of Two Battalions of the Elector's Guards, One of Grenadiers, Thirteen other *Bavarian-Battalions*, Five *French*; Four Regiments of *Curaffiers*, of Eight hundred Men each, and Three Squadrons of Dragoons, making, in all, about 18000 Men, all choice Troops, commanded by the above-mention'd Field-Marfhal of the Elector of *Bavaria*'s Forces, Lieutenant General *Larzemburgh*, and Count *Maffy*, Generals of Battalia, befides Two *French* Lieutenant-Generals. Their lofs was computed at 5000 Men; nor was that of the Confederates much lefs, which, however, was abundantly made up, by their gaining fo compleat a Victory, that gave them a free Paffage into the Electorate of *Bavaria*, and forc'd the Prince of that Name, to retire under the Cannon of *Augsburgh*.

The Elector was no fooner informed of the Defeat of his Troops at *Schellemburgh*, than he quitted his ftrong Camp, between *Dillingen* and *Lavingen*, and came to the other Side of the *Danube*, over-againft *Donawaert*, in his March to the River *Leche*, to prevent the Confederates cutting off his Retreat to his own Country. The fame Night he fent Orders to the Garrifon of *Donawaert*, to fet fire to the Town, to burn their Bridges and Magazines, and then retire; for which end they had put Straw in every Houfe: But the Confederates being advanc'd into the Suburbs, and laying their Bridge to pafs into the Town, the Garrifon did not think fit to ftay and execute their Orders, for fear of having their Retreat cut off, whereby the Burghers fav'd their Houfes, and the Confederates enter'd the Town without any Oppofition, finding in it Two thoufand Sacks of Meal, and great ftore of Oats, with all forts of Provifion and Ammunition, which the Enemy had not Time to deftroy.

Tow

Two Advantages of such Importance, as this signal Victory, and the Consequence of it, in the Reduction of the strong Town of Donauwert, without Blows, could not but induce His Grace to give notice of it to the several Courts of the Allies, amongst whom, the States-General receiv'd the Two following Letters from, which being of great weight, to illustrate the foregoing happy Successes, it would be an Injury to the Public, to be robb'd of the Satisfaction of their perusal.

The Duke of Marlborough's LETTER *to the* States-General, *about the Battle of* Schellembergh.

High and Mighty LORDS,

"UPON our Arrival at *Onderingen*, on *Tuesday*,
"I understood that the Elector of *Bavaria*
"had sent the best of his Foot to guard the Post
"at *Schellembergh*, where he had been casting up
"Intrenchments for some Days, because it was of
"great Importance: Therefore I resolv'd to attack
"him there; and marched Yesterday Morning,
"by 3 of the clock, at the Head of a Detachment of
"6000 Foot, and 30 Squadrons of our Troops, and
"3 Battalions of *Imperial-Grenadiers*; whereupon the
"Army began their March, to follow us, but the
"Way being very long and bad, we could not get
"to the River *Werntz*, till about Noon; and it was
"full 3 of the clock, before we could lay Bridges,
"for our Troops and Cannon; so that all Things
"being ready, we attack'd them about 6 in the
"Evening. The Attack lasted a full Hour. The
"Enemies defended themselves very vigorously,
"and were very strongly intrench'd, but, at last,
"were

(30)

"were obliged to retire, by the Valour of our
"Men, and the Good God has given us a com-
"pleat Victory.
"We have taken 15 Pieces of Cannon, with all
"their Tents and Baggage. The Count *d'Arco*,
"and the other Generals that commanded them,
"were obliged to save themselves, by swimming
"over the *Danube*. I heartily wish Your *High*
"*Mightinesses* good Success from this happy Begin-
"ning, which is so glorious for the Arms of the
"Allies, and from which, I hope, by the Assi-
"stance of Heaven, we may reap many Advan-
"tages. We have lost very many brave Officers;
"and we cannot enough bewail the loss of the
"Sieur *Goor*, and *Beinheim*, who were killed in this
"Action. The Prince of *Baden*, and General
"*Thungen* are slightly wounded. Count *Stirum* has
"receiv'd a Wound cross the Body, but 'tis hop'd
"he will recover. The Hereditary Prince of
"*Hesse Cassel*, Count *Horn*, Lieutenant-General, the
"Major-Generals *Wood* and *Pallandt* are likewise
"wounded. I can, at present, give your *High*
"*Mightinesses* no more Particulars, but will not fail
"to do it upon the first Opportunity.
"A little before the Attack began, the Baron
"of *Moltenburgh*, Adjutant-General to Prince *Eu-*
"*gene*, was sent to me by His Highness, with Ad-
"vice, That the Marshals of *Villeroy* and *Tallard*
"were march'd to *Strasburgh*, having promis'd the
"Elector of *Bavaria* a great Re-inforcement by the
"Way of the *Black-Forest*; and I have Advice by
"another Hand, that they designed to send him
"50 Battalions, and 60 Squadrons of their best
"Troops. Since I was witness how much the
"Sieur *Mortagne* distinguish'd himself in this whole
"Action, I could not omit doing him the Justice,
"to recommend him to your *High Mightinesses*, to
"make up to him the loss of his General; where-
"fore I have pitched upon him to bring this to
"Your

" Your *High Mightinesses*, and to inform you of the
" Particulars.

I remain, &c.

Ulmengen,
July 3. 1704.

The Duke *of* Marlborough.

P. S. The Detachment, abovesaid, was supported by Fifteen Battalions of the Left, and as many of the Right-Wing.

His Grace's Second LETTER *to the* States, *concerning the Success of the foregoing Action.*

High and Mighty LORDS,

"THO' I had the Honour to write to you,
" Yesterday, by Monsieur *Montague*, to in-
" form you of the Victory which God has been
" pleased to give us over the Enemies, on the
" 2d Instant; yet I judge it well worth the while,
" to send another Express, to acquaint you with
" the Fruits of our Success. As soon as the Elector
" of *Bavaria* had Intelligence of the Misfortune
" of his Troops, he quitted his Camp between
" *Dillingen* and *Lavingen*, and last Night appear'd
" over-against this Place, on the other Side the
" *Danube*, bending his March towards the *Lech*,
" fearing to be cut off from his own Country:
" We have Advice, that part of his Troops have
" already passed that River, as the rest certainly
" will, as soon as we have passed the *Danube*,
" which I hope to do to Morrow, our Men being
" hard at work, in laying Bridges over it.

" Yesterday-Morning the Elector sent Order to
" the Garrison of this Place, to set the Town on
" fire, as also to burn the Bridges, and the Maga-
" zines,

" zines, and to retire. Pursuant to which Order,
" they put Straw into all the Houses; but seeing
" us advance into the Suburbs, and fall to work,
" to lay Bridges, to pass over into the Town,
" they durst not stay to execute their Design,
" for fear of being cut off. The Burghers found
" means to save their Houses; the Garrison only
" burn'd the Bridge, and some of the Magazines,
" and retired early this Morning with great Pre-
" cipitation. We took possession of the Town,
" and found in it a Magazine of Powder, and 3
" Pieces of Cannon, 2000 Sacks of Meal, a great
" quantity of Oats, which will serve, in part, to
" store the Magazines which we design to make
" here, for the subsistance of our Army: And I
" am now of Opinion, That the *French* will find
" it difficult to join the Elector of *Bavaria*, with
" the Re-inforcement they design for him.

" The Prisoners we have taken, report, That
" there were on the *Schellembergh*, 16 Battalions of
" *Bavarians*, and 5 of *French*; some say 9, and
" others 15 Squadrons, all of their best Troops,
" the greatest part of which were either killed,
" drowned, or taken.

" Our Soldiers had also the good Fortune to
" find the Count *d'Arco*'s Plate in his Camp.

" I assure Your *High Mightinesses*, we shall be
" careful to make the best Advantage we can of
" this Success, to press the Elector as hard as pos-
" sible, notwithstanding he has the *Leche* before him,
" and to lose no Time to bring him to Reason.

I am, with all Respect,

Your HIGH MIGHTINESSES

Humble and Obedient Servant,

Donawert,
July 4. 1704.

(Signed)

MARLBOROUGH.

Having

Having taken possession of *Donawaert*, and left a Garrison in it, the Confederate-Army passed the *Danube*, over several Bridges of Boats, made for that purpose, and encamped at *Mortingen*, in the Elector of *Bavaria*'s Country, whose Army, (as has been before mention'd) was retreated on the other Side of the *Leche*, and encamped under the Cannon of *Augsburgh*. The Duke resolving to improve the Advantages he had gain'd, and to press the Enemy before they had recover'd themselves from the great Consternation they were under, gave Orders for passing the *Leche*, which being done, the Garrison of *Nieuburgh* abandon'd that Place, and retired to *Ingoldstadt*, the strongest Hold in all *Bavaria*. Whereupon a Detachment was sent to take possession of the former, under the command of General *Herbiville*, who was commanded to remain there, for the convenience of drawing Provisions out of *Franconia*, for the subsistance of the Army, while it continued in *Bavaria*.

Rain was the next Place that submitted to His Grace's Victorious Arms, wherein the Besiegers found 24 Pieces of Brass Cannon, and some Ammunition, besides a considerable quantity of Corn, the Garrison of 400 Foot, under the command of the Count *de Mercy*, Brigadier-General, being conducted to the Elector's Camp. At the Reduction of this Town, His Grace was given to understand, by Count *Vekien*, General of the *Palatine-Horse*, who was sent from Prince *Eugene* for that purpose, that the Marshals *Villeroy* and *Tallard*, with an Army of 45000 Men, had pass'd the *Rhine* about *Fort-Kiel*, giving out that they intended to succour the Elector of *Bavaria*, it was not doubted but one of them, at least, would attempt; and therefore His Highness desir'd a Reinforcement of Horse, that he might the better be able to observe the Enemies Motions. Thereupon Prince *Maximilian* of *Hannover*, was detach'd with 30 Squadrons of Imperial-Horse, with Orders to join Prince *Eugene* with all diligence; and His Grace sent likewise an Express, to acquaint the latter, that if he thought necessary, a further number would follow.

Much about this Time, His Highness receiv'd a Letter from the Emperor, written in his own Hand, to acknowledge his great Services, which being an Honour seldom done to any one under the Degree of a Crown'd-Head, ought to have that regard shewn to it, as to be inserted Word for Word. The Letter ran thus.

Illustrious and most sincerely Beloved,

"YOUR Deserts towards Me, and My House, and the Common Cause, are great and many, and the singular Application, Care and Diligence, which you have shewn in bringing up, and hastening the powerful Succours, which the most Serene and Potent Queen of *Great-Britain*, and the States General of the *United Provinces* have sent me to the *Danube*, are not to be ranked in the last Place. But nothing can be more Glorious, than what you have done in conjunction of your Army with mine, in the most speedy and vigorous Attack, and forcing of the Enemies Camp near *Donawaert*, on the 2d of this Month, since my Generals themselves, and Ministers, declare, That the success of that Enterprize, (which is more acceptable and advantagious to me, at this present Time, than almost any Thing else that could befall me) is chiefly owing to your Counsel, Prudence, and Execution, and the wonderful Bravery and Constancy of the Troops that fought under your command.

"Therefore,

(35)

"Therefore, altho' the Testimony of those great Men, and Fame it self, the Rewarder of Noble Actions, do highly and justly extol your Name, I, who reap the Advantage which this Victory brings to the Common Cause, have thought my self obliged to Honour and Illustrate the Glory you have gain'd, by the Testimony of my Letter, and to assure you, that I shall lose no Opportunity, to shew you, by Effects, how grateful, and well-inclined I am towards you. In the mean Time, that you carry on, with the same Alacrity and Industry, what you have so Valiantly and Vigorously begun, and that in conjunction with the Margrave of *Baden*, my Lieutenant General, and other Commanders of my Troops, you use your utmost Endeavours and Force, that the End may answer this Beginning; and that the War, which the *Bavarian* hath seditiously raised in the Bowels of *Germany*, may be brought to a speedy conclusion, is not what I do so much exhort you to, as I assuredly expect. For you cannot but be fully satisfied, that there is the highest Glory therein; and that this will be an Eternal Trophy to your most Serene Queen, in the *Upper-Germany*, where the Victorious Arms of the *English* Nation were never seen in the Memory of Man. I pray God to bless, with a prosperous Success, your Counsels and Enterprizes, and confirm to you, again and again, the most favourable Inclination, and Affection of my Mind towards you.

Given in my City of Vienna,
July *the* 12th, 1704.

His Grace, and Prince *Eugene*, finding that the Elector of *Bavaria* was still inflexible, notwithstanding several Offers made to him on their part, to draw off from the Interests of the Common

F 2 Enemy,

Enemy, and that it was impoſſible to attack him in his Fortified-Camp, under the Cannon of *Augsburgh*, without infinite Diſadvantage; and conſidering, beſides, that the Marſhal *de Tallard* was advancing with a conſiderable Body of Forces, they reſolved to attempt the reducing the other ſtrong Places in *Bavaria*, and to begin with *Ingoldſtadt*. Prince *Lewis* undertook to command, and carry on the Siege with the Imperial-Troops, and His Grace to cover it with the Auxiliary Forces, which, in caſe of need, might be joined by thoſe under Prince *Eugene*, who, by this Time, was advanced to *Dillingen*.

On the other Hand, the Marſhal *Tallard*, with about 22000 Horſe and Foot, being come to *Biberach*, on the 4th of *Auguſt*, in the Morning, he left his Troops, and went to the Elector's Camp, to confer with him, about the Conjunction of the Two Armies. Whereupon his Electoral Highneſs having left a *French* Garriſon in *Augsburgh*, marched, with the reſt of his Forces, to join the New Auxiliaries, as if he intended to paſs the *Leche* at *Biberach*, in order to attack the Confederate Army. But this Feint was only to cover his true Deſign, of paſſing the *Danube* at *Lawingen*, and to fall on the Army which Prince *Eugene* had brought from the Lines of *Biebl*, which was then encamp'd at *Hochſted*, before His Highneſs could be re-inforc'd.

This Intention was ſuſpected by the Prince, who having been at the main Army, in Conference with Prince *Lewis*, and the Duke of *Marlborough*, and taking notice, in his Way, of a Tract of Ground, very proper for a Camp, being a Height that reach'd from the Villages of *Munſter* and *Erlingloven*, to the Wood near *Appershoven*, with a Rivulet before it, ſent Orders to his Army to come and poſſeſs themſelves of that advantagious Poſt, which were put in execution.

In

In this Conference it was agreed to continue in their late Resolution of besieging *Ingoldstadt*, for which purpose, Prince *Lewis* march'd that Way, with 22 Battalions of Foot, and the Regiments of Horse of *Cronsfield*, and *Hohenz-Sollern*, the Curiassiers of *Merci*, and the Dragoons of *Castelli*. Prince *Eugene*, who had taken leave of my Lord Duke, in order to return to his Army, came back not many Hours after to His Grace's Quarters, upon Intelligence, that the Enemy had pass'd the *Danube* at *Lawingen*, whereupon, after those Two Generals had consulted together about 2 Hours, His Highness return'd to his Army, which he found ready to march, to go and possess themselves of the Entrenchments of *Schellembergh*, whither those that commanded in his absence, had already sent Workmen, to put them again into a State of Defence, not judging it safe to expect the *French* and *Bavarians* in the Camp of *Munster*, with an Army that did not exceed 18000 Men. But the Prince caus'd the Tents to be immediately set up again, contenting himself with sending the Baggage to *Donawaert*, rightly conjecturing, that the Enemy, who pass'd the *Danube* that Day at *Lawingen*, could not come near his Army that same Evening; and that it would not be impossible for him to maintain the important Post of *Munster*, till the Duke had joined, who, he supposed, was upon the March for that Intention.

Tho', upon Advice that the Enemy, who were well inform'd of his Weakness, design'd to attack them the next Day, he caused all his Infantry, and part of his Cavalry to march afterwards to the Camp at *Schellembergh*, keeping only 22 Squadrons of Dragoons of his own Army, and 28 Squadrons which the Duke-Regent of *Wurtembergh* had brought to his assistance, by order of the Duke of *Marlborough*. He passed the Night with those few Troops, in the Camp of *Munster*, keeping the

Horse

Horses ready saddled, with resolution to continue there, if possible, though without coming to an Engagement, 'till he had been join'd by His Grace, who, he had notice by an Express, would come up with him the next Day. Accordingly General *Churchill* join'd him betimes, with 20 Battalions; whereupon he re-call'd the Troops he had sent to *Schellembergh*, and in the Evening the Duke arrived with his whole Army.

This Junction being happily made on the 11th of *August*, the 2 following Days were spent in Preparations to attack the *French* and *Bavarians*, who were encamp'd on a very advantagious Post, on a Hill, their Right-Flank being cover'd by the *Danube*, and the Village of *Blenheim*, and their Left by the Village of *Lutzingen*: They had likewise before them a Rivulet, whose Banks were high, and the bottom marshy, so that it was thought, at first, to be unpassable, as, indeed, it was afterwards found to be in several Places. In these Circumstances, it was thought a very hazardous Enterprize, to attack so numerous an Army, and in so advantagious a Post, the Enemy being upwards of 60000 strong, and the Allies no more than 52. But there seem'd to be an indispensible necessity of falling immediately upon them, before they had Time to fortifie themselves: For besides that, the Confederate-Army should have wanted Forrage much sooner than *Ingoldstadt* could have been taken; the Generals of it were well informed, That the Marshal *de Villeroy*, leaving Monsieur *de Coigny* in the Camp near *Offenburgh*, with a Body of Troops sufficient to keep, within the Lines of *Biebl*, the *German* Forces that were there, was ready to make an Irruption into the Country of *Wirtembergh*, with another Body, which might have acted in concert with the Elector of *Bavaria*, and have been re inforced by Detachments from the Prince's Army, to fall afterwards on the Rear of the Lines

of

of *Biehl*, so that thereby the *French* Armies would have established a free Communication from the *Rhine* to the *Danube*, and have forced all to submit as far as the *Mein*; whilst the Elector, from his Camp at *Hochstedt*, might have ruin'd a great part of *Franconia*, and have brought Things to that pass, that the Auxiliaries, under His Grace, should not have been able to find either Subsistence of Winter-Quarters on the *Danube*, nor in the *Upper-Germany* Though, on the other Hand, that great and seasonable Supply, could not have left the Empire in the Winter, without exposing it to the utmost ruin, and leaving an entire Superiority to the *French*.

These prevailing Reasons made His Grace, and Prince *Eugene*, resolve to Fight, in pursuance of which Resolution, the Baggage was sent to *Rietlingen*, a Village between *Munster* and *Donawaert*.

The Confederate Army, the Strength of which has been related before, as well as that of the Enemy, had Fifty Pieces of Cannon, and the *French* had upwards of Ninety, which answer'd one another before the Attack was begun, with great execution. When on the 13th of *August*, a Memorable Day, on which, the Fate of the Empire, or rather of all *Europe* was to be decided, at Three Quarters past Twelve at Noon; His Grace who Commanded on the Left, and had to do with Marshal *Tallard*, who Commanded the Right Wing of the Enemy, gave the Signal for the Assailants to enter upon Action, whereupon, Major General *Wilks*, made the first Onset, with the five *English* Battalions of *How*, *Ingolsby*, *Marlborough Row*, and *North* and *Grey*, and four Battalions of *Hessians*, supported by the Lord *Cutts*, and Major General St. *Paul*, with Eleven other Battalions, and Fifteen Squadrons of Horse, under the Command of Major General *Wood*. The five *English* Battalions led on by Brigadier *Row*, who charged on Foot at the

Head

Head of his own Regiment, with unparell'd Intrepidity, Assaulted the Village of *Blenheim*, advancing to the very Muzzles of the Enemies Muskets, and some of the Officers exchanging Thrusts of Swords with the *French* thro' the *Palissadoes*. But being expos'd to a Fire, much superior to theirs, they were soon forced to Retire, leaving behind them one Third Part of their Men, either Killed or Mortally Wounded, the Brigadier that Commanded them being of the Number of the latter. In this Retreat, they were pursued by Thirteen Squadrons of the *French Gendarmerie* and *Carrabiniers*, who would have entirely cut them to Pieces, had not the *Hessian* Infantry stop'd their Carrier, by the great Fire they made upon them. The *French* being Repulsed and forced to Fly in their turn, were chased by five Squadrons of *English* Horse, who by this time had pass'd the Rivulet; but whilst the Enemy rallied themselves, some fresh Brigadiers superior in Number, came to their Assistance, charg'd the Assailants with great Vigour, and oblig'd many of them to Repass the Rivulet with great Precipitation. Here again, the *Hessian* Foot perform'd notable Service, putting the *French* to the Rout by their continual Fire, and regaining the Colours, which they had taken from *Row*'s Regiment.

Whilst *Row*'s Brigade Rallied themselves, that of *Ferguson*, Headed likewise by himself, Attack'd the Village of *Blenheim* on the Left, but with no better Success; and though both returned three or four Times, to the Charge with equal Vigour, yet they were both still Repulsed with like Disadvantage; so that it was found impossible to force the Enemy in that Post, without entirely Sacrificing the Confederate Infantry.

The *English* Foot having thus begun the Engagement on the Left, the Horse of the same Wing pass'd the *Rivulet*, with great Bravery over against

the

the Centre, or main Battalia of the Enemy, as did likewise that of the Right Wing, having made several Passages with diverse Pieces of Wood: After which, they drew up in Order of Battle, the *French* and *Bavarians*, giving them all the time that could be desired for that Purpose, keeping themselves very quiet on the Hills they were possess'd of, without descending into the Meadows towards the *Rivulet*, in so much, that even the second Line of the Horse had time to Form themselves: And *to this Capital Fault, the Confederates ought principally to ascribe their Victory.*

The Dukes Cavalry moving towards the Hill, that of the Marshal *Tallard* came down at last, and Charg'd his Men with a great deal of Fury, the *French* Infantry at the same time, that were Posted at *Blenheim*, making an incredible Fire on their Flank, which were advanc'd too near that Village from behind some Hedges; so that the first Line was put into such Disorder, that part of them Retir'd beyond the *Rivulet*. Hereupon, His Grace gave Orders for Lieutenant General *Bulow*, Commander in Chief of the Troops of *Lunenburgh*, to bring up his own Regiment of Dragoons, and two of the Troops of *Cell*, which charged the Enemies Horse with so much Vigour, that they broke them, and drove them beyond the second *Rivulet* called *Maulweyer*, and from thence to the very Hedges of the Village of *Blenheim*. This gave time to those that had given Ground, to Face about and Repass the *Rivulet*, which Troops form'd a second Line behind the above mention'd Regiment of Dragoons and some others that had join'd them, so that those Dragoons remain'd in the first Line, during the rest of the Action.

The Cavalry of the Left Wing having by this Success, gain'd the Advantage of Forming themselves entirely in Order of Battle, advanced leisurely to the Top of the Hill, and several times charg'd

charg'd the Enemies Horse, who were always Routed, but, who nevertheless Rallied every time, though at a considerable distance, which gave the Confederates opportunity to gain Ground. As the Duke, who was now in Person among them, was preparing for a fresh Attack, Marshal *de Tallard* caus'd Ten of his Battalions to advance, to fill the Intervals of his Cavalry, in order to make a last Effort, which His Grace perceiving, caused Three Battalions of the Forces of *Cell*, to come and sustain him. Then the Prince of *Hesse-Cassel*, General of the Horse, Lieutenant Generals, *Lumly*, *Bulow*, *Hompesch* and *Ingoldsby*, return'd with their Troops to the Charge, but the superior Fire of the Enemies Infantry, put their First Line into some Disorder, in so much, that it shrunk back, and remain'd for some time at about Sixty Paces distant from the Enemy, neither Party advancing against the other. At last, the Confederates push'd forward with so much Bravery and Success, that having broke and Routed their Adversaries Horse, the 10 Battalions, who found themselves abandon'd by them, were, for the generality, cut to pieces, none escaping, but a very few Soldiers, who threw themselves on the Ground, as dead, to save their Lives Marshal *de Tallard* rallied his broken Cavalry, behind some Tents that were still standing in his Camp, and seeing Things in this desperate Condition, resolved to draw off his Dragoons and Infantry out of the Village of *Blenheim*: Thereupon, he sent one of his *Aid-de-Camps* to Marshal *Marsin*, who with the Elector of *Bavaria*, commanded on the Left, to desire him, "To face the
" Enemy, with some Troops on the Right of the
" Village of *Overklaw*, to keep them in play, and
" favour the Retreat of the Infantry that was in
" *Blenheim*. But *Marsin* represented to the Messenger, that he had too much business in the
" Front of the Village where he was posted, (and
" where

" where he had to do with the Duke of Marlborough
" himself, who was come to the assistance of Prince
Eugene) as well as in the rest of the Line, to
be able to spare any Troops, he not being
Victorious, but only sparing his Ground In
the mean Time, Lieutenant-General *Ingoldsby*
made the other Generals, at the same Attack,
sensible, how easily they might entirely defeat
the *French* Cavalry, by charging them on the
Right-Flank. Which Advice being put in execution, with a great deal of Vigour, the Enemy
were presently disordered, and put to flight; part
of them endeavoured to gain the Bridge they had
over the *Danube*, between *Bleinheim* and *Hochstedt*.
The other part, among whom were the *Gens d'Arms*,
closely pursu'd by the *Luxenburgh* Dragoons, and
those that escap'd from being killed, threw themselves into the *Danube*, where most of them were
drowned. Those who fled towards *Hochstedt*, rallied once more, making a shew to succour the rest;
but the same Regiment of *Bothmar* faced them, and
kept them in awe for some Time, till it was join'd
by some Regiments, when they made the best of
their way to save themselves by flight. The Marshal *de Tallard* was inveloped with the Run aways,
and taken near a Mill, behind the Village of *Sonderen*, not far from the *Danube*, by Monsieur *de Bothenbourgh*, a *Hessian*-Lieutenant-Colonel, Aid-de-Camp,
to the Prince of that Name The Marquis *de Montfrout*, General of Horse, *de Seppeville, de Silly*, and
de la Vaitere, Major-Generals, Monsieur *de la Mossiere St Pollange de Ligondaux*, and several other Officers of Note, were also made Prisoners in this Rout.
While these Things pass'd at the Village at *Blenheim*, and in the Center, His Grace caused the
Village of *Overklaw*. Marshal *de Marsin*'s Quarters,
to be attack'd by the Brigade of *Berensdorf*, consisting of 10 Battalions. The Prince of *Holstein-Beck*,
who commanded them, as Major-General, pass'd

G 2 the

the Rivulets at the Head of 2 Battalions, with undaunted Resolution: But as the Imperial Cavalry, which was to have supported him, was above a Musket-shot from him, he was hardly got over, when 7 or 8 of the adverse Party's Battalions, fell upon him with great Fury, before he could form the Forces he had with him into proper Order, so that that of *Goor* was almost entirely put to the Sword, and the Prince himself desperately wounded, and taken Prisoner. The Confederates being sustain'd by some *Danish* and *Hannoverian* Cavalry, went to the Charge the second Time, which had no better success; but the third Time, His Grace, in Person having brought up some Squadrons, which were supported by others of the Body of Reserve, made them advance with some Battalions, beyond the Rivulet, whereupon the Enemy began to retire.

As soon as the Duke of *Marlborough* had perform'd this considerable Service, he repaired to the Center, where finding the Action decided in favour of the Allies, he caus'd part of the Victorious Cavalry to Halt, to observe the Motion of that part of the Enemy, which by this Time was drawn up beyond the Morass of *Hochstedt*. During this Halt, the Elector of *Bavaria*, whom Prince *Eugene* could make no Impression upon for some Time, but whose Bravery, at last, put them to the Rout, was perceiv'd making his Retreat from the Village of *Lutzingen*. Upon which, Orders were dispatch'd to the Baron *de Hompesch*, who, with several Squadrons, was pursuing the Fugitives towards *Morsilingen*, and had already overtaken and forced 2 of their Battalions to lay down their Arms: Orders, I say, were sent to him to face about, and march to join those that halted, as well to prevent the Electors falling upon *Hompesch* his Rear, as to form a Body, in order to charge that Prince, who march'd in great Haste, but excellent Order, with his Squadrons on the Left, and his Battalions on the Right. But before General *Hompesch* returnd from the Chace, the Right-Wing of our Army was perceiv'd at some distance behind the Elector, and appearing to be part of his Army, marching in such a manner, as might have easily flank'd us, had the Duke immediately charg'd him. His Grace, with great Prudence, sent out a Party to view them, during which Time, the Elector continued marching off with great Precipitation, till he reach'd the Morass of *Marselingen*.

The *French* Horse being entirely defeated, and the Confederates Masters of all the Ground, which was between the Enemies Left, and the Village of *Blenheim*, the 28 Battalions, and 12 Squadrons of Dragoons, which were in that Village, found themselves cut off from the rest of their Army, and despairing of being able to make their Escape, after a weak Attempt to repulse His Grace, whose Infantry that surrounded them, capitulated at about 8 of the clock at Night, laid down their Arms, deliver'd their Colours and Standards, and surrender'd themselves Prisoners of War, on Condition, that the Officers should not be search'd.

This Defeat cost the Enemy, by their own Accounts, 40000 Men, in which number they include 4 or 5000 they lost in their precipitate Retreat to the *Black Forest*, either by Desertion, or the Pursuit of the *Hussars* and *Peasants*, and the Consequences of it was the Reduction of all *Bavaria*, and such other Places as had been wrested from the Empire, by the Elector of that Name. General-Officers, Colours, Standards, Kettle Drums, Cannon, Tents, Pontoons, Coaches, Mules, Cases of Silver, Bridges of Boats, and other Utensils of War were taken without number, and likewise stood the Allies in 4485 Men killed, 7525 wounded, and 272 lost, or made Prisoners

As the Courts of *England* and *Holland* bore a great part in the Triumphs of this Day, so His

Grace

Grace, at the first beginning of the Enemies Flight, took his Pocket Book, and wrote the following Letter to his Dutchess, on Horse-back, which Letter he dispatch'd forward to *England*, from the Field of Battle, by Colonel *Parke*, which was as follows.

"I Have not Time to say more, than to beg of you to present my humble Service to the QUEEN, and to let Her know, that the Army has had a compleat Victory. Monsieur *Tallard*, and Two other Generals, are in my Coach, and I am following the rest. The Bearer, my *Aid-de-Camp*, Colonel *Parke*, will give Her Majesty an Account of what has passed: I shall do it in a Day or two, by another Hand, more at large.

MARLBOROUGH.

His Grace's LETTER *to Mr. Secretary* Harley, *sent the next Day, by another Hand, upon the same Subject.*

SIR,

"I Gave you an Account on *Sunday* of the Situation we were then in, and that we expected to hear the Enemy would pass the *Danube* at *Lawingen*, in order to Attack Prince *Eugene*. At 11 that Night, we had an Express from Him, that the Enemy were come over, and desiring he might be Reinforc'd as soon as possible: Whereupon, I order'd my Brother *Churchill* to Advance at One of the Clock in the Morning with 20 Battalions, and by Three the whole Army was in Motion. For the greater Expedition,

(47)

"tion, I order'd Part of the Troops to pass over
"the *Danube*, and follow the March of the Twen-
"ty Battalions; and with most of the Horse and
"Foot of the First Line, pass'd the *Lech at Rain*,
"and came over the *Danube* at *Donawaert*; so that
"we all joined the Prince that Night, intending
"to advance and take this Camp at *Hochstedt*. In
"order whereunto, we went out on *Tuesday* early
"in the Morning, with 40 Squadrons to view the
"Ground, but found the Enemy had already po-
"ssess'd themselves of it. Whereupon, We re-
"solved to Attack them, and accordingly we
"March'd between three and four in the Mor-
"ning Yesterday, from the Camp at *Munster*,
"leaving all our Tents standing. About Six We
"came in view of the Enemy, who we found,
"did not expect so early a Visit. The Cannon
"began to Play about half an Hour after 8. They
"form'd themselves into 2 Bodies, the Elector
"with Monsieur *Marsin* on the Left; and Monsieur
"*Tallard* and his Troops on the Right; and had
"Two little Rivulets besides a Morass before them
"which We were obliged to pass over in their view
"and Prince *Eugene* was forced to take a great
"Compass to come to the Enemy, so that it was
"One of the Clock before the Battle began. It
"lasted with great Vigour till Sun-set, when the
"Enemy were obliged to Retire; and by the
"Blessing of God, We obtained a compleat Victory.
"We have cut off great Numbers of them, as well
"in the Action, as in the Retreat, besides above
"30 Squadrons of the *French*, which I have push'd
"into the *Danube*, where We saw the greatest Part
"of Them Perish. Monsieur *de Tallard*, with se-
"veral of his General Officers, being taken Pri-
"soners at the same Time; And at the Village of
"*Bleinheim*, which the Enemy had Intrench'd and
"Fortyfied, and where they made the greatest
"Opposition, I obliged 28 entire Battalions, and

"12

" 12 Squadrons of Dragoons, to surrender them-
" selves Prisoners at Discretion. We took likewise
" all their Tents standing, with their Cannon and
" Ammunition; as also, a great Number of Stand-
" ards, Kettle Drums, and Colours in the Action;
" so that, I reckon the greatest Part of Monsieur
" *Tallard*'s Army is taken or Destroyed: The Bra-
" very of all Our Troops on this Occasion, can-
" not be Expressed; the Generals as well as the
" Officers and Soldiers, behaving themselves with
" the greatest Courage and Resolution. The Horse
" and Dragoons having been obliged to Charge 4
" or 5 Times The Elector and Monsieur *Marsin*,
" were so advantagiously Posted, that Prince *Eu-
" gene* could make no Impression on them, till the
" third Attack, at near 7 at Night, when he made
" a great Slaughter of Them. But being near a
" Wood side, a good Body of the *Bavarians* retired
" into it, and the Rest of that Army retreated to-
" wards *Lawingen*, it being too late, and the Troops
" too much tyred to pursue them far. I cannot say
" too much in Praise of that Prince his good Con-
" duct on this Occasion. You will please to lay
" this before Her Majesty, and His Royal High-
" ness; to whom I send my Lord *Tunbridge* with
" the good News. I pray, you will likewise
" inform your self, and let me know Her Majesty's
" Pleasure, as well relating to Monsieur *de Tallard*,
" and the other General-Officers, as for the disposal
" of near 1200 other Officers, and between 8 and
" 900 common Soldiers, who being all made Priso-
" ners by Her Majesty's Troops, are entirely at
" Her Disposal, but as the Charge of subsisting
" these Officers must be very great; I presume
" Her Majesty will be Inclined, that they be Ex-
" changed for any other Prisoners that offer.
 " I should likewise be glad to receive Her Ma-
" jesty's Directions, for the Disposal of the Stand-
" ards and Colours, whereof, I have not yet the
" Number;

"Number; but guess there cannot be less than an
"100; which is more than has been taken in any
"Battle these many Years.
"You will easily believe that in so long and
"vigorous an Action, the *English* who had so great
"a share in it, must have suffer'd as well in Offi-
"cers as Men; but I have not yet the Particulars,

I am,

Your most Obedient Humble Servant,

MARLBOROUGH.

His Grace's LETTER to the States-General, upon the same Occasion.

High and Mighty LORDS;

"I Had the Honour to write to your High Migh-
"tinesses, on *Sunday* last, to inform you of
"our Resolution to besiege *Ingoldstadt*, and of the
"Situation of the Enemy. That same Day, in
"the Evening, we understood that they had passed
"the *Danube* at *Lawingen*, upon which, at Mid-
"night, I order'd General *Churchill*, with 20 Bat-
"tallions, who had passed the *Danube* that same Day,
"to re-inforce Prince *Eugene*, and at 3 in the Mor-
"ning I began to march with the rest of the Army;
"part of which, that we might make as much haste
"as possible, took the same Way with General
"*Churchill*, and the Horse, with the First Line of
"the Foot, passed the *Lethe* at *Rain*, and the *Da-
"nube* at *Donawaert*. We join'd Prince *Eugene* the
"same Night, and encamp'd with our Right at
"*Apperrshosen*, and the Left at *Munster*, with a De-
"sign, next Morning, to possess our selves of the
"Camp at *Hochstedt*; but when Prince *Eugene* and
"I came

H

" I came to view the Ground, we found that the
" Enemy had already possess'd it: Upon which,
" we resolv'd to march towards them, which we
" did Yesterday, the Army being in motion by 2
" in the Morning, which the Enemy did not ex-
" pect. We came in sight of them by 6, and be-
" tween 8 and 9 we began to cannonade one an-
" other; but the Enemy having 2 Rivulets, or
" Brooks before them, and a sort of a Morass, the
" Horse were oblig'd to file off, and Prince Eu-
" gene having a great Turn to take, it was 1 of the
" clock before we could come to engage. The
" Enemy form'd themselves into 2 Bodies: The
" Elector, and Monsieur *Marsin* on the Left, and
" Monsieur *Tallard*, and all his Troops, on the
" Right. It fell to my share to engage the latter,
" so that at last the Battle grew hot, and continu-
" ed till Sun-set, when it pleased God to give the
" Allies one of the greatest and most compleat
" Victories that has been known.

" It is Impossible to express the Bravery of our
" Troops, as well Generals and Officers, as com-
" mon Soldiers, who deserve all possible praise
" Our Cavalry charged 4 or 5 Times: But Time
" does not allow me to be particular; their whole
" Army was put to the rout We have made a
" great Slaughter of them, and taken their Camp,
" with their Cannon and Ammunition On my
" Side we push'd above 30 Squadrons into the *Da-*
" *nube,* where most of them were drowned; and
" we have taken Monsieur *de Tallard,* with many
" of the General-Officers. In the Village of *Blein-*
" *beim,* which the Enemy had fortified, I have
" made 26 Battalions, and 12 Squadrons Prisoners
" at discretion; besides which, we have taken a
" great number of Standards and Colours.

" I know not yet the Particulars of all that pas-
" sed on the Right, but Prince *Eugene*'s good Con-
" duct, and the Bravery of his Troops was parti-
" cularly

" cularly observable in this glorious Action; for
" which I will delay no longer to congratulate
" Your *High Mightinesses*, referring you for the Par-
" ticulars, to Colonel *Panton*, one of my Adjutant-
" Generals, who having been in the Action, can
" tell the Particulars by word of Mouth.

I am, &c.

Aug. 14. *From the
Camp at* Hochstedt.

The Duke *of* MARLBOROUGH.

The States-Generals ANSWER.

My LORD,

" YOUR Excellency's welcome Letter, of the
" 14th Instant, from the Camp at *Hochstedt*,
" was delivered to us by Colonel *Panton*, who has
" related to us what passed in the memorable Bat-
" tle fought the Day before.
" We affectionately thank Your Excellency for
" the Readiness and Dispatch with which you was
" pleased to communicate so good News to us:
" Your First Exploit, this Campagne, at *Schellem-*
" *bergh*, gave us Ground to expect something bet-
" ter, but we durst not extend our Hopes to so
" great and-compleat a Victory, as this which you
" have obtained over the Enemy, with the Arms
" of the Allies.
" This Battle will set the Greatness of your Me-
" rit in its true Lustre: A Battle the Glory of
" which the greatest Captains of former Ages may
" envy you, and the Memory of which can never
" perish in succeeding Ages. We most humbly
" congratulate Your Excellency upon it; rejoi-

H 2 " cing

"cing upon the Glory you have acquired by it,
"as well as for the advantage that must ensue up-
"on it to the Common Cause.

"This Action will instruct *France*, that their
"Forces are not always *Invincible*, and will prove
"such a Blow, as their King never felt in the
"whole Course of his Reign. We render Thanks
"to God for it, who has been pleas'd to bless this
"your Couragious Enterprize; and we beseech
"him to prosper all your great Designs: Assuring
"you, that none can be with more Esteem and
"Sincerity, than we are,

Your, &c.

Given at our Court at the Hague.

His Grace not only receiv'd the foregoing Congratulation from their High Mightinesses, but had also, in his return to the *Rhine*, another Testimonial of his great Services, in another Letter from his Imperial Majesty, who, on Account of them, tho' with great Reluctance on the Duke's Side, who would by no means give his Acceptance of that Title, without his Royal Mistresse's Approbation, had created him a Prince of the *Holy Empire*, the Investiture of *Mindelheim*, being afterwards put into his possession, by His Grace's Proxy, Mr. *Stepney*. This was written in the Emperour's own Hand, after this manner.

Most Illustrious Cousin, and most Dear Prince,

"I Do gladly call by these Names your *Dilecti-*
"*on*, whom I have freely, and of my own
"Accord, admitted among the Princes of the
"*Holy Roman Empire*. Not so much in considerati-
"on of Your *Noble Family*, as upon account of
"your personal Merit, and your great Deserts
"towards my August House, and the *Holy Roman*
"*Empire*

"*Empire.* I have been willing that this public
" Monument, of the supreme Honour, in *Germa-*
" *ny*, which I have so deservedly conferr'd upon
" you, should remain, that it may be more and
" more made appear to all the World, how much,
" as I freely own it, I, and all the Empire, owe
" to the most Serene QUEEN of *Great-Britain*,
" for having sent Her powerful Assistances, as far
" as *Augsburgh* and *Bavaria* it self, under your Con-
" duct, when my own Affairs, and those of the
" Empire, were so much shaken and disorder'd, by
" the perfidious Defection of the *Bavarians* to the
" *French*, and also to your *Dilection*, upon account
" that Things have been so prudently, so vigo-
" rously, and successfully transacted: For not on-
" ly Fame, but likewise the Generals of my Forces,
" the Companions and Sharers of your Labours
" and Victories, attribute the same to your Coun-
" sels, and the Valour and Bravery of the *English*,
" and other Forces, who fought under your Con-
" duct. These Actions are so great, and particu-
" larly that of *Hochstedt*, past Ages having never
" seen the like Victory obtained over the *French*,
" that we may rejoice to see, not only the most
" pernicious Efforts of the Enemy repulsed, and
" the Affairs of *Germany*, which were somewhat
" tottering, and those of all *Europe* secur'd and set-
" led again, but likewise that it may be reasonably
" hop'd, that the full and perfect Liberty of the
" Christian World shall be rescued from the Power
" of *France*, which was so imminently impending
" over it. Being entirely persuaded, and sure, that
" your *Dilection* will, without Intermission, apply
" all your Care and Industry towards that End.
" There remains nothing else for me, but to wish
" you a prosperous Success, and that I assure you
" of further Marks of my Gratitude upon all Occa-
" sions, which I shall be ready to express.

Given in the City of Vienna, *Aug* 28. 1704.

The

The Dukes *Second* LETTER *to the* States-General, *concerning the Battle of* Hochstedt.

"I Gave my self the Honour to write to your
"High Mightynesses on *Thursday* last, by
"Colonel *Panton*, one of my Adjutants Generals, to
"impart to you the Happy Success of the Arms of
"the Allies in *Germany*, and the glorious Victory
"which we have obtained over the Enemy, of
"which, we feel every Day the good influence
"The Number of Prisoners increases Hourly,
"and we reckon to have now about 11000, besides
"1200 Officers. I must confess, that great Num-
"bers is very troublesom to us, there being few
"Places in this Country to put them in. This
"obliges me to desire your High Mightynesses,
"that they may be disposed of in the Places of
"the United Provinces: Mean time, we shall
"endeavour to ease our selves of them in this
"Country, as soon as possible, for nothing else
"stops us here.

"As the Face of Affairs in this Country is
"wholly changed at Present, Prince *Eugene* and I
"have imparted to Prince *Lewis* of *Baden* our Sen-
"timents, that to amuse our selves with the Siege
"of *Ingoldstadt*, at present would be but losing of
"Time, and that we believe it will be more ad-
"vantagious for the good of the common Cause,
"to join all our Forces to streighten more and
"more the Enemy, and oblige the *French* to quit
"*Germany*, and repass the *Rhine*: For then, not
"only *Ingoldstadt*, but also the whole Country of
"*Bavaria* must fall of themselves. We have an
"instance of it, in the Case of the City of *Augs-
"burgh*, which the Enemy quitted Yesterday Mor-
"ning. Their Deputies are come hither to desire
"our Protection, and a Detachment is Marching
"thither to take Possession thereof; we Hourly
expect

"expect an Answer from the Prince of *Baden* on
" this Subject.
" This Day we have return'd Thanks to God,
" through the whole Army, for his Favour towards
" us, which appears the more conspicuous, in that
" the Enemy own, that their Army consisted of
" 82 Battalions, and 147 Squadrons, which were
" advantagiously Posted: Whereas, we had but
" 64 Battalions, and 166 Squadrons, of which
" Number, 1500 Horse were with the Prince of
" *Baden.* This Evening we are to make Public
" Rejoycings by a General Discharge of our Ar-
" tillery and small Arms throughout the Army.
" I have nothing farther to add, but I cannot
" conclude without repeating to Your High
" Mightyness, that the Valour and good Conduct
" of the *Baron de Houpesche*, and your other Gene-
" rals, and also the Bravery which the Officers and
" Soldiers of your Troops have express'd upon
" this Occasion, deserve the greatest Encomiums.
" I therefore flatter my self, that in filling up the
" vacancies your High Mightynesses, will have a
" particular Regard for such who have been in the
" Action, and for the Recommendation of their
" Generals, who were Eye Witnesses of their Be-
" haviour.

From the Camp at
Steinheim, *Aug* 17. 1704.   (Sign-d)

The Duke *of* MARLBOROUGH.

The Dukes *Third* LETTER *to the* States-
General.

High and Mighty LORDS,

" I Gave my self the Honour to write to your
"   High Mightynesses on *Sunday* last from
" *Steinheim.* The next Day after, the Marshal *de*
" *Tallard*, with the other Officers of Note, was
" sent towards *Franckfort* and *Hanau*, under a Guard
                                                    " of

"of Dragoons. We have made the Repartition
"of the other Prisoners, who are sent into the
"Neighbouring Places, that they may be more
"easily Guarded, till they are sent away. Their
"Number is greater than at first believed, since
"they exceed 13000 Officers and Soldiers, inclu-
"ding about 3000, who lifted themselves in the
"Confederate Troops. On *Tuesday* the Army de-
"camp'd, and March'd to *Gundelfingen*. Yesterday
"we advanced to *Ober Elchingen*, and this Day to
"this Camp, which is about half a League from
"*Ulm*. We have found great Numbers of Officers
"Buried in the Villages through which we March-
"ed, and some Citizens of *Ulm* assure us, that
"when the Enemy March'd from thence, they
"carryed away above 7000 Wounded, amongst
"whom, were about 1000 Officers. They burn'd
"a great many Waggons, to make use of the
"Horses upon *Brankars*. [This is a sort of a LIT-
"TER] Our *Hussars* and several Parties of Horse
"follow them very closely, who together with
"the *Boors*, have Kill'd a great Number of the E-
"nemies Soldiers, whom they found stragling
"We begin to streighten *Ulm*, expecting the Ar-
"rival of the Prince of *Baden*, who passed the
"*Danube* this Day at *Donawaert*, and as soon as he
"is come, and that we have Regulated what Troops
"are to carry on this Siege, I shall advance towards
"the *Rhine* with the Forces, which I have the Ho-
"nour to Command. This Morning a Deputy
"from the City of *Memingen* came to our Camp,
"to desire our Protection, and Reports that the
"Electoress of *Bavaria* was gone through that
"Place with Five of Her Children, under a Guard
"of Fourteen Squadrons, to joyn the Elector,
"who according to our last Advices, was about
"*Dutlingen*, with the Marshal de *M*—— I am, &c.

From the Camp at
Sefellingen, Aug 21 170—

The Duke of M———ROUGH.

As

As the forgoing Letters contain a Journal of the Dukes motions, some Days after the Battle, so it will be superfluous to follow Him Step by Step, till we bring him to cover the Siege of *Landau* at *Croon-Weisnbourgh* where he arrived the 12th. of *October* following. Let it suffice therefore, that having receiv'd the Submission of the Magistrates of *Augsburgh*, to whom His Grace was pleas'd to say, They had nothing to fear from the Troops of Her *Britannick* Majesty, and the *States-General*, who were only sent against the Enemies of the Empire and their Allies; and afterwards, had the News of the Surrender of *Ulm* and *Memmgen*, seen the Articles of Capitulation between the Electoress of *Bavaria* and Count *Wratislaw*, about Her giving up that Electorate to the Empire, and been present at great part of the Siege of *Landaw*, that was carried on by the King of the *Romans* in Person, and under him by Prince *Lewis* of *Baden*; upon Advice that the *French* intended to send a Detachment from the *Netherlands* to secure *Triers*, His Grace sent some Battalions, and a Party of Dragoons to possess *Homburgh*, and Fortifie that Post. This Detachment was follow'd by another, and by the Duke in Person, who in four Days March arrived at *Hermerdill*, within 6 Leagues of *Triers*, where three Deputies of the City waited on Him, and made Him acquainted that the *French* having still 300 Men in the Fort St. *Martin*, they were apprehensive of some ill Usage, if His Grace did not prevent it. Whereupon, he March'd the next Morning before break of Day, and about 11 the same Day, appear'd in sight of *Triers*; so that the Enemy abandon'd that Fort in hast.

Being in Possession of that Important Post, He Summon'd a great Number of Pioniers to Work on the Fortifications, and view'd the Ground about the *Saar*, in order to mark out a Camp for the Horse to cover those Work men: He went towards *Traerback*;

I.

erback, to make a narrow Inspection into the strength of the Place, and give the necessary Directions for the Siege of it; the Care of which, was committed to the Prince of *Hesse*. He returned the next Day towards *Landaw*, where he found the Besiegers, Masters of the Counterscarp, and afterwards arriv'd at *Croon-Weissenbourgh*, somewhat displeas'd with the slowness of the Siege, and considering that the *French* had sent all the Horse of their Houshold from their Camp at *Haguenau*, to put them into Winter Quarters, His Grace order'd the *English* Cavalry to March from *Croon-Weissenbourg* towards *Holland*.

The Siege of *Landaw* being ended by a Surrender of the Town, after two Months open Trenches, with the loss of Two Thousand Men Killed on the part of the Imperialists, and Four Thousand on that of the *French*. The Duke of *Marlborough* took his leave of the King of the *Romans*, and the other Generals, and having order'd the *English* Foot to Decamp, and March towards the *Rhine*, to be Embark'd there for *Holland*, and taken the necessary measures for the Winter Quarters of the rest of the Forces under his Command, resolved to Crown his Glorious Campagne, by an Important Negotiation with the King of *Prussia*, in Favour of the Duke of *Savoy*; which He not only accomplish'd by prevailing with His Majesty, to continue the 8000 *Prussians* which he had in *Italy* in that Service; but by laying down such Schemes to the Court of *Berlin*, as put by their pursuit of their Pretensions about His Majesty's Right of Inheritance, to the late King *William*'s Estate, to a more convenient Opportunity This being one of the great Services that could be done at this Juncture, when that King was taking measures to assert his just Rights, was acknowledged as such, by the whole Confederacy in general, and not only His Majesty of *Prussia* dismiss'd Him with Presents of an inestimable Value, as a

Token

Token of his Esteem for his Person, and great satisfaction in his Graces Negotiations, but the States-General order'd a particular Deputation of the Council of State, to attend him with their Thanks and Acknowledgments at His Arrival at the *Hague*, where he receiv'd the same from all the Ministers of the Foreign Princes that resided there, on the part of the Grand Alliance.

At his entrance the next Day into that Illustrious Assembly, which was conven'd for that purpose, the President for that Week Monsieur *Ittersum*, Address'd himself to His Grace in the Name of the Deputies of the several Cities and Provinces in these Words.

"Your Highness is happily Arrived in these
"Provinces, laden with Laurels and fresh Ho-
"nour, from the remotest part of *Germany*, whe-
"ther the same Success that has attended you on
"the *Maese*, the *Demer* and the *Scheld* Triumphantly
"follow'd you to the *Rhine* and *Danube*. The Victo-
"ries you have gain'd on the latter, are pregnant
"Instances of your great Skill and Experience
"in Military Affairs, and are so many Repetitions
"of what had before been done on the Former.
"Wherefore this State which is next under God,
"endebted to your Prudence and Care in the Con-
"duct of their Troops, for the many Advantages
"they have lately gain'd over the Common Ene-
"my, Congratulates you by Me, upon your Pre-
"servation of the Empire, the Reduction of *Ba-
"varia*; the Recovery of the Towns, you have
"rescued out of their Hands; and your safe Arri-
"val in these Parts, where your Presence is high-
"ly acceptable, and where their High Mighti-
"nesses are prepared to enter into such further
"Measures with you, as shall be most Conducive
"to the Re-establishment of the Publick Peace, and
"to the Honour and Welfare of the High Allies,
"among whom, they shall always in a particular

"manner

" manner have at Heart, that of Your Highnesses
" Mistress the Queen of Great *Britain*.

The Dukes ANSWER.

High and Mighty LORDS,

" AS the Honour that is this Day done me, is
" infinitely Superior to any Services of
" mine, so I cannot but acquaint your High
" Mightiness's that I shall always think it owing to
" the Bravery of your Troops, without whose A-
" ssistance, my endeavours to succour *Germany*,
" would have been of no Effect. I must likewise
" do this Justice to the Troops of the Empire,
" that they very much Contributed to their own
" Preservation, under the Conduct of their In-
" comparable Leaders, and if any thing that has
" been done by Me, or the Troops of my most
" Gracious Mistress shall be of Importance enough
" to bring the Enemy to Reason, in a safe and
" Honourable Peace, I shall think my self abun-
" dantly Compensated, as well as the Queen, who
" enter'd into this War for no other End.

Affairs being settled in *Holland*, in relation to the
ensuing Campagne, His Grace took Ship for *England*, where having been graciously receiv'd at
Court, by the Queen, and his Royal Highness, he
was complimented on the part of the House of
Peers, by the Lord-Keeper, in the following
Speech.

My Lord Duke of Marlborough,

" THE happy Success that hath attended Her
" Majesty's Armies, under Your Grace's
" command in *Germany*, the last Campagne, is so
truly

" truly Great, so truly Glorious in all its Circum-
" stances, that few Instances, in the Histories of
" former Ages, can equal, much less excel the
" Lustre of it.

" Your Grace has not overthrown young unskil-
" ful Generals, raw and undisciplin'd Troops, but
" Your Grace has conquer'd the *French* and *Bava-*
" *rian* Armies: Armies that were fully instructed
" in all the Arts of War; Select Veteran Troops,
" flush'd with former Victories, and commanded
" by Generals of great Experience and Bravery.

" The Glorious Victories Your Grace has ob-
" tain'd at *Schellembergh* and *Hochstedt*, are very
" Great, very Illustrious in themselves; but they
" are greater still in their Consequences to Her
" Majesty, and Her Allies.

" The Emperor is thereby reliev'd; the Empire
" it self freed from a dangerous Enemy, in the
" very Bowels of it; the exorbitant Power of
" *France* is check'd; and, I hope, a happy Step
" made towards reducing that Monarch within
" his due Bounds, and securing the Liberties of
" *Europe*.

" The Honour of these Glorious Victories,
" Great as they are, (under the immediate Bles-
" sing of Almighty God) is chiefly, if not alone,
" owing to Your Grace's Conduct and Valour.

" This is the unanimous Voice of *England*, and
" all Her Majesty's Alllies.

My LORD,

" THIS Most Honourable House is highly
" sensible of the Great and Signal Services Your
" Grace has done Her Majesty, this Campagne,
" and of the Immortal Honour you have done the
" *English* Nation; and have commanded me to give
" you their Thanks for the same.

" And

" And I do accordingly give Your Grace the
" Thanks of this House for the great Honour Your
" Grace has done the Nation, and for the Great
" and Signal Services you have done Her Majesty,
" and this Kingdom, the last Campagne.

To which the Duke reply'd.

My LORDS,

" I Am extremely sensible of the great Honour
" Your Lordships are pleas'd to do me. I
" must beg on this Occasion to do right to all the
" Officers and Soldiers I had the Honour of ha-
" ving under my Command; next to the Blef-
" sing of God, the good Success of this Campagne
" is owing to their extraordinary Courage.
" I am very sure, it will be a great Satisfaction,
" as well as Encouragement to the whole Army,
" to find their Services so favourably accepted.

The Commons likewise had the following Answer to their Deputation, with Thanks, sent to attend His Grace at his Apartments in St. *James's*-
Palace.

Gentlemen,

" IT'S a great Satisfaction to me, to find that
" my Faithful Endeavours, in discharging
" my Duty to the Queen, and to the Public, are
" so favourably accepted. I beg leave to take this
" Opportunity of doing Justice to a great Body
" of Officers and Soldiers, who accompanied me
" in this Expedition, and all behaved themselves
" with the greatest Bravery imaginable. And, I
" am sure, this Honour done us by the House of
" Commons, in taking so much Notice of it, will
" give

"give a general Satisfaction and Encouragement
"to the whole Army.

Some few Days after, the Commons took into consideration the great Services that had been perform'd by the Duke of *Marlborough*, the last Summer, and to consider of some means to perpetuate the memory of them: They came to this unanimous Resolution.

"That an humble Address be presented to Her
"Majesty, expressing the great Sense this House
"hath of the Glorious Victories obtain'd by the
"Forces of Her Majesty, and Her Allies, under
"the Command of His Grace the Duke of *Marl-*
"*borough*: And humbly desir'd Her Majesty, That
"She would be graciously pleas'd to consider of
"some proper Means to perpetuate the Memo-
"ry of the great Services perform'd by the said
"Duke.

Gentlemen,

"I Am very well pleas'd with your Address,
"and I will take into consideration, as you
"desire, and send you my Thoughts upon it, in
"a little Time.

Five Days after, Mr. Chancellor of the *Exchequer* acquainted the House, That he had a Message sign'd by Her Majesty: And he deliver'd it to Mr. Speaker, who read the same to the House, and was as followeth.

ANNE, R.

"HER Majesty having taken into Conside-
"ration the Address of this House, rela-
"ting to the great Services perform'd by the
Duke

" Duke of *Marlborough*, does incline to grant the
" Interest of the Crown, in the Honour and Man-
" nor of *Woodstock*, and Hundred of *Wootton*, to him
" and his Heirs; and desires the Assistance of this
" House, upon this extraordinary Occasion.

" The Lieutenancy and Rangership of the Parks,
" with the Rents and Profits of the Mannor and
" Hundreds, being granted for Two Lives, Her
" Majesty thinks it proper, that Incumbrace should
" be clear'd.

Upon which, the House brought in a Bill, and desired Her Majesty to advance Money for the clearing of the Incumbrance of the said Mannor and Hundreds, in order to the present Settlement thereof upon the Duke of *Marlborough*, and his Heirs.

The Duke was very serviceable, by his Interest, during this Session of Parliament, in preventing the Tacking the *Occasional Conformity-Bill* to one for Money; and tho' he had all along given his Vote in the House of Peers, against such a scandalous Evasion of the Penal-Laws, as the Practice endeavour'd to be exploded by that useful Bill; was not wanting, in Address, to draw off many Members, that were equally desirous it should pass, with himself. But as this was misconstrued by those who call'd themselves *The Church-Party*; so some Removals that succeeded it, wherein His Grace's Advice was suspected to have a great Share, render'd him more and more obnoxious to them. Whereupon the *Whigs*, who had before, in their Weekly Papers, traduc'd and ridicul'd him, by calling him, *Sine clade Victor*, till after this Campagne; were pleas'd, thence-forward, to take him into their Favour, and, by way of contradiction, make a very Idol of him.

The Parliament being broken-up, at the Close of which, Her Majesty, her self, was pleas'd to
call

call the *TACK, A Dangerous Experiment*, the Duke of *Marlborough* return'd again to the *Hague*, and having regulated the Operations of the Army, set out for the Place of their Encampment near *Mastricht*, where having view'd the *English* Troops that had taken up their Stations along the *Maeze*, he pass'd that River the 17th of *April*, 1705, and bent his March, according to his Agreement with the Prince of *Baden*, towards the *Moselle*, and went from *Coblentz*, to confer with that Prince, at his Residence at *Radstat*, giving Orders, in the mean Time for the Troops to continue their March. Having settled Matters with His Highness, he arriv'd, some Time after at *Triers*, and assembled all the Troops in that Neighbourhood, and pass'd the *Moselle* at *Igel*, with the *English*, while the *Dutch*, and others in the Pay of *Great Britain* and *Holland*, pass'd the *Saar* at the same Time, and join'd the *English*.

His Grace advanc'd by the most difficult Defile of *Taverny*, where it was expected that Marshal *Villars*, who, with a numerous Army, lay near *Sirk*, would have oppos'd his March, which he might have done with great advantage; but he did not attempt it, so that the Confederates encamp'd within a Mile of *Sirk*, and the next Morning made a Motion, and took the Camp at *Elst*, the Enemy retreating before them to *Conings-Macheren*, possessing themselves of a very advantagious Post, which they made yet stronger, by casting up Entrenchments, and felling down Trees, so that it was impossible to attack them in that Camp, with any probability of Success. Which, indeed, was not the *English* Generals Design, for he was advanced so far only to cover the Siege of *Saar-Louis*, which was to have been carried on by a Detachment of Imperial Troops, that Prince *Lewis* had promised to bring from *Lauterburgh*, and by some Forces in the Pay of *England* and *Holland*. The Duke dispatch'd frequent

quent Expresses, to quicken the March of those Forces, and to exhort the Princes, who had promis'd to furnish Artillery, Horses and Waggons, to send the same with all speed; but all these lively Remonstrances had no effect, and the Imperialists, who were to have been on the *Rhine*, on the 9th or 10th of *June*, were not arrived the 28th, nor were there either Horses or Artillery provided.

In the mean Time, the Forces of the States-General being very much weaken'd by the Detachments sent to the *Moselle*, it was thought fit that the Remains of the Army, under the command of Monsieur *Auverquerque* should stand on the Defensive, and entrench themselves near *Maestricht*, expecting the *French* would be obliged to send a strong Re-inforcement from thence to the Marshal *Villars*, but they were deceived in their Expectation, for the Enemy being informed how Things passed on that Side, resolved to make their advantage of it; and coming out of their Lines, march'd and invested *Huy*, the Town of which Name they were Masters of the same Day, and the next, storm'd Fort St. *Joseph*, but were vigorously repuls'd in Three Attacks. Three Days after they possess'd themselves of Fort *Picard*, and another called the *Red-Fort*; and then batter'd the Castle with abundance of Fury, when the necessary Preparations for an Assault being made, and the Breaches so wide, that the defence of the Place, any longer, seem'd impossible, the Governour beat the *Chamade*, but could obtain no other Conditions, than that the Garrison should have the Honour to march out at the Breach, with their Arms, and then lay them down, and surrender themselves Prisoners of War.

The News of the taking of *Huy*, reaching the Duke of *Marlborough*'s Army, the Deputies of the States represented to his Grace, That it was impossible to subsist any longer in his Camp; and that

that the *Germans*, by their Slowness, having defeated all their Projects on the *Moselle*, it was to no purpose to continue any longer in those Parts, when the Army might be much better employ'd in the *Netherlands*, in stopping the Progress of the Enemy. So that, in a Council of War, held at *Triers*, it was resolved, That the Confederates should march back to the *Maeze*, except 7000 *Palatines*, in the Pay of *England* and *Holland*, who were left at *Triers*. According to this Resolution, his Grace marched for the *Netherlands*, and the *Imperial*, *Prussian*, and *Wirtembergh* Troops, who had but just before joined them, moved towards the *Upper-Rhine*.

Marshal *de Villars*, likewise, having now no Enemy now to fear, made a Detachment to reinforce the Elector of *Bavaria* in the *Netherlands*, and another to strengthen the Marshal *de Marsin* in *Alsace*, advancing with the rest of his Army toward the *Saar*. Upon his approach, the Governour of *Saarbach* quitted the Castle, and blew up the Fortifications, and Monsieur *Aubach*, who commanded the *Palatine* Troops in *Triers*, by an unpardonable Oversight, did the same, for even before any Enemy appeared in sight, he destroyed all the Magazines the *English* and *Dutch* had erected there, at an incredible Expence, blew up the Fortifications, burnt the Boats designed to make Bridges, and fled from that important Post. After which, *Villars* marched to join *Marsin*, and, in conjunction with him beat the *Imperialists* from the Lines of *Croon-Wissenbergh*.

In the mean Time, the Duke of *Marlborough*, by his diligent March, arrived Time enough to save the Citadel of *Liege*, which the *French*, after the Reduction of *Huy*, had laid Siege to, so that the face of Affairs was immediately chang'd in the *Netherlands*, for the Enemy, upon Advice of his Grace his approach, sent back their Artillery to

K 2 *Namur*,

Namur, and retired in great Precipitation to *Tongeren*. On the other Hand, his Grace continuing his March, arriv'd at *Maestricht* the 27th of *June*, and having taken Measures with Monsieur *d'Auverquerque*, and the other Generals, to march towards the Enemy; they decamp'd for that purpose, but the *French* thought fit to prevent them, and retired from *Tongeren*, nearer to their Lines. On the 2d of *July* the Duke pass'd the *Maese*, and advanced to *Haneff*, while the Forces, under Monsieur *Auverquerque*, march'd at the same Time to *Theys*, upon the *Jaar*. The Enemy having Notice of this March, decamped in haste, and, as it were, fled into their Lines, having sent away most of their heavy Baggage the Day before.

The *French* having thus secured themselves within their Lines, the Confederate Generals thought fit to take the Castle of *Huy*, before they proceeded further, and to that End made a Detachment under General *Scholten*, to invest that Place, while the Duke of *Marlborough*, and Monsieur *d'Auverquerque*, made each a small Motion to cover the Siege. Two Days after the Batteries began to play against Fort *Picard*, and the Dispositions being made for attacking it, the Allies soon made themselves Masters of the Cover'd Way, and were resolutely climbing up the Fort, which the Enemy perceiving, fled into the Castle. They had quitted the *Red-Fort* 2 Hours before. The next Day a Battery was brought to play against the Castle, and another was erected in Fort St. *Joseph*, so that a considerable Breach being made, the Enemy beat a Parley, and demanded to march out, and be conducted to *Namure*, which being refused, they surrendred upon the same Conditions as had been granted to the *Dutch* 2 Months before.

After the Reduction of *Huy*, he resolved to undertake more considerable Actions; and as nothing appeared more Glorious and Advantagious, in it

Consequence,

Consequence, than the attacking the Enemies Lines, his Grace sent General *Hompesch* to propose it to the States, who return'd Answer, That having an entire Confidence in the Conduct and Prudence of that Renowned General, they left it wholly to him, to do whatever he should think fit, for the Good of the Common Cause. Upon this, his Grace held a General Council of War, wherein that Undertaking was debated, but nothing being resolved on the first Time, a second Council was called, when some of the *Dutch* Generals oppos'd it; but Monsieur *d'Auverquerque*, the Prince of *Hesse*, Count *Noyelles*, and some others, gave unanswerable Reasons, why it ought to be undertaken, so that the Attack was entirely resolved on.

The Enemy were posted along their Lines, with near 100 Battalions, and near 146 Squadrons, and the Allies having 92 Battalions, and 146 Squadrons, the Two Armies were pretty equal. It was therefore resolved to make a Feint, to divide the Enemies Forces; and, accordingly, the Army under Monsieur *d'Auverquerque* made a Motion on the other Side of the *Mehaigne*, and the Duke of *Marlborough* made another at the same Time, as if he intended to support him in the Attack of the Lines, about *Messelin*, where they were not so strong as in other Places. This Stratagem succeeded to those Two Generals Wish, for these Motions, particularly the passing the *Mehaigne*, gave great Jealousie to the *French*, so that they bestow'd their chief Attention on that Side. Whereupon the Duke having made the necessary Dispositions, on the 17th of *July*, about 4 in the Morning, gave Order for the whole Army to get ready to march that Evening: And Count *Noyelles*, and General *Scholten* were directed to advance with the Two Bodies under their Command, about 9 of the clock directly to *Wangen* and *Elixhim*, which Two Posts they were to to attack, if the Posture of the Enemy permitted it; and about 10 his Grace's Army were to strike their Tents, and follow, marching directly towards the Lines, before the Two Bodies, aforesaid, were to force their Passage.

The Darkness of the Night somewhat puzled the Guides, that conducted those Detachments, so that it was half an Hour past 4 in the Morning, and broad Day before they came near the aforementioned Posts, which, according to Information, were found to be but thinly guarded. Count *de Noyelles* caus'd the Castle of *Wangh*, which defended a Stone-Bridge, that was there at the *Geete*, to be attack'd; but the *French* immediately abandon'd that Post, and gave an Opportunity to the Grenadiers, that were order'd on that Service, to march forwards, and attack the Barrier of that Line, which the Guards there did not defend much better than the other had done the Castle, and so the Troops enter'd the Line, on that Side, with little or no Opposition, although the Enemy had 12 Squadrons of Dragoons encamped behind *Oastmalen*, (within a Cannon-shot of the Place where the first Detachment enter'd) which immediately mounted their Horses, but durst not advance to defend their Barriers. At the same Time 3 Battalions possess'd themselves of the Bridge and Village of *Hethshenn*, a quarter of a League from *Wangh*, on the Left, which was done with as little Opposition: Nor did Lieutenant-General *Scholten* meet with greater Resistance at the Villages of *Over-hespen* and *Neer-hespen*: So that being Masters of those Bridges and Barriers, and having made several other Bridges, the Horse went over them, and immediately rang'd themselves in order on the Height, extending their Right towards the Village of *Hackendoven*, and some Battalions drew up along the Line, and behind the Horse.

Whilst

Whilst the Workmen were busy'd in making Passages through the Line, 10 of the Enemy's Squadrons and 4 Battalions, were perceived between the Villages of *Gouchancourt* and *Eſtmale*; but they gave Time to the Confederate Forces to extend themſelves, endeavouring only to advance to the Village of *Elixheim*. The Count *de Noyelles* caus'd the Troops he had with him to go over as faſt as poſſible: And thereupon the Duke of *Marlborough* arriving with his whole Army, his Cavalry went over the Line with extraordinary Expedition, as the reſt had done, and ſo they all made up towards the Enemy, who by this time were reinforced to the number of 50 Squadrons and 20 Battalions, and advanced with great Reſolution behind the hollow Way that goes from *Elixheim* to *Tirlemont*. This obliged the Confederate Horſe to make a ſtand a few Minutes, till ſome Battalions advancing, lined the *Hollow Way*, and firing upon the Enemy's Horſe, obliged them to retire out of the Reach of their Muskets, and to form themſelves before their Infantry, which gave an Opportunity for the Cavalry to paſs the *Hollow Way* In the mean time, the *French* caused 8 Pieces of Cannon with treble Barrels, to advance, with which they made a terrible Fire on the Confederate Horſe; but the Duke of *Marlborough* being come in Perſon at the Head of freſh Squadrons, and ſeeing that the Enemy were continually receiving Reinforcements, and that their Infantry was going to join them, his Grace reſolved to charge them with Horſe only, which was done with that Ardor and Courage, that the Cavalry of the Two Crowns being ſoon broken and put to flight, they went to rally themſelves behind their Infantry, whilſt his victorious Horſe poſſeſs'd themſelves of the Cannon and Ammunition Waggons The Enemy being join'd with ſome Squadrons, and having interlined ſome Battalions with them, moved again towards the Confederates; but the

the latter being likewise reinforced, and sustained by their Infantry, made Advances to receive them.

The Right of the Confederate Horse coming too near the Hedges of the Village of *Eismale*, which were lined with *French* and *Bavarian* Foot, were somewhat disorder'd by their Fire, and oblig'd to shrink back; but having soon after extended themselves more towards the Right, to make way for some Battalions that marched against the Enemy's Foot, they both charg'd with that Bravery and Briskness that the Enemy's Horse was soon defeated and cut in Pieces, and their Infantry being left along in the Plain, had much ado to get away in Disorder, between the Villages of *Heilsheim* and *Gershoven*, where they met with the rest of the Army, and formed themselves as well as they could. In the mean time the Duke of *Marlborough* caused the rest of his Troops to enter the Lines, and extended the Right of his Army towards the Grü Geete before *Tirlemont*, in which Town they took the Battalion of *Monluch*, which upon the first Summons surrender'd at Discretion. In this Action the Marquis *d'Alegre* and the Count *de Horne*, Lieutenant-Generals, a Major General, Two Brigadiers, and several other Officers of all Ranks, besides abundance of private Men, were made Prisoners, 10 Pieces of Cannon, 9 Standards, 4 Colours, and 1 Pair of Kittle-Drums, were likewise taken; and the News of so momenteous an Advantage being of too great Importance not to be dispatch'd immediately to the States General, Lieutenant-General *Hompesch* was immediately after the Reduction of *Tirlemont*, sent for that purpose with this Letter from his Grace.

High and Mighty LORDS,

"I Congratulate your High Mightinesses upon
" our happy Entrance into the Lines, an
" th

' the Defeat of a considerable Body of the Enemy,
' who offered to dispute the same. We began our
' March about 10 at Night, and Count *de Noyelles*
' who commanded a Detachment of 38 Squadrons
' and 20 Battalions; which I had sent to surprize
' the Posts of *Neechespen* and *Heilsheim*, had all the
' desired Success, and distinguish'd himself in a
' particular Manner; as did also the Prince of
' *Hesse*, and all the other Generals, who were in
' the Action. The Troops did also express such
' Bravery, as was even beyond our Hopes. The
' Enemies being repulsed, I caus'd the Forces to
' advance towards this Place, where I obliged the
' Battalion of *Monluc* to surrender themselves Pri-
' soners. I thought this good News deserved to
' be sent to your High Mightinesses by a Person
' of Note, and I have chosen Lieutenant-General
' *Hompesch*, who had a great share therein, to in-
' form you of the other Particulars, referring to
' my next to give your High Mightinesses an
' exact Account of the Prisoners, Cannon, and
' Standards, taken from the Enemy. I intend to
' advance to morrow towards *Louvain*. I am with
' an inviolable Respect,

Your HIGH MIGHTINESSES

Most Humble, and most Obedient Servant,

From the Camp at Tirle-   (S'gn'd)
mont, July 18 1705.

The Prince *and* Duke *of* MARLBOROUGH.

After the Defeat of the Body commanded by
Monsieur *d'Allegre*, the Elector of *Bavaria* and
Marshal *de Villeroy*, consulted for the safety of the
rest of the Army, and decamping in the sight of the
Confederates, pass'd the *Geete* and the *Dyle* with

all imaginable Diligence, and pich'd their Tents in the strong Camp at *Park*, with their Left at *Roselaer*, and their Right against the Height of *Louvain* at *Wineselen*: From whence the Elector writ to the Baron of *Mulbrecht*, his Favourite, after this manner. Dear Baron, *God forgive those who suffered themselves to be surpriz'd, the whole Army is here, and the Evil is not so great as to be past Remedy. The Country of* Brabant *may be saved, as well as* Antwerp, *if it pleases God. I am well, but exceedingly fatigued.* On the other hand, the Duke of *Marlborough* passed the *Great Geete*, and encamped with the Right at *Rosbeeck*, and the Left behind *Tirlemont*, and that of Monsieur *d'Auverquerque* extended it self with the Right to *Grain*, and the Left to *Blixbeim*. In this Camp his Grace receiv'd the following Letter from the States, in Answer to his dated at *Tirlemont*.

SIR,

" WE do not believe it is necessary to use
" many Words to convince your Excel-
" lency what Joy your Letter of the 18th past caus'd
" amongst us, since it gave us the News of your
" glorious Entring with the Army within the
" Lines, as well as of the Defeat of part of the
" Enemy's Forces: A happy Success for which we
" have offered up many Vows. The Lieutenant-
" General Baron *d'Hompesche*, who brought us the
" Letter, has given us a full Account of all that
" pass'd on that Occasion. Our Generals allow,
" that this Victory, under God, is entirely due
" to your Excellency's Care, Prudence, and Va-
" lour, having surmounted and conquer'd those
" Difficulties and Obstacles, which, for above
" Two Years have appeared unsurmountable and
" invincible. This gives new Lustre to your Lau-
" rels, at the same time that it adds to their Num-
" ber. We heartily congratulate your Excellency
" upon

"upon it, and do not less Interest our selves in
"your Glory, than in the Advantages you procure
"to the Publick We pray to God to bless all
"your Designs, and all your Enterprizes more and
"more. We cannot but entertain good Hopes of
"them for the future, and will use our utmost
"Endeavours to facilitate the Execution of them.
"We will never forget the good Services you ren-
"der to our State, and the Esteem we have for
"your Person, and your Merit encreasing every
"Day. We shall ever be,

SIR,

*Your Excellencies most Affectionate to render
you Service,*

The States-General of the United Provinces
of the Low Countries,

At the Hague,
Aug 22. 1711.

F. V. REEDE.

By their Order,

F. FAGEL.

The Emperor likewise upon the same Occasion was pleased to declare to Colonel *Richards*, one of the Duke's Adjutants, who brought him an Account of the Enemy's Defeat abovemention'd, That *his Grace's Services to the Common Cause in General, and particular to his Family, were such that they should never be forgotten by him, nor his Posterity.* The next Day the Confederate Army moved, and in their March took about 1200 Prisoners, who could not follow the precipitate March of the fugitive Enemy, and encamped the same Evening within Cannon-shot of *Landau*. But, tho' by this Success, the Troops of the Two Crowns were forced to abandon *Diest*, *Sichem*, *Arschot*, and some other small Places, yet the suffering them to possess themselves of the strong Post of *Park*, which was look'd upon by those who had not implicite Value for all his Grace's Actions as a great Oversight in the Duke, who they say had it in his Power to have posted himself there before them) hindred the further Progress of the Campaign: For that General afterwards endeavouring to force some Pass upon the *Dyle*, could not succeed therein, so that He marched from thence to *Meldest*.

The Enterprize on the *Dyle* appearing impracticable, his Grace sent the Baron *de Hompesche* to propose a new Project to the States-General, which their High Mightinesses approv'd by Directions to their Deputies in the Army, to make two or three Marches, without calling a Council of War, to favour the Design formed by the Duke. While Baron *Spaar* was ordered to make a Diversion for the same purpose, by Attacking the Enemy's Lines in *Flanders*, which he succeeded in by possessing himself of Four Forts, and taking several Officers and 200 private Men, Prisoners, but afterward retired upon account of their advancing against him with a superior Force, carrying away with him several Hostages for the Payment of Contributions.

In the mean time, the Duke having left Two Battalions at *Tirlemont*, and as many at *Diest*, marched to *Genape*, whence he detach'd General *Church* with 20 Battalions to *Fishermont*, where his Grace joined him the next Day. This sudden March kept the Enemy in continual Alarms, not knowing where the Storm might fall: However, the Elector of *Bavaria* and Marshal *Villeroy* only stretched their Right to *Over-Ysche*, and kept their Left at *Nether-Ysche*, with the little River *Ysche* before them, by which they covered both *Louvain* and *Brussels*.

(77)

The next Morning, (viz. the 18th of *August*) by break of Day, the Allies filed off with the Right-Wing, in Two Columns, and pass'd the long narrow Road of *Hulpen*, where they were not a little surpriz'd to find no Enemy, on account of the difficulty of that Pass. About Noon the whole Army was drawn up, in sight of the Enemy, whom the Duke of *Marlborough*, and Monsieur *d'Auverquerque* having viewed, they were both of Opinion to attack them immediately, before they had Time to recover the Consternation, which was apparent enough in their Army. But the Artillery not being yet come up, (as some was) through Monsieur *Slangenburgh*'s Fault, who design'd to thwart the Duke, (because the Attack of the Lines was undertaken without his Privity or Consent.) and having also persuaded some other *Dutch* Commanders to join with him, they made a Report to the Deputies of the States, That the Enterprize was neither Adviseable nor Practicable; whereupon the Deputies absolutely refused to consent to it. His Grace submitted, tho' with great Regret, as appears by the Expostulatory Letter he writ next Day to their Principal, which was made public at the *Hague*, and occasion'd great Murmurings amongst the People. That *Letter* ran thus,

High and Mighty LORDS,

"According to what I had the Honour to
" write to Your *High Mightinesses*, the 13th,
" the Army march'd on *Saturday*, and encamp'd
" that Day at *Corbais*, and St. *Martin*'s, and the
" next Day at *Genap*. On *Munday* we came to *Fisher-*
" *mont*, and Yesterday we were in Motion before
" break of Day, and having pass'd several Defiles,
" we came into a pretty large Plain, having found
" the Enemy, as we expected them, between *O-*
" *ver-Ysche*, and *Neer-Ysche*, with the little Rivulet
" *Ysche*

"*Yser* before them. At Noon, or a little after, our whole Army was drawn up in order of Battle, and having view'd, with Monsieur *d'Auverquerque*, the Four Posts which I design'd to attack, I flatter'd my self, already considering the Goodness and Superiority of our Troops, that I might soon have congratulated Your High Mightinesses upon a Glorious Victory: But, at last, when the Attack was to begin, it was not thought fit to engage the Enemy. I am confident that Messieurs, the Deputies of Your High Mightinesses, will acquaint you with the Reasons that were alledg'd to them, *Pro* and *Con*; and they will, at the same Time, do Monsieur *d'Auverquerque* Justice, by informing you, that he was of the same Opinion with me, *That the Opportunity was too fair to be let slip.* However, I submitted, though with much Reluctancy.

"I shall speak this Day to Messieurs the Deputies, and to Monsieur *d'Auverquerque*, that they may give Orders for the Attack of *Leewe*, and for carrying on, at the same Time, the levelling of the Lines.

I am, with all manner of Respect,

Your HIGH MIGHTINESSES

Most Obedient Servant,

At the Camp at Lower-Wovre, *Aug.* 19. 1705.

The Prince *and* Duke *of* MARLBOROUGH.

P. S "My Heart is so full, that I cannot forbear representing to Your High Mightinesses, upon this Occasion, that I find my Authority here, to be much less, than when I had the Honour

nour to command your Troops, laſt Year, in *Germany*.

On the other hand, the *Dutch-Deputies* endeavour'd to juſtifie their Conduct, by a Letter they likewiſe wrote to their High Mightineſſes, which is alſo induſtriouſly diſpers'd, and for the ſake of Impartiality, ought not to be left out in this place, but to be communicated to the Public, in the following manner.

High and Mighty LORDS;

"WE made ſeveral Marches ſince the 15th
" Inſtant, according to the Duke of
" *Marlborough*'s Project, communicated to us. Yeſ-
" terday we broke up from *Brain la Leu*, as we
" had the Honour to ſignifie to Your High Migh-
" tineſſes, on *Munday* laſt, That our Deſign was
" to march further along the *Dyle*, with an In-
" tent to paſs the *Lane* and *Yſche*, and afterwards
" endeavour to make our ſelves Maſters of *Lou-*
" *vain*, or gain ſome greater Advantages for the
" Arms of the States, and the High Allies, by
" fighting the Enemy, if a *fair Occaſion* offer'd.
" Having paſs'd the *Lane*, where we wonder'd to
" find no Enemy to diſpute ſo difficult a Paſſage,
" we met with more Obſtacles at the *Yſche*; for,
" beſides the Report of *Three Generals*, which had
" view'd (*Slangenburgh*, *Zalich*, and *Dompre*) and
" ſaid there was no Ground for the Horſe, either
" to paſs, or be drawn up; we found the Paſſes
" ſo difficult, and the whole Enemies Army ſo
" well poſted to defend them, that we thought it
" was not to be attempted, without having firſt
" heard the Sentiments of Monſieur *d'Auverquerque*,
" and the other Generals, and Lieutenant-Gene-
" rals. We found them all, except Monſieur *Au-*
" *verquerque*, to be unanimouſly of Opinion That
" the

" the attacking of the Enemy, in the said Posts,
" would be attended with the greatest Difficulty
" and Hazard, to the Common Cause; alledging,
" That considering the Enemy could not be at-
" tack'd but with the greatest Disadvantage on
" our Side, we should, in case of a Defeat, be re
" duc'd to the greatest Straits imaginable, partly,
" because being so far advanced into the Enemy's
" Country, we should neither have had Places nor
" Hospitals to send our wounded Men to; and
" partly, because, in such a Case, the Enemy
" might easily have cut off our Convoys of Bread
" Besides which, the said Generals were of Opi-
" nion, That the Affairs of our High Allies, and
" our Republick, justly weigh'd, were not yet re
" duc'd to such a Condition, as to attempt, (as
" they call'd it) so *Desperate a Work*.

" We own, That my Lord Duke of *Marlborough*
" was of Opinion, as well as Monsieur *Auverquer-*
" *que*, That the Attack was practicable, and might
" be attended with Success; but we could not
" resolve to consent to a Thing of so great Im-
" portance, contrary to the Opinion of all the
" Generals of that Army, to which Your High
" Mightinesses have done us the Honour to de-
" pute us.

" And we hoping that we have fully satisfied the
" Intention of Your High Mightinesses, contai-
" ned in your Resolution of the 5th Instant, to
" permit the Duke of *Marlborough*, without the
" holding a Council of War, to make 2 or 3 Mar-
" ches, for the Execution of some Design, formed
" by his Grace. We therefore, for the future,
" shall regulate our Conduct, according to our
" Instructions, and Your High Mightinesses' Reso
" lution, of the 26th of *June* last, except Your
" High Mightinesses should be pleased to send us
" further Orders. And we cannot conceal from
" Your High Mightinesses, That all the Generals
" of

of our Army think it very strange, that they should not have the least Notice of the said Marches.

"This Day we came to encamp here, and design suddenly to march again, in order to besiege *Sout Leuwe*, so soon as the necessary Preparations shall be made ready. Wherewith,

HIGH and MIGHTY LORDS,

veren, Aug. 19. 1705.

(*Signed*)

ROUWENOORT,
VAN HEMSKIRK,
N. V. SCAAGEN.

What were their High Mightinesses Sentiments of this Affair, is left to the Reader's Conjecture, tho' 2 Days after the Reduction of *Sout Leuwe*, and the levelling of the Lines from *Wasseigne*, to that Place, his Grace went to *Turnhout*, to meet Monsieur *Buys*, Pensioner of *Amsterdam*, who was sent to confer with him, on the Part of the States General. What pass'd in that Interview, is not truly known, but it must be confess'd, there is room to intimate, that Mr. *Buys* assured his Grace of the Readiness of his Masters to give him all reasonable Satisfaction for the Disgust he had taken at some Passages at *Over-Ysche*, and to make him, for the future, more easie in his Command, by removing those who were most inclined to contradict him. Nor will this Surmise appear groundless, if we consider that the *English* Court, and, indeed, the Generality of the People, did at this Time so warmly espouse the Duke of *Marlborough*'s Resentment, that a Pamphlet, entituled, *The Dutch Politicks*, in which severe Reflections were made on the *Hollanders* in general, and in particular the State-

M   Deputies,

Deputies, for not suffering his Grace to fight the Enemy, was publickly sold, and escaped uncensur'd; and, which is more, the Earl of *Pembroke*, Lord President of the Council was named to go Envoy-Extraordinary to *Holland*, in order, as it was supposed, to expostulate the Matter with the States, but their High Mightinesses prevented his Lordship's Journey, by giving satisfaction to the Duke, and removing General *Slangenburgh*, who, from that Time, as well as the Deputies, never acted under the same Characters.

Nothing material happen'd, this Campagne, on the Side of the Allies, but the taking of *Sandvliet*, which, his Grace having given Orders to be invested, left the Army, and made a Journey to *Vienna*, upon an Invitation from the new Emperor, *Joseph* the *First* of that Name, to come thither, and concert the Operations of War for the ensuing Year; where he was receiv'd with extraordinary Marks of Distinction, after he had all the Honour pay'd him by the respective Princes, through whose Territories he pass'd, that could be expected by a Person of the highest Merit, having been presented with a Diamond-Ring of great value, by the Emperor; a Sword set round with Diamonds, by the King of *Prussia*; a fine Calash, and six Horses, by the Elector of *Hannover*, and other rich Presents by the Elector *Palatine*, and that of *Triers*.

From thence he return'd to the *Hague*, where having dispatch'd all Things previous to his Imbarkation, and found the States ready to comply with the Proposals he made, for bringing the Common Enemy to Reason, he arriv'd at *London*, during the Session of Parliament, and was not only graciously receiv'd by the Queen, but had the Thanks of the House of Commons, *for his great Services perform'd to Her Majesty, and the Nation, in the last Campagne, and for his prudent Negotiations*

as with Her Majesty's Allies. To which he was
pleased to reply:

Gentlemen,

"I Am so sensible of the great Honour that is
"done me by this Message, that I cannot
"have the least concern at any 𝔓𝔯𝔦𝔳𝔞𝔱𝔢 𝔐𝔞𝔩𝔦𝔠𝔢,
"while I have the satisfaction of finding my faith-
"ful Endeavours to serve the Queen and the King-
"dom, so favourably accepted by the *House of*
"*Commons.*

By *Private Malice*, the Reader is here to understand, some Passages are hinted at in a Pamphlet
called *The Memorial of the Church of England*, that
made free with his Grace's Character, and other
persons in eminent Posts about the Queen, which
Pamphlet, upon Her Majesty's having complain'd
in Her Speech to both Houses of Parliament, occasion'd great Enquiries, with a Promise of a Reward for the discovery of its Author, tho' to no
manner of effect, he remaining at that Time conceal'd, tho' since known.

But the House of Lords did not think fit to do
his Grace the same Honour, by congratulating him
on his taking his Seat among them, tho' my Lord
Haversham, in his way, seem'd to insinuate, he had
done Things that deserv'd their Thanks, if his
Lordship's manner of summing up the Merits of
the Campagne, may not be said to have Two
Handles.

"THE First Thing I shall speak to, (*said that
Noble Peer, in his Speech to the House of Lords, Nov. 15.)
"*is, The present Confederate War,* in which we are
"engag'd; and because the best way of judging
"what we may reasonably expect for the future,
"is to consider the Actions that are pass'd, give

"me leave a little to take notice to your Lord-
"ships of *the Operations of the last Campagne*. I shall
"not say much of our *Forcing the* French *Lines*, and
"our *Beating the* French *Troops afterwards*, tho' that
"was a very great and brave Action, but because
"there was such a *Mixture of Victory and Misfor-*
"*tune*; and that this is such a chequer'd Piece,
"I purposely forbear taking further notice of it.

"But there were Two other Actions, which, I
"think, take in your whole Campagne, *the March*
"*of our Army to the Moselle*, and the *Business of Over-*
"*Yssche*; in both which, give me leave to say, (not
"to give it a harder Term) we were not used as
"we might have reasonably expected. Our Ge-
"neral, with a great deal of Conduct, *covered*
"*Prince* Lewis *of* Baden's *Army*, nor can it be
"doubted, he might easily have joined us, if he
"had pleased, without the least danger from the
"French; which, if he had done, by the best Ac-
"count I could ever get, (and I think I have
"a very true one) we had been, at least, *Five*
"*and twenty thousand stronger than the* French *there*;
"but being disappointed of being joined by Prince
"Lewis, and of the Assistance we expected from
"him, *that great Design proved abortive*.

"The next was the Business of *Over-Yssche*, when
"by the Conduct of my Lord Duke of *Marlbo-*
"*rough*, we had a fair Opportunity of *putting an*
"*End to the War at once, the* Dutch *held our Hand*,
"*and would not let us give the deciding Blow*.

"Thus ended your Campagne, tho' it began
"with more promising Hopes of Success, than
"this next I believe will: You had then an Ene-
"my to deal with, whose Counsels were distract-
"ed, whose Troops were broke, and the Courage
"of his Army sunk, &c.

Whatever the Intent of the foregoing Speech
was, the Result of it ended in a Joint-Address

both Houses, for Her Majesty to keep up a good Correspondence with Her Allies, especially the *Dutch*, for which the Duke of *Marlborough* had Orders given him, by Her Majesty, as well as the Envoy-Extraordinary, who resided with them on the Part of *Great-Britain* The Session being ended, his Grace return'd to his wonted Employment, and the Army of the States having been drawn together near *Tongeren*, to the number of 60 Battalions, and 90 Squadrons, and being join'd by the *English*, arriv'd in the Army on the 12th of *May*, 1706. Here he resolv'd, in Conjunction with Monsieur *d'Auverquerque*, and the other Generals, to lose no Time, but to push the Campagne forward, before Marshal *Marsin* could come from the *Moselle*, to strengthen the *French* Army on that Side; who, after a successful Expedition into *Germany*, was upon full March to join the Duke of *Bavaria* and *Villeroy*. These Two Generals had drawn together the Armies of the Two Crowns, near *Louvain*, and pass'd the *Dyle* the 19th Instant, and posted themselves between *Tirlemont* and *Judoigne*, with the *Gheete* before them; whereupon the Duke of *Marlborough* sent Orders to the *Danish* Troops, who were advancing from their Quarters, to hasten their March, resolving to make towards the Enemy, (without staying for the *Hessian* and *Hannover* Troops, who were at that Time upon the *Rhine*) and either oblige them to retire, or bring them to a Battle. This was not hard to effect; for they having drain'd all their Garrisons, and depending on their Superiority, had taken a Resolution to attack him before those Troops came up. This the Duke had notice of, and was very well pleased that they would afford him an Opportunity, which he doubted would have cost him some trouble, and therefore to save them the trouble, he advanced towards them. In the mean Time the heavy Baggage was sent by the Way of *Borgworm* to *Tourine*, and on *Sunday* the 23d, N. S. the Army went in Quest of the *French*, in order of Battle, taking their Rout between *Meerdorp* and *Bonef*. In this March they discover'd some of the Enemy's Hussars, and about Ten in the Morning the Main Body of the Army, which was advanc'd as far as *Ramilly*, *Offuz*, and *Taviers*, Villages situate between the *Mebaigne* and the *Yause*, where they had posted a Body of 18 or 20 Battalions that had entrench'd themselves. In the mean time their Army was drawn up in Battalia, as was that of the Allies by their Generals; the Right Wing of the first extending as far as the *Mebaigne*, and their Left to *Judoigne*, and the Posture of the last in their Right near *Foltz* on the *Yause*, with a little Morass in the Front, and the Left near *Branchu* on the *Mebaigne*.

The Enemy had posted a Brigade of Foot next to the *Mebaigne*, and filled the Space betwixt that and *Ramillies* with upwards of 100 Squadrons, among which were the Troops of the *French* King's Houshold: At *Ramillies* they had about Ten or Twelve Pieces of Treble Cannon. From thence to *Anterglise*, they had formed a Line of Horse at some Distance behind them.

His Grace judging by the Situation of the Ground, that the stress of the Action would be on the Left, order'd that besides the number of Horse belonging to that Wing, the *Danish* Squadrons, being Twenty in Number, should also be posted there. It was about Two in the Afternoon before the Confederate Army could be form'd into the Order, it was thought fit to engage in, and then they began the Attack on their Left with Four Battalions, which push'd the Brigade abovemention'd from their Post on the *Mebaigne*. Monsieur d'*Auverquerque* about the same time charged with the Horse of that Wing. The Success was doubtful for about half an Hour, which the Duke of *Marlborough*

borough perceiving, order'd the rest of the Horse of the Right Wing (except the *English*, who were 17 Squadrons, and kept for a Body of Reserve) to support those on the Left.

Here, while his Grace was rallying some, and giving his Orders to some, he was in very great Danger, being singled out by several of the most Resolute of the Enemy, and falling from his Horse at the same time, had either been kill'd, or taken Prisoner, if some of his own Foot, that were near at hand, had not come very seasonably to his Assistance, and oblig'd the *French* to retire. After this, the Duke had still a greater Escape from a Cannon-Ball that took off Col. *Brinfield*'s Head, as he was remounting his Grace

The Village of *Ramellies* was attacked by a Detachment of 12 Battalions, commanded by Lieutenant-General *Schultz*, which enter'd at once with great Vigour and Resolution. His Grace hasten'd the Line of Foot thither to support them, which, though it was at a great Distance, yet came up soon enough to beat the Enemy quite out of the Village; and at the same time charged the rest of the Foot that were posted behind the *Geete*, while the *English* Horse were order'd to support them.

By this time the Enemy's Right Wing of Horse being entirely defeated, the Horse of the Duke's Left Wing fell upon the Foot on their Right, of whom they slew great Numbers, cutting in Pieces about Twenty of their Battalions; whose Colours they Took, and likewise Cannon. The rest of the Enemy's Infantry were entirely broken, though the Horse of their Left Wing seemed to make a stand, to gain time for their Foot to retire, but were charged so quick, and with so much Bravery, by the *English* Horse, led on by his Grace in Person, that they altogether abandon'd their Foot, and the Confederate Dragoons pushing into the Village

lage of *Autreglise*, made a terrible Slaughter of them; the *French* King's own Regiment of Foot, called the Regiment *de Roy*, begging for Quarter.

Then their Left Wing being attack'd in Flank, the *English* Regiments of *Churchill* and *Mordaunt*, getting over the Morass towards the end of the Action, and charging them there, likewise was put to the Rout, some flying towards *Namur*, and others elsewhere; so that the Victory was entire on the side of the Allies, who took more than 5000 Prisoners, and kill'd 8000 upon the Spot, not including those that died of their Wounds after the Battle Among the Prisoners of Note, were Messieurs *Pallavicine* and *Mezeeres*, Major-Generals; the Marquis *de Bar*, Brigadier-General of Foot; the Marquis *de Bame*, Son to the Marshal *Tallard*, who died afterward of his Wounds, a Nephew of the late Duke of *Luxemburg*; the Earl of *Clare*, and several other Officers of Distinction. Among the other Spoils, likewise were all their Artillery, Two Pieces excepted, amounting to 90 Pieces of Cannon, 80 Colours and Standards, all the Enemy's Baggage, Arms, Waggons, Muskets, Swords, Carcasses, innumerable, being found scatter'd along the Road promiscuously. The Kettle Drums and Standards of the *French* King's Houshold Troops were likewise taken.

The Victors also had many Officers of Note kill'd and wounded, who with Private Centinels, amounted to 2066 of the first, and 3564 wounded, so that this Advantage, how great soever it prov'd in the Events of it, was not so cheaply bought, as is usual for Accounts on the side of those that Conquer to give out. His Grace having dispatch'd Colonel *Richards* with the News of this important Defeat to the Queen from the Field of Battle after he had done pursuing the Enemy, which was continued till Ten at Night, caus'd the Army to march to *Bevechien*, where they halted the 24th for the

Refreshment of the Troops, after which a [motion] being made the next Morning for passing the *Dyle*, in order to attack the Enemy next morning, that with the Remains of their scatter'd [men] were encamped near *Louvain*. The Duke [of Marlborough] receiv'd Advice in the Night, that [they] had prevented him by a precipitate Retreat to [it]. Whereupon the Bridges being laid over [the *Dyle*] near *Louvain*, that City made its Submission, and receiv'd a Confederate Garrison of 500 [men], from whence his Grace wrote the following Letter to the States.

High and Mighty LORDS,

"MOnsieur *d'Auverquerque* having sent Monsieur *de Wassenear* to inform your High Mightinesses of the Victory, which God was graciously pleased to give us over the Enemy, on *Sunday* last: I deferr'd my Congratulations till to day, that I might be able at the same time to acquaint your High Mightinesses, with the Success of our Design to pass the *Dyle*, which we had determined to attempt the next Morning; but the Enemy thought fit to spare us that Trouble, having left us an open Field by their Retreat towards *Brussels*; so that with double Joy I have the Honour to write this Letter to your High Mightinesses from *Louvain*, where for *the Good of the Common Cause* I had *long wish'd* to be. 'Tis certain all the Generals, Officers, and Soldiers, did all that was possible for Men to do on this glorious Occasion, and their Conduct and Bravery, cannot be sufficiently extolled: I make no doubt, but your High Mightinesses Deputies, and Monsr *d'Auverquerque* have given this just Honour to your own Troops, and that your High Mightinesses will seek Occasions to

" to acknowledge and reward the Merit of so ma
" ny brave Men.
" I have chosen Colonel Chaselos to carry th
" acceptable News to your High Mightinesses,
" well for his Merit the last Campaign, as for th
" Service he has now done the State. He will in
" form your High Mightinesses from Point b
" Point, of all that has pass'd, and of the presen
" Condition of the Enemy, whom we are reso
" ved to follow. I taking the utmost Pleasur
" by giving Proofs of inviolable Regard for you
" High Mightinesses Interest, to satisfy you, th
" I am with very much Respect,

Your HIGH MIGHTINESSES

Most Humble and most Obedient Servant,

Loovain, May
25. 1706.   (*Signed*)

The Prince *and* Duke *of* MARLBOROUGH

The States having with wonderful Satisfaction
receiv'd this Letter from the Duke, tho' he seem'd
to give them a Touch of the Aversness of some
People to attempt the Passage of the *Dyle*, return'd
for Answer.

S I R,

" THE News brought the Day before Yester
"   day by the Adjutant General *de Wassenaer*,
" of the great and signal Victory which the Army
" of the Allies, under your wise and couragious
" Conduct, has, by the Blessing of God, gained
" over that of the Enemy, has filled our Hearts,
" and the Hearts of all the good Subjects of our
" Commonwealth with unspeakable Joy, which
" is now redoubled by the Confirmation of it in
" your Excellency's Letter of the 25th of the last
                                          " Month

Month, which was delivered to us, before the Arrival of Colonel *de Chanclos*; and at the same time acquaints us with your glorious Entry into *Louvain*, from whence we have a long time as much wish'd to hear from you, as your Excellency has desired to be there, for the Good of the Common Cause. We do in Return congratulate with your Excellency, for the happy Success of this great and glorious Action; a Success principally due, next to the Divine Benediction to your Conduct, and your Valour, which will render your Glory immortal. It is a particular Satisfaction we receive from the Testimony which you have given of the Courage and Bravery of our Troops. We never doubted, but they would follow the Steps of so great a Leader as your Excellencies In the mean time this Testimony is extremely advantagious to them, and gives us great Pleasure. We will not forget the Services which they have perform'd upon this great Occasion. We pray God to bless more and more, all your Designs and all your Enterprizes And since your Glory after the Battles of *Schellemberg*, of *Hochstedt*, and of *Ramillies*, cannot be encreas'd by the Greatness of Victories, we desire it may be augmented by their Number. We pray you to believe that the Esteem we have for your Excellency's Person, and rare Merit, cannot be greater. We are

Your Excellency's most Affectionate to serve you,

The *States-General of the* United-Provinces *of the* Low-Countries,

G. de Stauylt de Seroskercke.

By their Command,

F. FAGEL.

(92)

The *French* having abandon'd *Louvain*, and retired over the Canal of *Bruffels*, my Lord Duke follow'd them without any loss of Time; and having decamp'd from *Bethlem*, came to *Dighem* the 26th, and in his March receiv'd a Letter from the Marquis of *Deynfe*, Governour of *Bruffels*, where all Things were in the utmost Confusion, intimating that the States of *Brabant*, and the Magistrates of that City, design'd to wait upon him to make their Submission. But as no body was better able to give a good Account of those Transactions than his Grace himself, we shall insert here the following Letter, to preserve the Memory, and first one from that General to Mr Secretary *Harley* in these Words:

SIR,

"I Hope Colonel *Richards* will be with you in a
" Day or two, with the good News of our
" Victory over the Enemy, which by the Event
" appears to be much greater than we could well
" have expected. For on *Monday* Night, while we
" were making our Dispositions to force the Paf
" sage of the *Dyle* by Break of Day the next Morn
" ing, we had Advice, that the Enemy having
" abandoned *Louvain*, were retir'd towards *Bruffels*,
" so that we made Bridges and passed the River
" without any Opposition. We encamp'd that Day
" at *Bethlem*, and continued our March next Morn-
" ing early. About Ten of the Clock, I received
" the enclosed Letter by a Trumpet from the Mar-
" quis *de Deyfne*, Governor of the Place. Where-
" upon I sent Colonel *Pawton*, one of my Aids de
" Camps, with a Compliment to him and the
" States to let them know I should be glad to see
" them in the Afternoon. About Four of the
" Clock they came to my Quarters near *Dighem*
" with Two other Deputations. One from the
                                    " Sovereign

"Sovereign Council of *Brabant*, and the other
"from the Burgomasters and City of *Brussels*.
"They all shewed great Satisfaction at their being
"delivered from the *French* Yoke, and expressed
"themselves with a very becoming Respect to Her
"Majesty on this Occasion. As soon as they were
"gone, I writ a Letter in Conjunction with the De-
"puties of the Army, to the States, whereof you
"have here a Copy. I was advis'd to it, as necef-
"sary, not only to enable them to assemble, but
"likewise to prompt them to declare immediate-
"ly for King *Charles*, before the Enemy came to
"make a Stand. We writ Two other Letters of
"the like Tenor to the Sovereign Council and to
"the City, which have all the good Effect we
"could wish: For Yesterday in the Afternoon the
"Three Deputations returned with the Letters,
"whereof you have likewise Copies, owning his
"Catholick Majesty in Form. They repeated
"again the great Sense they have of Her Maje-
"sty's Goodness, in relieving them from the Op-
"pression of the *French* Government; and I can
"assure you, there seems to be an universal Joy
"among all sorts of People. The Magistrates of
"*Mechlen*, and those of *Aloft*, have likewise been
"with me, and made their Submissions. The
"Enemy have abandoned *Liere*, and carry'd all
"their Artillery and Stores to *Antwerp*, which, I
"reckon is now the only Place in *Brabant* we are
"not Masters of. The Army passed the Canal of
"*Brussels* yesterday, and came and encamped at this
"Place, where we Halt to Day and to Morrow,
"to refresh the Troops, who have marched Six
"Days together without any rest. Nothing could
"excuse the giving them so great a Fatigue, espe-
"cially after a Battle, but the necessity of pursu-
"ing the Enemy, and getting hither. However,
"I shall send a Detachment to morrow to possess
"themselves of *Aloft*. I leave my Brother *Churchill*

to

"to command at *Brussels*, with Four Battalions,
"and Four Squadrons. Our hasty Pursuit of the
"Enemy, oblig'd them to leave a great number
"of wounded Officers there, who were made
"Prisoners of War; among others, the Count de
"*Horne*, a Lieutenant-General, and the Earl of
"*Clare*, a Major General; but the latter died on
"*Wednesday* of his Wounds. There are likewise
"great numbers in other Places.

"On *Sunday* we shall continue our March to
"*Aloft*, and so on towards *Ghent*, to press the
"Enemy, while the Consternation continues a-
"mong them. I cannot help saying That, I
"think, a Victory was never more compleat, nor
"greater Advantages made of the Success, in so
"short a Time I hope God will continue to
"bless Her Majesty's Arms, till the Enemy be
"reduc'd to the Necessity of accepting a Firm and
"Solid Peace. Besides the great Slaughter that
"was made, in the Battle, of their best Troops,
"we have an Account, from all Parts, of great
"Numbers of Deserters, that are gone to *Luge*,
"*Maestricht*, and other Frontier Places, since the
"Action, whereby their Army must be much
"weaken'd.

I am, &c.

At the Camp at Grim-
bergh, May 28. 1706.

MARLBOROUGH.

His

(95)

His Grace, *and the* States-Deputies LETTER *to the* States *of* Brabant, *ran thus.*

Gentlemen,

"GOD having bless'd the Arms of the Allies,
" in behalf of His Majesty, King *Charles*
" the *Third*, and the Retreat of the Army of
" *France*, having given us an Opportunity of ap-
" proaching your Capital, I come to assure you
" of the Intention of the Queen, my Mistress,
" as the Deputies do on the part of the States
" General their Masters, and in the first place to
" tell you, That Her Majesty, and their High
" Mightinesses have sent us to maintain the just
" Rights of His said Catholick Majesty *Charles* the
" *Third*, to the Kingdoms of *Spain*, and to all that
" depends thereon, and that Her Majesty the
" Queen, and their High Mightinesses, nothing
" doubting but that you being likewise con-
" vinced of the lawful Sovereignty of his said
" Majesty, will with Pleasure embrace this Oc-
" casion of submitting your selves to his Obedi-
" ence, as faithful Subjects. We can assure you,
" Gentlemen, at the same Time, on the part of
" the Queen, and the States, That His Catholick
" Majesty will maintain you in the entire Enjoy-
" ment of all your ancient Rights and Privileges,
" as well Ecclesiastical as Secular; and that we
" will be very far from making the least Innovati-
" on in what concerns Religion; and that His Ca-
" tholick Majesty will cause those Concessions to
" be renewed which are termed, *The joyful Entry
" of Brabant*, in the same manner as they were
" granted by his Predecessor, *Charles* the *Second*, of
" Glorious Memory. As to our selves, we assure
" you, That the Army shall be employ'd every
" where in such manner as you desire it; and that
"we

" we will most earnestly seek, in every Thing,
" the Opportunity of shewing the Respect, and
" sincere Esteem, wherewith we have the Honour
" to be,

GENTLEMEN,

Your most Humble and most Obedient Servants;

At the Camp of Beaulieu, May 26. 1706.

The Prince *and* Duke *of* Marlborough.
FERDINAND VAN COLLEN.
Sieur GOSLINGA.

The Answer of the Three Estates, to which the foregoing Letter was directed, contained in substance, " That they had receiv'd, with all possible
" Respect: The Letter which his Highness, and
" their Excellencies did them the Honour to write
" to them the 26th Instant, and should, without
" any loss of Time, communicate in the usual and
" requisite Form; in the mean Time they were
" come to return them a Thousand most humble
" Thanks for the obliging Offers, and the most
" honourable Marks they had receiv'd of the Pro-
" tection which his Highness, and their Excel-
" lencies were pleased to grant them on the part
" of Her Majesty, the Queen of *Great-Britain,* and
" their High Mightinesses, the States-General, as
" also the sincere Assurances given them; That his
" Catholick Majesty, King *Charles* the *Second,* would
" maintain them in the full Enjoyment of the an-
" cient Rights and Privileges, both Ecclesiastical
" and Civil, without permitting the least Innova-
" tion to be made in any Thing that related to
" the Church; and that His said Majesty would
" cause the Concession, known under the Name

" of *The joyful Entry of Brabant*, to be renewed in
" the same manner, as was done by King *Charles*
" the *Second*, of Glorious Memory: That they did
" not doubt, but the other Members of the States,
" in the Day of the General Assembly, would ex-
" press, (as they did at this present) their perfect
" Submission and Obedience, which should be fol-
" lowed by that Loyalty and fervent Zeal, which
" they had always shewn for him, whom God had
" granted to them, to be their Masters and So-
" vereign: That they were also penetrated with
" a lively Sense of all the Goodness and Favours,
" wherewith his Highness, and their Excellencies
" in particular, had been pleased to honour them,
" and humbly pray'd they would be fully per-
" suaded they had the Honour to be with E-
" steem, &c.

The other Two Letters from the Sovereign Council, and from the Burgo-Masters and Sheriffs of the City of *Brussels*, being to the same effect, are purposely omitted, but in order to the *Danish* Nation, whose Troops signaliz'd themselves wonderfully at the Battle which occasion'd this amazing Revolution, must be inserted in its proper place, it being written the Day after the preceding Letter to Mr. Secretary *Harley*, This was in the following Terms.

SIR,

BEING informed, that the Letter which
" I did my self the Honour to write to
Your Majesty, the next Day after our Victory, happen'd to fall into the Hands of the Enemy, I take the liberty to address this Second Letter to Your Majesty, to congratulate you, with all Submission and Respect, upon the happy Success which God has been graciously plea-
sed

"sed to give the Arms of the High Allies, over
"the Enemy; the Particulars of which I forbear
"to repeat, well knowing that Your Majesty has
"had a full Account of them from other Hands.
"We have already reap'd all the Fruits of it, that
"we could wish for in so short a Time. The
"Capital City of *Brussels*, and all the other Towns
"of *Brabant*, *Antwerp* excepted having submit-
"ted to his Catholick Majesty, King *Charles* the
"Third.

"After the Troops have had a little Refresh-
"ment, we shall advance again towards the Ene-
"my, without giving them Time to recover them-
"selves, relying entirely on the Blessing of Hea-
"ven, and the Bravery of the Troops, particu-
"larly those of Your Majesty, who distinguish'd
"themselves so eminently, and acquired so much
"Glory in the Battle, that I cannot excuse my
"self from writing this Second Letter to Your
"Majesty, to do Justice to the Duke of *Wirtem-
"bergh*, who, that Day, gave shining Proofs of
"his Capacity and Valour, as also to all the other
"Generals, Officers, and Soldiers of Your Maje-
"sty's Troops, under his Command, who well
"deserve all the Praises I can give them; and if
"I may presume to say it, All the Regard Your
"Majesty can shew for such brave Men. I have
"not been wanting to do them that Justice to
"the Queen, and His Royal Highness; and I
"hope Your Majesty will excuse the Liberty I
"take in recommending them to your Favour,
"and also in beseeching Your Majesty to believe,
"that I am inviolably, with the most submissive
"Respect, SIR,

Your Majesty's most Humble and most Obedient Servant,

From the Camp at Grim-
berg, May 29. 1706.

The Prince *and* Duke *of* MARLBOROUGH.

The

The Day after the Date of the preceding Letter, the Duke of *Marlborough* caus'd the Army to march towards *Ghent*, which arriv'd, and took Post at *Meerlebeek*, near that Place, the same Day, from whence his Grace return'd an Answer to the last Letter sent him from the States, after this manner.

High and Mighty LORDS,

"I Return you my most humble Thanks for the
"Letter Your High Mightinesses have done
"me the Honour to write to me, bearing Date
"the 27th past. The satisfaction you express of
"the Services we have done to your Republick,
"affects us with a due Sense thereof, and will en-
"courage us more and more to continue to use
"our utmost Efforts for the Common Cause.
"Since my last from the Camp of *Grimberg*, we
"are come near *Ghent*, having sent a Detach-
"ment of 2000 Grenadiers, and 1000 Horse, un-
"der the Command of the Duke of *Wirtembergh*,
"with the Pontons, to lay a Bridge over the
"*Scheld* at *Gavre*, to endeavour thereby to cut
"off the Retreat of the Enemy, whose Army was
"then encamp'd near the City; but as soon as
"they had notice of our Design, they abandon'd
"the same, and march'd Yesterday Morning, at
"3 of the clock, towards their old Lines, near
"*Courtray*. Yesterday, after our arrival in this
"Camp, in the Afternoon, the Magistrates of
"the City came to make their submission, and
"we have written to them, in concert with Mes-
"sieurs the Deputies, a Letter to the same effect,
"as we did to the City of *Brussels*, and we doubt
"not but they will follow their Example. The
"Prince of *Ventimiglia*, Governour thereof, who
"has been left in the Castle, with a Battalion of

"*Spaniards*,

" *Spaniards*, had sent to us some Proposals, but I
" am persuaded he will surrender, as well as the
" Marquiss of *Deynse*, Governour of *Brussels*. We
" are sending a Detachment to *Bruges*, to receive
" their submission; and I have just now written
" Two Letters, One to the Marquiss *de Terracina*,
" Governour of the Citadel of *Antwerp*, wherein
" are Four *Spanish* Battalions, and the Other to the
" Magistrates, to exhort them to submit. Quar-
" ter-Master-General *Cadogan* is entrusted with
" those Letters, from which I expect a good Suc-
" cess. I will with all speed impart to Your High
" Mightinesses the Answers I shall receive.

I am, with all possible Respect, &c.

At the Camp at Meerle-
beck, June 1. 1706.   (*Signed*)

The Prince *and* Duke *of* MARLBOROUGH.

Another LETTER, *from His* Grace, *to the* States-General.

High and Mighty LORDS,

" According to what I gave my self the Ho-
" nour to write to Your *High Mightinesses*,
" the 1st Instant, the Castle of *Ghent* was obliged
" to surrender the next Day. The *Spanish* Battali-
" on, consisting of 400 Men, with the Colonel
" the Marquiss *de los Rios*, and all the Officers be-
" ing made Prisoners of War, but all the Soldiers
" except 50, declared for King *Charles*. The Sum-
" mons we sent to *Bruges*, and the County of
" *Franc*, has had the desired effect. The Magi-
" strates came hither this Morning, to make their
" submission, and acknowledge their lawful Sove-
" reign

" reign in due Form. We caused 2 Battalions of
" the Troops of *Flanders*, to march there into, and
" another was sent to *Damme*, which the Enemy
" had abandon'd. But what is more surprizing
" still, having Yesterday caused *Oudenard* to be
" summon'd, and upon their Refusal, order'd Lieu-
" tenant-General *Scholten* to march thither with 7
" Battalions, 4 Pieces of Cannon, and 2 Mortars;
" the Garrison consisting of 3 Battalions, has im-
" mediately capitulated, and a *French* Battalion
" therein has obtained leave to retire. The other
" 2 Battalions being *Spaniards*, and the Governour,
" have declared for King *Charles*; and at this In-
" stant I am informed, that our Men are got into
" the Place. This Morning I receiv'd a Letter
" from Brigadier *Cadogan*, whom I sent to sum-
" mon *Antwerp*, whereby it appears, that we had
" been rightly informed of the Strength of that
" Garrison, since he acquaints me, That there are
" 5 *French*, and as many *Spanish* Battalions therein.
" However, he informs me, That they seem'd
" dispos'd to surrender upon honourable Terms,
" whereupon, having advised with Messieurs the
" Deputies, and Monsieur *d'Auverquerque*, and con-
" sider'd the Importance of that Place, and how
" precious Time is to us, we have sent a full Pow-
" er to the Brigadier aforesaid, to grant them
" reasonable Conditions, of which we expect an
" Account to Morrow.

" The Hand of God appears visibly in all this,
" striking the Enemy with such a Terror, as obli-
" ges them to deliver up many strong Places,
" without offering the least Resistance.

" This has encourag'd me to summon the Towns
" of *Dendermonde* and *Ostend*, and, for that pur-
" pose, I have sent Detachments with Letters for
" the Governours We shall soon know what this
" will produce, and I shall not fail to impart it
" to Your *High Mightinesses*. We have made our
" Bridges,

" Bridges, and the necessary Dispositions to pass
" the *Scheld* and the *Lys* to Morrow, to encamp
" between *Deynse* and *Nivelle*. The Enemies are
" retired beyond *Courtray*.

I am, &c.

June 3. 1706.

The Prince and Duke of MARLBOROUGH

P.S. "I am inform'd, from Monsieur *Scholten*,
" That the 3 Battalions of the Garrison of *Oude-*
" *nard*, are all marched away, the *French* to *Cour-*
" *tray*, and the others towards *Mons*.

On the 4th the Army march'd from *Meerlebek*,
and encamp'd between *Deynse* and *Nivelle*, where
the Magistrates of *Oudenard* came to wait upon the
Duke, to desire his Protection, and assure him of
their Fidelity to His Catholick Majesty, *Charles*
the Third. On the 5th they decamp'd again, and
march'd, and took Post with their Left at *Arsele*,
and the Right at *Canegbem*; and that Morning
Baron *Schilde*, Treasurer of *Antwerp*, with an Offi
cer of the Garrison of that Place, came to his
Grace, with Letters from the City, and the Marquiss *de Terracine*, Governour of the Castle, praying that those Gentlemen might have leave to go
to the Elector of *Bavaria*, to receive his Directions
upon the Conduct they were to observe, in relation
to the Summons which had been given them But
the Duke did not think fit to grant their Request,
but sent them back to *Antwerp*, with Answers to
the Letters they brought, and immediately detach'd
my Lord *Orkney* with a 1000 Horse, to join Brigadier *Cadogan*, and invest the Place, with Direction
to form the Siege, as soon as his Lordship could be
joined by 16 Battalions, who were order'd to march
for that purpose from *Flanders*, In the mean Time

Orders

Orders were sent to Brigadier Ca**gan** to give the Garrison no more than Four Hours to consider of the Capitulation that was offered them, which was actually sign'd on the 6th, by which the Garrison that consisted of Six *French*, and Six *Spanish* Battalions, were allowed to march out in Three Days, and be conducted to *Quesnoy*.

When the Garrison was to march out according to the Articles, one *Spanish* and one *Walloon* Regiment, both entire took on with the Confederates; and of the other Regiments of those Countries, there were scarce 150 left; when they passed by *Brussels*, most of the Officers and Soldiers entred into the Service of his Catholick Majesty; as did likewise the Marquis of *Winterfield*, Lieutenant-General and Governor there, who commanded the Garrison in the City of *Antwerp*, and the Baron *de Wrangle*, a General, Men of the First Quality, and of great Credit among the Troops.

Monsieur *d'Auverquerque* on the 15th following, marched with a Detachment to form the Siege of *Ostend*, and Lieutenant-General *Fagel* had order at the same time to attack the Fort of *Plassendale*, which was taken that Evening by Assault, the Garrison being put to the Sword. Those Troops advanced afterwards, and took the Bridge of *Sauswoode*, thereby securing the Sluces. They set forward the next Day for *Ostend*, which was closely block'd up on the side of the Sea by a Squadron of Ships under Sir *Stafford Fairborne*. The Batteries were finish'd, and the Trenches open'd against the Town, the First of *July*, which being terribly batter'd both by Sea and Land, beat a Parly on the 6th, and had leave for the Garrison to march out with their Swords, upon Condition that they should not bear Arms against King *Charles* III. for the space of Six Months, from the Date of that Agreement; but no mention being made of the Shipping, they all fell into the Confederates Hands,

Hands, there being at that time Three *French* Men of War, with others of the *Spanish* Nation, as well as Privateers, which, with the Merchant-men, were all made Prize.

Monsieur *d'Auverquerque*, after the Taking of *Ostend*, having joined the Duke of *Marlborough* at *Harleback*; that Prince after taking Possession of *Courtray*, which the Enemy had abandoned; and on the 11th advanced to *Helchin* on the *Scheld*, and being joined by the Troops of *Prussia* and *Hanover*, with 3000 *Palatines*, made all the necessary Dispositions for a Siege. This the *French* were sensible of, and by means of their Sluices render'd the *Lis* un-navigable below *Menin*. But General *Salisk* was order'd with a strong Detachment, to break down the Dams and Sluices between *Armentiere*, *Lisle*, and *Menin*, to free the Course of that River, that the Boats laden with Artillery and Ammunition might come up from thence to *Courtray*. At length the Siege of *Menin*, in *French Flanders*, was pitch'd upon, and the Place was invested by General *Salisk*, on the 23d, but for want of Artillery could not open the Trenches till the 5th of *August*, on which Day the Duke of *Marlborough* receiv'd the Two following Letters from King *Charles* III by way of Acknowledgment of his great Services.

My Lord Duke and Prince,

"YOU could never have given me more con-
"vincing Proofs of your Zeal and Concern
"for my Service, and the Good of the Common
"Cause, than by interposing your good Offices
"with the Queen your Mistress, in order that the
"Fleet and Forces which she had design'd for my
"Service, might use the Diligence they have
"shewn to come hither. My City of *Barcelona*
"wherein I have chose to continue, to encourage

the Garrison and Inhabitants to a long and vigorous Defence, was reduced to such Extremities, that without the Arrival of this Fleet and Succours, it was to be feared that the Enemy, who were actually lodged on the Point of the Counterscarp, and had made sufficient Breaches, would have taken the Place in a very little time. I do hereby acquaint you with so fortunate an Event; and while I hope that the rest of the Campaign will answer this noble Beginning, I flatter my self to hear, likewise, in a short time good News from you, and the glorious Operations you have performed by your own Valour, and that of the Troops under your Command. The Queen your Mistress and Messieurs the States-General, could not oblige me more than in sending hither the Count *de Noyelles* and Brigadier *Stanhope*. I assure you that their Persons have always been, and always will be acceptable to me, and do not question but you interested your self in the Choice of Both, as you do in every Thing, that may promote my Interests and those of the Common Cause. Whereupon I pray God to keep you, *my Lord Duke and Prince*, in his holy Protection, and I assure you of my perfect Esteem and Gratitude.

rcelona, May 10 1706.

CHARLES, R.

My Lord Duke and Prince,

BY these few Lines, which you shall receive with a Letter of the 10th Instant, I have been willing to share with you, the new Joy I have of seeing my City entirely freed from the Siege. Never was Retreat made with so much Precipitation, as that the Enemy made just now, having left us all their Artillery, consisting of

"140 Pieces of Brass Cannon, and a vast Quan-
"tity of all manner of Ammunition and Provisi-
"ons; beyond Belief, I do not doubt but yo[u]
"shall receive from other Hands the Particula[rs]
"of this Siege, whereof I write this the shorte[r]
"Praying God to keep you, *my Lord Duke a[nd]*
"*Prince,* in his holy Protection.

Barcelona, May   CHARLES, R.
12. 1706.

His Grace likewise had Dispatches from the Ea[rl]
of *Peterborough* on the same Subject, which he r[e-]
turn'd Answer too, to this Purpose.

My LORD,

"Though we have no direct Account of you[r]
"Lordship's Progress since the Relief [of]
"*Barcelona*, yet the Advices from several othe[r]
"Parts, as well as the Enemies Frontiers, agree [so]
"well, and we are naturally so inclined to be-
"lieve readily what we wish, that I perswade m[y]
"self there is no Reason to doubt of your havin[g]
"some time since brought the King to *Madrid* A[nd]
"this goodNews has been indulged here with t[he]
"greatest Satisfaction, I do with no less Pleasu[re]
"take this fresh Opportunity of Congratulatin[g]
"your Lordship on the glorious Occasion, whic[h]
"is by all Hands chiefly attributed to your Valo[ur]
"and good Conduct. The whole Confederac[y]
"full of Joy for the Advantages this wonder[ful]
"Success will produce to the Publick; and I a[m]
"sure you I am no less so for the Addition it [has]
"made to your Lordship's Glory, in which [no]
"Man alive takes more Part than I do. A[fter]
"such surprizing Events, there is nothing th[at]
"may not expect from you, therefore I hope yo[ur]
"Lordship will not think us unreasonable in o[ur]
"Hop[e]

Hopes, that we shall soon hear of the entire Reduction of *Spain* to the Obedience of their Lawful Sovereign, for which you seem'd design'd by Providence to be the happy Instrument; and I heartily wish you all manner of Success in the accomplishing this great Work. We have reduced *Ostend*, and are now making all possible Diligence in the necessary Preparations for the Siege of *Menin*, and hope, with the Blessing of God, we shall not end our Campaign there. I am, with Truth and Respect,

My LORD,

Your Lordship's most Faithful Humble Servant,

MARLBOROUGH.

The Town of *Menin*, after it had been batter'd for several Days with extraordinary Fury, thought to Capitulate on the 23d, when they were allow'd to march out with all Marks of Honour. The Garrison consisting of 12 Battalions of Foot, and 3 Squadrons of dismounted Dragoons, who were conducted the next Day to *Duway*.

This Conquest being happily settled, the Duke of *Marlborough* gave Orders for the besieging of *Andermonde*, on the 29th of *August* in Form, General *Churchill* being to command in that Attack. Three Days after, which, his Grace arriv'd in the Camp, where he wrote to the States-General the following Particulars.

High and Mighty LORDS,

I Arrived here last *Thursday* Night, with Monsieur *de Gislinga*, and Monsieur *de Geldermalsen*, to hasten the Attack of this Place, and am very glad I can acquaint your High Mightinesses, that

"this

" this Morning about Ten a Clock the Garrison
" beat a Parley demanding honourable Conditi-
" ons; but my Brother return'd Answer, that he
" could grant them no other Terms, than that
" they should remain Prisoners of War, yet that
" their Baggage would be left them, provided
" they did declare themselves, and deliver up one
" of the Gates in Two Hours time. They rejected
" this Proposal, and the Hostages having been sent
" back, Orders were given to renew the Attack,
" whereupon the Garrison desired a further Cessa-
" tion of Arms for an Hour, at the Expiration of
" which they surrendered, and about Five deliver-
" ed up the Gate of *Mechlen*. They are to march
" out next *Tuesday*, in order to be conducted to
" *Holland*.

" I heartily Congratulate your High Mighti-
" nesses upon this happy Event, in which the Hand
" of God has visibly appear'd: It having been ob-
" serv'd, that for several Years past, there has not
" been in this Country, so favourable a Season for
" such an Enterprize. I am with entire Devotion
' and Respect,

High and Mighty Lords, &c.

From the Camp before Den-   (Sign'd)
dermonde, Sept. 5. 1706.

The Prince and Duke of MARLBOROUGH

The next Thing the Confederates had to do, was
to form the Siege of *Aeth*, which was undertaken
by Monsieur *d'Auverquerque*, who invested it with
Forty Battalions and Thirty Squadrons, which
actually encamped before the Place, on the 16
of the same Month. The Trenches were opened
the 20th, and the Works carried on with so much
Success, that on the 29th a Lodgment was made

on the Cover'd-way, and in the Night between the last of *September*, and the first of *October*, they took Possession of the Counter-guard before the Bastion which was attack'd, which obliged the Garrison to beat a Parley; the Consequence of which was, that Monsieur *d'Auverquerque* gave them to understand, That they were to expect no other Terms than to be Prisoners of War, but out of Courtesy he would allow the Officers their Swords and Baggage, and Soldiers their Snapsacks, giving them half an Hours time to consider of it. The Governor at first would not agree to it, upon which Hostilities were renew'd; but they accepted the Conditions at last, and surrender'd accordingly. The Garrison consisted of 2100 Men, of whom 500 were kill'd and wounded during the Siege, which was much about the same Number as it cost the Allies.

Thus concluded this glorious Campaign, and the Duke left the Field, and came to the *Hague*, where he was highly caress'd on Account of his great Services, and communicated to the States the following Letter and Answer, written by and to the Elector of *Bavaria*.

The Elector of Bavaria's Letter to the Duke of Marlborough.

" THE most Christian King, *Sir*, finding that
" some Overtures of Peace, which he had
" caused to be made by private Ways, had, in-
" stead of producing the Effects of making known
" his Dispositions for promoting a General Peace,
" been look'd upon by ill designing Men, as an
" Artifice to disunite the Allies, and make Ad-
" vantage of the Misunderstanding that might be
" created among them, has resolved to shew the
" Sincerity of his Intentions, by renouncing all
" secret

"secret Negotiations, and openly proposing Con-
"ferences, in which Means may be found, for
"Re-establishing the Tranquility of *Europe*.

"The *Most Christian King* is pleased to commis-
"sion me to inform you of this, and I desire
"you to acquaint the Queen of *England* with it.
"I give the like Notification on the Part of the
"*Most Christian King*, to the States General, by
"a Letter that I have written to their Field De-
"puties; and he would do the like with regard
"to the other Potentates that are at War with
"him, had they Ministers so near at Hand as
"you are, to receive the like Intimation, he
"having no Design to exclude any of the said
"Potentates from the Negotiations that shall be
"begun in the Conferences he proposes.

"Further, For advancing a Good so great and
"necessary to *Europe*, which has too long suffer'd
"the inevitable Calamities of War, he consents,
"That a Place may forthwith be chosen, be-
"tween the Two Armies, and after their sepa-
"ration, between *Mons* and *Brussels*, in which
"you, Sir, with whom the Interests of *England*
"are so safely entrusted, the Deputies, the States
"shall be pleased to nominate, and the Persons
"whom the King of *France* shall impower, may
"open their Intentions upon so important an Af-
"fair.

"I am extremely pleased, Sir, to have such an
"Occasion to write to you this Letter, being
"persuaded it will leave no room for making
"a Doubt of the Sentiments of His *Most Chri-*
"*stian Majesty*, which may be so beneficial to all
"*Europe*

"It will be a pleasure to you to give an Ac-
"count of this to the Queen of *England*, without
"loss of Time, and to whomsoever else you
"shall think fit. I shall expect your Answer, Sir,
"to communicate it to the *Most Christian King*;
"and

"and shall always be ready, Sir, to do you Ser-
"vice.

Mont, Octo-
ber 21. 1706. (Signed)

M. EMANUEL, Elector.

The Dukes ANSWER.

SIR,

"HAving communicated to the Queen, my
" Mistress, what your Electoral Highness
" did me the Honour to write to me in your Let-
" ter of the 21st of last Month, of the Intentions
" of the most Christian King, to endeavour to
" re-establish the Tranquility of *Europe*, by Con-
" ferences to be held for that purpose, between
" Deputies on both Sides   Her Majesty has com-
" manded me to answer your Electoral Highness,
" That it is a Pleasure to Her, to be informed of
" the King's Inclinations, to agree to the making
" of a solid and lasting Peace with the Allies, as
" being the sole End that obliged Her Majesty to
" continue this War till now: She will be very
" glad to conclude it in concert with all Her
" Allies, on Conditions that may secure them from
" all Apprehensions of being forc'd to take up
" Arms again, after a short Interval, as happen'd
" last Time   Her Majesty is also willing I should
" declare, That She is ready to enter jointly with
" all the High Allies, into just and necessary Mea-
" sures, for setling such a Peace, Her Majesty
" being determined not to enter upon any Nego-
" tiation, without the participation of Her said
" Allies: But the way of Conference that is pro-
" posed without more particular Declarations on
" the part of *His Most Christian Majesty*, does not
" seem

(112)

"seem proper to Her for attaining a truly solid
"and lasting Peace: Their Lordships, the States-
"General, are of the same Opinion. Wherefore
"your Electoral Highness will rightly judge, That
"'tis necessary to think of other more solid Means
"to attain so great an End; to which Her Ma-
"jesty will contribute, with all the Sincerity that
"can be wish'd, having nothing so much at
"Heart, as the relief of Her Subjects, and the
"Tranquility of *Europe*. Your Electoral Highness
"will always do me the Justice, to be persuaded
"of the respect with which I have the Honour
"to be,

SIR,

Your most Humble, and most Obedient Servant,

The Prince *and* Duke *of* Marlborough.

The Letters from the Elector, above-mention'd, to the Deputies of the States, being to the same purport with that to his Grace, I shall not here transcribe them, but only insert an Extract of the States Resolution hereupon, which was communicated to the Congress of foreign Ministers, the Day after it was made, in these Words.

Friday, Nov. 19. 1706.

"MOnsieur *Tullecken*, and others, Deputies of
"their *High Mightinesses*, for foreign Af-
"fairs, reported to the Assembly, That Monsieur
"*Van Collen*, and *Cuper*, Two of their *High Migh-*
"*tinesses* Field Deputies, did, in a Letter directed
"to Mr. Register *Fagel*, dated the 23d of *October*
"last, send one from the Elector of *Bavaria*, da-
"ted the 20th of the same Month, written to their
"*High Mightinesses* Field-Deputies, and delivered
"to

"to the said Messieurs, *Van Collen*, and *Cuper*, who
"only were then with the Army; by which Let-
"ter, the Elector of *Bavaria* proposes, in the Name
"of *The Most Christian King*, the holding of a Con-
"ference between the Two Armies, or between
"*Mons* and *Brussels*, to treat of a Peace with the
"States, and their Allies: That they, the said
"Deputies of Foreign Affairs, having had that
"Letter communicated to them, judg'd it for the
"good of the States, and of the Common Cause,
"to keep that Affair secret, till the Arrival of the
"Prince and Duke of *Marlborough*, who was ex-
"pected here in few Days after, considering that
"the said Prince and Duke had received from
"the Elector of *Bavaria*, a Letter of the same
"Tenour: That the said Prince and Duke be-
"ing arriv'd here, they, the said Deputies, had
"discoursed and concerted with him, and there-
"upon drawn up, in writing, a Form of an An-
"swer that might be given to the Elector of *Ba-
"varia*, by Messieurs *Van Collen*, and *Cuper*, who
"had receiv'd it, which Form, (or Draught)
"when approved by their *High Mightinesses*, the
"said Prince and Duke had agreed to answer on
"the same Foot, on the Part of Her Majesty of
"*Great-Britain*, (*which Letter of the Elector of Ba-
"varia, and the Form of the Answer they laid before
"the Assembly*) on all which their *High Mightinesses*
"having deliberated, thank'd the said Deputies
"for their good Management on this Affair; and
"it is besides thought good, by these Presents,
"to repute the said Form of an Answer as agreed,
"and to require and authorize the said Messieurs,
"*Van Collen*, and *Cuper*, to write and sign it, in the
"Terms it was drawn up in; after which it shall
"be sent to the Field-Marshal, Monsieur *d'Auver-
"querque*, that he may send it by a Trumpet, to
"the Elector of *Bavaria*.

Q "That

"That, moreover, both the said *Letter* and An-
"swer shall be communicated to the Ministers of
"the High Allies, that are Members of the Grand
"Alliance, to whom it shall be represented, That
"their *High Mightinesses* being firmly resolved to
"observe their Alliances in every Part, and to
"do nothing derogatory from the same, in regard
"thereto, would not be wanting to impart to
"them the Propositions that have been made to
"them, and what they have resolved thereon.
"That Peace cannot but be extremely agreeable
"to them, and to all the other Allies, without
"doubt, if it can be had on such Terms, as may
"reasonably promise for its being firm and lasting;
"but that the Conference proposed, without a
"more particular Discovery of the Intention of
"*France*, and without a probable Certainty or Ap-
"pearance of good Success, does not seem to
"their *High Mightinesses* to be a proper Means for
"attaining it, but rather a Means to divert the
"Thoughts of War, and of the great Preparati-
"ons the Enemy make, and to lull some of the
"Allies asleep, by the Hopes of Peace: That
"their *High Mightinesses*, for their own Parts, are
"resolved to stick to the Measures they have ta-
"ken, and to the Alliance made, which God has
"hitherto so wonderfully bless'd, and to execute
"and observe sincerely, what was stipulated and
"promis'd by the Treaties, and therefore not to
"enter into any Negotiation of Peace, but jointly
"with their High Allies; and not without com-
"municating to them faithfully, conformable to
"the said Treaties, the Overtures that may be
"made to them on this Subject; expecting that
"the High Allies will do no less on their Part.
"And Monsieur *Tulecker*, and the other Deputies
"of the States for Foreign Affairs, are required
"by these Presents, and commission'd to enter
"into Conference with the said Ministers, on the

said Subject, and to make a Report of all that passes to this Assembly.

The Grand Pensionary, and the Duke of *Marlborough*, spoke in behalf of the foregoing Resolution, and both concluded for a continuance of the [War]: They also desired the Ministers to write to [their] Principals, to exert their best Efforts for carrying on the War effectually, and to take Example [by] *England* and *Holland*, who were determin'd to make a most vigorous Campagne. The Assembly was exceedingly charmed and satisfied with the sincere, obliging and honest Communication of the aforesaid Premises, and concluded to do their utmost to prevail with the Princes they belong'd to, to augment their Forces accordingly.

Some Days after this Assembly was held, the Duke took his Leave of the States, and went for *England*, where, on the 4th of *December* following, a Committee of the House of Commons, then sitting, gave their Attendance upon him, with the Thanks of that Venerable Body of Senators, for his eminent Services to Her Majesty, and Her Kingdoms, in the great and glorious Victory and Successes obtain'd over the Enemy, the foregoing Campagne. Whereupon his Grace was pleas'd to make them this Answer.

Gentlemen,

"IF any Thing could add to my satisfaction, in the Services I have endeavour'd to do the Queen and my Country, it would be the particular Notice the House of Commons is pleas'd to take of them, so much to my advantage.

On the 5th the Lord Keeper made the following Speech to the Duke, upon the very same Occasion.

My Lord Duke of Marlborough,

"I Am commanded by this House, to give you[r] Grace their Acknowledgments and Thank[s] for the eminent Services you have done since the last Session of Parliament, to Her Majesty, and your Country, together with their Confe[-] derates in this Just and Necessary War.

"Tho' your former Successes, against the Pow[-] er of *France*, while it remained unbroken, gav[e] most reasonable Expectation, that you wou[ld] not fail to improve them; yet what your Grac[e] has performed this last Campagne has far excee[-] ded all Hopes, even of such as were most Af[-] fectionate and Partial to their Country's Inte[-] rest, and your Glory. The Advantages you have gain'd are of such a Nature, so conspi[-] cuous in themselves, so undoubtedly owing t[o] your Courage and Conduct, so sensibly an[d] universally beneficial in their Consequences t[o] the whole Confederacy, that to attempt to a[-] dorn them, with the colouring of Words woul[d] be in vain and inexcuseable, and therefore [I] decline it; the rather, because I should ce[r-] tainly offend that great Modesty which alon[e] can and does add a Lustre to your Actions, an[d] which in your Graces Example, has successful[ly] withstood as great Tryals as that Vertue has m[et] with in any Instance whatsoever; and I be[g] leave to say, That if any Thing could mo[ve] your Grace to reflect with much satisfaction [on] your own Merit, it would be this, That so A[u-] gust an Assembly does, with One Voice, Prai[se] and Thank you: An Honour, which a Jud[g-] ment so sure as that of your Grace's, to thi[nk] rightly of every Thing, cannot but prefer [to] the Ostentation of a publick Triumph.

The Duke of Marlborough's ANSWER.

My LORDS,

"I Esteem this as a very particular Honour which your Lordships are pleas'd to do me; no body in the World can be more sensible of it than I am, nor more desirous to deserve the Continuance of your Favour and good Opinion.

What further related to his Grace, during this Session of Parliament, was, that the House of Lords, after he had honour'd the City of *London* with his company, upon a solemn Invitation from that body corporate, were pleas'd to distinguish themselves by an Address to the Queen in his Favour, to perpetrate his Memory, by setling and continuing his Titles and Honours, with his Right of Precedence in his Posterity, by Act of Parliament, with Her Royal Allowance, in answer to which, Her Majesty sent the following Message.

ANNE, R.

"Nothing can be more acceptable to me than your Address, I am entirely satisfied with the Services of the Duke of *Marlborough*, and therefore cannot but be pleased you have so just a Sense of them.

"I must not omit to take notice, That the respectful manner of your Proceeding, in desiring my Allowance for bringing in the Bill, and my Direction for the Limitation of the Honours, does give me great satisfaction.

"My Intention is, That after the Determination of the Estate which the Duke of *Marlborough* now has in his Titles and Honours, the same
"should

" should be limitted to his eldest Daughter, (*his only Son, the Marquiss of* Blandford, *being living when he was first created a Duke*) " and the Heirs Male of
" her Body, and then to all his other Daughters
" successively, according to their Priority of Birth,
" and the Heirs Male of their respective Bodies,
" and afterwards in such manner as may most ef-
" fectually answer my Design and yours, in per-
" petuating the Memory of his Merit, by conti-
" nuing, as far as may be done, his Titles and
" Name to all Posterity.

" I think it would be proper, That the Honour
" and Mannor of *Woodstock* and the House of
" *Blenheim*, should always go along with the Ti-
" tles, and therefore I recommend that Matter to
" your Consideration.

Then the *Duke* express'd himself thus, upon this Occasion.

My LORDS,

" I Cannot find Words sufficient to express the
" Sense I have of the Great and Distinguish-
" ing Honour which the House has been pleased
" to do me in their Resolution, and their Appli-
" cation to Her Majesty. The Thoughts of it
" will be a continual Satisfaction to me, and the
" highest Encouragement; and the thankful Me-
" mory of it must last as long as any Posterity of
" mine.

" I beg leave to say a Word to the House in re-
" lation to that Part of Her Majesty's Gracious
" Answer, which concerns the Estate of *Woodstock*,
" and the House of *Blenheim*; I did make my
" humble Request to the Queen, That those might
" go along with the Titles, and I make the like
" Request to your Lordships, That after the
" Dutchess of *Marlborough*'s Death; (upon whom
" they

" they are settled in Jointure) that Estate and
" House may be limitted to go always along with
" the Honour.

The Duke of *Marlborough*, who in most of the preceeding Years made a shining Figure by his Military Atchievements, bespeaks the Reader's Attention in the Year 1707. chiefly by his important Negotiations. For the Management of which, his Grace having been detained Nine or Ten Days at *Margate* by contrary Winds, embark'd there the 13th of *April*, N. S. with intent to land at *Ostend*; but the Wind changing again, made the *Brill* the 16th at Night, from whence the next Day he arrived at the *Hague*, to the great Joy of the Allies, who expected him with the utmost Impatience, and having dined with Mr. *Stepney*, the *British* Envoy Extraordinary, who was lately return'd from *Brussels*, made a Visit to the Grand Pensionary, and another to the President of the Assembly of the States-General. On the next Day, after he had receiv'd the Compliments that were wont to be paid him on the like Occasion, he went to the Congress of Foreign Ambassadors, &c. to whom he signified, that the Queen of *Great Britain* could hearken to no Peace, but what might firmly secure the General Tranquility of *Europe*. He likewise conferr'd with the Deputies of the States, who waited on him for that End at his own House, where on the 19th in the Evening he had another long Conference with them, upon several important Affairs; and among other Things told them, " That the Troubles of *Saxony*, into which
" the King of *Sweeden* had lately broken with a
" considerable Army, occasioning a great Distra-
" ction in the Empire, and infinite Prejudice to
" the Common Cause, the Queen his Mistress,
" had thought fit to send him thither, to pay a
" Compliment to that Prince, and endeavour to
engage

" engage to remove the juſt Jealouſies his long
" Stay in the Heart of *Germany*, gave to ſome of
" the High Allies: For which purpoſe he had the
" neceſſary Power from her *Britannick* Majeſty
" and deſired to have the ſame from the States
Whereupon the Penſionary, having on the 20th of
the ſame Month, acquainted the States of *Holland*
and *Weſt-Frieſland*, with the Neceſſity of the ſaid
Journey, they eaſily concurr'd in thoſe Meaſures,
and his Grace ſet out the ſame Evening for *Leipſig*
by the Way of *Hanover*. On the 22d he arriv'd at
the laſt of thoſe Places, where having had ſeveral
Conferences with the Elector of that Name, and
his Miniſters. He took his Leave of that Court the
24th following in the Evening, and was met on
the 26th at *Hall* by Mr. *Robinſon*, (now Lord Biſhop
of *Briſtol*, and Lord Privy-Seal) Envoy Extraordinary from Her *Britannick* Majeſty to the King
of *Sweden*, Count *Zinzendorf* of the ſame Quality
from the Emperor, and Monſieur *Cranenburgh* the
Dutch Miniſter. After Dinner, the Duke received
the Compliments of the Magiſtrates and of the
Univerſity, and then proceeded to *Alt-Ranſtadt*,
the King of *Sweden*'s Head Quarters, accompanied
by the Miniſters before mention'd. Here he went
directly to Count *Piper*'s Quarters, and after ſome
Conferences with the prime Counſellor, came directly to thoſe which his *Swediſh* Majeſty had given Orders to be prepared for him The next
Morning his Grace was congratulated upon his
Arrival, by the Miniſters and General Officers,
and about Ten of the Clock had his Audience of
the King, to whom he preſented the Queen's Letter, and made the following Compliment in *French*.
Sir, *I preſent to Your MAJESTY a Letter not from
the Chancery, but from the Heart of the QUEEN
my Miſtreſs, and written with Her own Hand. Had
not Her Sex prevented it, ſhe would have croſſed the Sea
to ſee a Prince admired by the whole World. I am in
the*

[i]n Particular more Happy *than the* QUEEN, *and wish I could serve some Campaigns under so great a [Gene]ral as Your* MAJESTY, *that I might learn [wha]t I yet want to know in the Art of* War. To [th]is the King, with a plainess that is natural to [him], and abhorrent of any Thing that bears the [leas]t Resemblance of Flattery, was pleased to re[ply] in *High Dutch*, by an Interpreter.

My Lord Duke,

THE Queen of *Great-Britain*'s Letter, and your Person, are both highly acceptable to me, and I shall always have the greatest Regard for the Interposition of her *Britannick* Majesty, and the Interests of the Grand Confederacy, having with extreme Reluctance been forc'd to give the least Umbrage to any one Member of it; but your Excellency cannot but be sensible of the just Occasion that has brought me and my Troops hither; and you may assure the Queen, my Sister, that my Intentions are to depart from hence as soon as the Satisfaction required on my side is given me, till when I am determined to remain in this Electorate, without doing any thing to the Prejudice of the Common Cause in General, or the Protestant Religion in Particular.

After Dining with his Majesty, the Duke had a second Audience, at which assisted Count *Piper* and Monsieur *Harmelin*, the Two Chief *Swedish* Ministers, and Mr. *Robinson*; and which being over, his Grace went to wait upon King *Augustus* at *Leip[si]ck*, upon an Invitation from that Prince, with [w]hom he had a private Conference, and then re[tu]rn'd to Count *Piper*'s Quarters the next Day, [w]here he dined. In the Evening he likewise sup[p]ed with Velt-Mareschal *Rienschild*, who return'd

R his

his Visits on the 29th, when he had his Audience of Leave of the King of *Sweden*. Before it was ended, King *Stanislaus* came in and was complimented by his Grace, who soon after took his Leave, waited upon the King of *Poland* at *Leipsick*, and thence without making any stay, proceeded on his Journey to *Berlin*, very well satisfied with his Reception and Negotiations at the Court of *Sweden*. Though some People thought fit to observe, That his Majesty's speaking to him in *High-Dutch*, and by an Interpreter as well as taking no manner of Notice of his Grace's Heroick Actions in return to the Compliment upon his own, was no great Inducement for the Satisfaction that is before express'd.

On the 30th, the Duke arriv'd at *Charlotenburgh*, the King of *Prussia* having sent Monsieur GRUMKOW, one of his chief Ministers, to desire him to advance that Way. His Grace supped that Night with the King, and was lodg'd in the Apartment belonging to the Margrave. On *Sunday, May* the 1st, he went to Divine Service with the King, who had given particular Orders to Monsieur *L'Enfant* to preach in *French* on that Occasion. On the 2d his Grace left *Charlotenburgh*, in order to return towards *Hanover*, where he arrived on the 3d; and the Day following, after a private Conference with his Electoral Highness, dined with that Prince. In the Afternoon he set out for the *Hague*, which he reach'd on the 8th of the same Month, after having received the highest Marks of Distinction in the several Courts through which he passed, since his first Departure from thence. The next Morning his Grace was complimented by the Foreign Ministers, and other Persons of Quality upon his Return; and in the Evening communicated to the Deputies of the States General the Assurances he had received from the King of *Sweden*. This entirely dissipated the Jealousy some of the Allies had entertained of that Monarch's Designs; which were industriously fomented by the Emissaries of *France*, who, on the other hand, left no Stone unturn'd to engage the young *Northern* Hero in an open Rupture with the Emperor, for which that King did not want plausible Pretences; one of which was an insolent Affront received from Count *Zobor* in the Presence of his Majesty's Envoy, Count *Strablenheim*. The former daring to say, while the Discourse ran upon the Affairs of *Europe*, That *Three Rogues occasion'd a great deal of Mischief in the World*. For though he named but Prince *Rogotsky* for one, and King *Stanislaus* for another, yet he used such Expressions, as plainly shew'd he meant the King of *Sweden* for a Third; whereupon the *Swedish* Envoy thought himself obliged to give him a Box on the Ear. The other Grounds of Complaint was, his Imperial Majesty's conniving at the Escape of Twelve hundred *Muscovites* through his Territories into *Germany*, and the Affairs of Religion in *Silesia*; which all the Instances of the Queen of *Great-Britain*, and other Protestant Powers, in behalf of those abus'd People, had never been redress'd without his Majesty's Intervention in their behalf, but these Things were happily blown over by the Duke of *Marlborough*'s Journey as above-mention'd.

The Duke of *Marlborough* having found all Things ready for opening the Campaign, left the *Hague* for *Brussels*, where being arrived on the 13th of *May*, he immediately held a Council with Monsieur *d'Auverquerque* and the States Deputies the Result of which was, that Orders were sent to the Confederate Troops to march to their Rendezvous at *Anderlecht*. Eight Days after his Grace joined the Army, which the same Day made a Motion, and encamp'd with the Right at *Bellengen*, the Left at *Lembeck* and *Hall* in the Rear; and upon Intelligence that the *French*, who had been

R 2 drawing

drawing together at the same time, continued quiet in their Lines, his Grace advanc'd nearer to them in order to meet them half-way for a Battle, which they had given out they would offer to the Confederates, or if they declined it, to lay Siege either to *Mons* or *Charleroy*. But on the 14th of *May*, certain Information was given, That the Enemy were come out of their Lines, and encamp'd at *Hasne* or *Paul*, and *Pironne*, where they had been review'd by the Elector of *Bavaria* and Duke of *Vandome*

Hereupon the Allies advanced the next Morning to *Seignies*, and the Enemy, who by this Motion, thought they would take the Camp of *Bois Seigneur-Isaac*, marched at the same time to *Pietra*. On the 27th the Duke of *Marlborough*, accompanied by several Generals, and Twelve Squadrons of Horse, took a View of the Ground, and Avenues that led to the *French* Camp, and upon Advice that they were posted in the Plain of *Fleurus*, a Council of War was held, wherein it was resolved to march to *Nivelle*, in order to attack them, and accordingly a Detachment was sent to view the Pass at *Rongueres*, through which they were to advance. The Generals, who were sent thither, reported, That the Enemy suspecting their Design, had secur'd that important Post, and would undoubtedly make it their Endeavour upon the first Motion of the Confederates, to hinder them from marching through that Pass, or else would Charge the first Troops that should get through with so much Advantage, that it would not be adviseable to move that Way. This Report being maturely weigh'd in a Council of War, and the Generals wisely considering at the same time, that the *French* had drained all their Garrisons, and muster'd all their Forces, with no other Design than to plunder the open and wealthy great Cities of *Brabant*, particularly *Louvain* and *Brussels*, in case the Allies should
-undertake

undertake any Siege, which they might have done in less Time, than the bringing up of the heavy Artillery would require; it was resolved to march back to *Brussels*, which prudent Advice was pursued with so much Diligence, that on the 26th the Confederate Army return'd from *Soignies* to the Camp of *Hall*, pass'd the next Day the Canal of *Brussels* at *Diggem*, and encamp'd at *Beaulieu*, where they rested the 30th; after which they march'd on the 31st to *Bethlehem*, laid Bridges over the *Dyle*, which they pass'd the 21st, and posted themselves at *Meldert*. The Enemy seeing their Design disappointed, advanced to the strong Camp at *Gemblours*, without daring to venture an Engagement, though much superior; and so both Armies continued above Two Months in their respective Camps, during which time, no Action worth Recording passed between them.

At last, upon certain Advice that the *French* had detach'd Thirteen Battalions and Twelve Squadrons towards *Provence*, where the Duke of *Savoy* was besieging the strong Fortress of *Toulon*, his Grace in Concert with Monsieur *d'Auverquerque* and the States-Deputies, resolv'd to march from *Meldert* towards *Genap*, from whence he might with less Disadvantage force the Enemy in their Camp at *Gemblours*. Accordingly, on the 9th of *August*, N. S. the Disposition was made for the Army to pass the *Dyle* at the Abbey of *Florival*, and late in the Evening Orders were given for the March of the Heavy-Baggage towards *Brussels*, and the laying Four Bridges on the *Dyle*; and at the same time a Body of Troops that were encamped near *Louvains* under Major General *Week*, and the Regiment of *Borbmar*, were order'd to march to *Florival*'s, and the Battalions in *Brussels* to advance to *Waterloe*. The 10th in the Morning the Artillery passed the *Dyle* at St *Jorisweert*; and about Three in the Afternoon the Duke of *Wirtemberg* marched

with

with 14 Squadrons to *Pieterhau*, with Orders
stay there till Morning, to observe the Enem[y]
and afterwards form the Rear-Guard. At 4 t[he]
whole Army decamp'd from *Meldert*, and acco[r]
ding to the Disposition that had been made, pas[s]
the *Dyle* at *Florival*; and having march'd all Nig[ht]
was, the 11th, at break of Day, about the Heigh[t]
of *Waveren*, where they made a short Halt, a[nd]
then continued their March towards *Genap*, whe[re]
they encamped, with their Right at *Promell[e]*
and their Left at *Davieres*, after a March of
Leagues. Here they had Intelligence, That t[he]
Enemy, upon notice of the Duke of *Wirtemberg[h]*
advancing with his Detachment to *Pieterbaus*, an[d]
of the Confederate Armies being in Motion, we[re]
extremely alarm'd, that their Troops were imme[e]
diately order'd to their Arms, and that they c[ut]
down several Trees in the Roads and Passage[s]
that led to their Camp, having no certain Info[r]
mation which way the Allies were gone, till abo[ut]
Midnight, when they began their March with a[ll]
possible haft, towards *Fleruss*, and *Hispenay*, inten[ding]
ding to be that Evening at *Goffilsers*, and gain th[e]
strong Camp at *Pieton*.

On the 12th, early in the Morning, the Con[?]
federate Generals receiv'd Advice, that the *Fren[ch]*
Army had made but a short Halt at *Goffilsers*, an[d]
reach'd *Seneff* about Midnight; the Elector of *B[a]*
varia taking his Head-Quarters in the Castle o[f]
Vanderbeck, and the Duke of *Vendosme* in the Farm
of *Rél*, between *Vanderbeck* and *Seneff*, having the
River *Pieton* before them. The Duke of *Marlborough*
and Monsieur *d'Auverquerque* having conferr'd there
upon it was resolved to march directly to *Nivelle*
in order to attack the Enemy, and accordingly
the Confederate Army march'd about 1 in the Af[-]
ternoon, and came into that Camp the same Even[-]
ing, their Right extending to *Valsanpont*, and their
Left to the River *Sonne*, at *Arquennes*. It being too

...e to attack the Enemy that Night, the necessary Preparations were made for doing it the next morning; and because it was rightly foreseen, [that] the Enemy would endeavour to retire in the [night], to gain the Camp at *Cambron*, all possible [care] was taken to prevent their Retreat. The [Count] *de Tilly*, with 40 Squadrons of Horse and [Dra]goons, commanded by the Earl of *Albermarle*, [and] the Major-Generals, Count *d'Erbach*, and *Ross*, [and] a Detachment of 5600 Grenadiers, commanded by Lieutenant General *Scholten*, and Major-[Ge]neral *Zoutland*, was order'd to post himself be[tw]een the Two Armies, with the Left at *Cornelisz*, [an]d the Right towards the Road from *Brack* to *Ni*-[vel]le, and in case the Enemy decamped, to fall up[o]n their Rear, and keep them in play, till the [w]hole Army could come up. Those Troops [m]arch'd with all imaginable Alacrity, notwith[st]anding which, they could not reach their re[sp]ective Posts before Midnight, and on the other [H]and, the *French* foreseeing the Duke of *Marlbo*-[rou]gh's Design, and judging that it would be im[p]ossible for them to avoid an Engagement, if [t]hey continued in that Camp till the next Day, [r]esolv'd to decamp in the Night.

They made the necessary Dispositions for that [p]urpose, about 7 of the clock, when the Confe[d]erate Army was coming into the Camp at *Nivelle*, [a]nd about 9 their Left began to retire towards *Marimont*, without beat of Drum, or sound of Trumpet. The 13th. a little before break of Day, Count *Tilly* advanc'd with his Detachment direct[l]y to the Enemy, saw their Army on a full March, [a]nd observ'd that they made their Retreat in good order, from Hedge to Hedge; and that the Coun[t]ry being very difficult, it was next to an im[p]ossibility to come at them: He sent Notice there[o]f to the Grand Army, and that he was march[i]ng to endeavour to attack their Rear, as he was

directed

directed: Whereupon 20 Battalions, and 30 Squadrons, with Count *Lottum* at the Head of them, were detach'd to support him. The Horse being commanded by Lieutenant-General *Dospr*, the Sieur *Schulemburgh*, and the Earl of *Athlone*, Majors General, and the Infantry by Lieutenant-General *Fagel*, and Major-General *Welderen*.

Count *Tilly* follow'd the Enemy with exquisite Diligence, and had several Skirmishes with their Rear, but having pursued them 3 or 4 Hours, as far as the Plains of *Marimont*, and observing that it was to no purpose to fatigue the Troops, he returned to the Camp. The Country being cut by many deep Roads, was favourable to the Retreat of the *French*, who posted therein some Infantry, which hinder'd the Confederate Horse from making Openings to follow them. The Duke of *Marlborough*, likewise, who was in the Pursuit, with a Detachment, return'd to his Camp, where he resolv'd to continue that Day, to give Time to the Troops to rest themselves, after the fatiguing March they had made; and because it was uncertain whither the Enemy bent their Course towards their Lines, or *Cambron*, Monsieur *d'Auverquerque* sent one of his Aid-de-Camp, with 150 Hussars, to post himself on the Hill of the *Great Roulx*, from whence they plainly discover'd their March, being about half a League from them. That Officer reported, That their Van-guard was advanc'd to St. *Dennis*, having the River *Haisne* behind them, which was confirm'd by the Spies, who added, That the Elector of *Bavaria* had his Quarters at St. *Dennis*, and the Duke of *Vendosme* at *Castreaux*.

The Generals concluded, from this March, that the Enemy did not design to retire within their Lines, but rather to possess the advantagious Camp at *Cambron* whereupon Orders were given for the Army to decamp from *Nivelle*, the 14th, about 6

the clock in the Morning, which had all the
way a most violent Rain to retard them, that ren-
d'd the Roads so very bad, that it was late when
Right came to *Soignies*, nor could the Left
until the 5th, in the Morning, although a
Pioneers had been at work ever since the 12th
ight, to repair the Roads from *Arquennes* to
nes. The Confederate Soldiers suffered very
ch in this March; but the Enemy still labour'd
der greater Disadvantages for having lain on
ir Arms, at St *Denms*, all Night, they pass'd on
ir March early the next Morning, in the same
nfusion as before to *Chievres*, where they arrived
out the same Time as the Allies came to *Soignies*.
sides the Fatigue this precipitate Retreat occa-
n'd a wonderful Desertion among the *French*; for
ir Soldiers being without Bread for above 2
ays, and without Rest for 3, not having Time
put up their Tents between *Seneff* and *Chievres*,
ove 8000 of them went over to the Confe-
rates, and at least as many more to *Brussels*, and
her Places. They likewise were in want of all
rts of Necessaries during their whole March from
mbleurs, their Baggage being sent off from thence,
ith their Artillery to *Charleroy*, upon their first
otion, to avoid an Engagement.
The great Rains which continued some Days,
ving made the Ways altogether unpassable, obli-
d his Grace to give over the Pursuit of the
nemy, and confin'd him and his Troops to the
amp at *Soignies*; and in the mean Time the Ene-
y fortified the Approaches to theirs, in the best
anner the Weather would permit. And tho' the
rmy was soon after re-inforced with 6 Battalions,
d 2 Regiments of Horse, from the Flying-Camp
Count *la Motte*, yet they retired farther behind
Marque, with their Right at *Pont a Tresin*, and
ir Left under the Cannon of *Lisle*. Whereupon
e Allies advanc'd towards them, and encamped

S with

with their Right at Rollegem, and their Left at Helchin, near the Scheld, subsisting all this while upon the French Territories.

Eight Days after they were possess'd of this Camp, the Duke of Marlborough having notice, That the French had made a Disposition to forrage that Morning at Templeuve, and the Villages near it, march'd out at break of Day, with 20000 Foot, 5000 Horse, and 12 Pieces of Cannon, in order to attack the Guard which cover'd them, and endeavour, by those Means, to bring them to a general Action; but the Enemy were inform'd of it, and did not think fit to venture out of their Camp. His Grace thereupon order'd his Troops to forrage those Places, which was done without the least Opposition, tho' under the Cannon of Tournay, within a League of the Enemies Camp, and 3 from the Confederates.

At last the Duke finding it impossible to bring the cautious Generals of the other Side, to a decisive Engagement, left the Camp at Helchin, where he form'd the Scheme of besieging Lisle the following Campagne, on the the 4th of October, and upon his Arrival at the Hague, the 6th of the same Month, made a Visit to the Grand Pensionary and Monsieur de Slingerland, Secretary of the Council of State. In the Afternoon of the following Day his Grace had a Conference with the Deputies of the States-General, wherein he communicated the Orders he had receiv'd from the Queen his Mistress, to repair to Francfort, and confer with the Electors of Mentz and Hannover, about the Operations for the ensuing Year; and the next Day after having again been in Consultation with those Deputies, set out for the Army, to give the necessary Orders for their marching into Winter Quarters. Where immediately after his arrival, the Troops designed for the Garrisons of Menin, Courtray, and Oudenard, went into those Places, and

...se for other Places filed off likewise for their ...spective Winter Quarters, as soon as they had ...d the *French* Army was separated

...rom hence his Grace set out for *Germany* the ...of *October*, and came to *Francfort* the 21st fol... ...g, where having engag'd the Princes of the ...ire to furnish their respective Quota's early, ...the War might be carried on with vigour in ...se Parts; and concerted with the Imperial ...isters the necessary Measures for Prince *Eugene* ...make the following Campagne with him in ...ders, he departed from thence the 29th, for ...*Hague*, where he was welcom'd at his return, ...the States-General, after he had been highly ...ess'd at the several Courts through which he ...s'd, in particular by the Elector *Palatine*, who ...t him at *Bruck*, about a League from his Ca... ...of *Bensberg*, where his Highness gave him a ...endid Dinner, under a very magnificent *Pervisan* ...nt, erected for that purpose; and after he had ...cluded several important Affairs, that were of ...utmost Consequence to the Grand Alliance

On the 4th of *November*, the Duke embark'd for ...land, and arriv'd at S*t James*'s the 7th of the ...me Month, where he was very graciously re...v'd by Her Majesty, and the Prince of *Den*... ...k, who were fully appriz'd of what was owing ...him for his Zeal for the Common Interest; ...some People that were well acquainted with ...litary Affairs, and knew how to lay hold of all ...vantages, spoke but indifferently of his Grace's ...vices in the Field this Campagne, and whatso... ...r he might deserve for his Negotiations, alledg'd, ...at the Dexterity of the Enemy prevented him ...every Design, and that he was not without his ...lts, in particular, want of Intelligence which ...ne of the most requisite Thing for a General, ...t would be accomplish'd in the Art of War. ...this Mind a Majority of both Houses of Par-

S 2   liament

liament were thought to be, since neither gave him their Thanks, and the House of Lords, which his Grace himself was a Member of, had their Debates interspers'd with some Glances at his Conduct. All that bore Reference to him during the Session, was, That upon an Enquiry into the State of the Nation, and the Misfortunes of the Battle of *Almanza*, and Siege of *Toulon*, the Earl of *Rochester* having commended the Earl of *Peterborough*'s Conduct and Courage, while he was employ'd in *Spain*, and enumerated his Services, for it had been a constant Custom, That when a Person of his Rank, that had acquir'd so much Honour abroad in so eminent a Post, as his Lordship had, return'd Home, he had either Thanks given him, or was called to an Account: Urging that the same ought to be done in the Earl of *Peterborough*'s Case. The Lord H— who spoke next, enlarg'd likewise on the Earl of *Peterborough*'s successful Services, but dextrously put off the Returning him Thanks, till the whole Tenure of his Conduct had been examined, to which the *Earl himself profess'd, He had nothing more at Heart*. The Lord *Haversham* was not silent, but having highly Extolled the same Lords Valour, Skill and Successes, made aside Wind Reflections the Earl of *Galway*, who succeeded the Earl of *Peterborough* in his Command: Averring, *That 'tis no wonder our Affairs in* Spain *went so ill, since the Management of them had been entrusted to a Foreigner.* Hereupon, several Members of that August Assembly (*the* QUEEN *present*) shew'd the necessity of carrying on the War, till the *Whole Monarchy* of *Spain* was recovered, and King *CHARLES* setled on the Throne, and among the rest the Earl of *Peterborough* himself said, *They ought to give the Queen Nineteen Shillings in the Pound, rather than make Peace on any other Terms,* adding, *That if it were thought necessary, he was ready to return to* Spain, *and serve even under the Earl of* Galway. This naturally brought

the consideration of Means and Ways to retrieve the Affairs of *Spain*, in Relation to which, the Earl of *Rochester* affirm'd, That *they seem'd to neglect the Principal Business and mind Accessories*, adding, He *remember'd the saying of a great General, the Old Duke of* Schombergh, (viz.) That the Attacking *France* in the *Netherlands*, was like taking a Bull by the Horns, *and therefore his Lordship proposed, That they should stand on the Defensive in* Flanders, *and send from thence* 15 or 20000 *Men into* Catalonia. That Noble Peer was seconded by the Earl of *Nottingham*, who complained of *Spain* being in a manner abandon'd. But the Duke of *Marlborough* shew'd with some Warmth, the Danger of such an Undigested Counsel, and the Necessity of *Augmenting*, rather than *Diminishing* the Forces in *Flanders*. The two chief Reasons his Grace urg'd were. First, *That most of the Enemies strong Places there, might be kept with one Battalion in each; whereas, the great Towns of* Brabant, *which the Allies had Conquer'd, required Twenty Times that Number of Men for their Preservation.* Secondly, *That if our Army in the* Netherlands *was weakened, and the* French *by their great superiority, should gain any considerable Advantage, which it was not improbable they might, the Discontented Part in* Holland, *who were not a Few, and bore with Impatience the necessary Charges of the War, would not fail crying out for Peace.* Hereupon, the Earl of *Rochester* said, " He wonder'd that No-
" ble Peer who had been ever *Conspicuous* for his
" *Calmness* and *Moderation*, should then be *out* of his
" *Temper*; adding, that there being an absolute
" Necessity to succour *Spain*, His Grace would o-
" blige their Lordships, if he would let them know
" where they might get Troops to send thither,
" and the more, because the Earl of *Peterborough*
" had that very Day assured them, that he had
" heard Prince *Eugene* say, That *the German Soldiers had rather be Decimated than sent to* Spain. The Duke of *Marlborough* very prudently answer'd the Reproach

proach of having shew'd some *Warmth*, by saying, *The Thing was of too great Importance to be spoken of without Concern*: And as for the Question proposed by the Earl, he answer'd it thus, *That if altho' it was improper to disclose secret Projects in so great an Assembly,* (to which that Day many Strangers had been admitted by the Favour of the Queens Presence) *because the Enemy would not fail of being informed of Them, yet to gratifie their Lordships, he could assure them, that Measures had already been concerted with the Emperour, for the Forming an Army* of 40000 *Men,* (whom he specified under the Command of the Duke of *Savoy,*) *and for sending Powerful Succours to King* CHARLES, adding, *That it was to be hoped, that Prince* Eugene *might be prevail'd with, to go and Command in* Spain, *in which Case, the Germans would gladly follow Him thither. The only difficulty which His* Grace said, *might be Objected against this Scheme, was the usual* slowness of the Court of Vienna; to which purpose, he took notice, That *if the* 7000 German *Recruits, which the Emperour had promised for the Army in* Piedmont, *had arriv'd Time enough, the Enterprize against* Toulon, *might have been attended with Success. But that it was to be hoped, and He durst engage his Word for it, that for the future, His Imperial Majesty would punctually perform his Promises* Upon this the Debate ended in an Address to Her Majesty that She would do Her utmost to oblige such of Her Allies as had hitherto fail'd in their Parts, to Act for the future as those, who had a real Concern for Restoring and securing Peace, and Liberty to *Europe.*

The Session of Parliament being ended, the Duke's Presence was as necessary in the Field, as it had been in the Cabinet, and the Armies on both Sides in the *Netherlands,* (soon after he had dispatch'd his Affairs at the *Hague*) took Post in their respective Places of Encampment. The *French* at *Soignies*, where the Dukes of *Burgundy* and *Berry,* and the Chevalier St. *George*, after his pretended Invasion of *Scotland*, joined them, while the Confederates made a Motion from *Billinghen*, and advanced the Right to *Herfelingen*, and the Left to *ll* and *Tulse*, the Head-Quarters being at St. *Renello*, which brought the Two contending Parties very near, and gave Hopes of a sudden Engagement to the latter, but the Enemy, to amuse our Generals, sent again for their heavy Baggage, and forrag'd for 2 Days, from whence it was concur'd, that they did not intend to march on the *th* of *June*, as some Deserters had reported; which made our Generals resolve to send their Army to forrage next Morning, and the Forragers went out accordingly by break of Day. But an Hour after Advice came, That the Enemy had began that Night, at 10, to send back their Baggage to *Mons*, and decamped the 7th of *June*, without any Noise, about 11, marching towards *Nivelle*. Whereupon the Foragers were immediately recalled; and that no Time might be lost, the Infantry March'd just about Noon from St. *Renello*, and were followed by the Cavalry. About Four they Form'd four Columns, intending to Encamp with their Right towards *Anderlecht*, and the Left at *Luke*; but upon Advice, that the *French* had not Encamped at *Nivelle*, but had continued their March by *Bois Seigneur Isaac* to *Brainela Lieu*, the Duke judged that they could not have any other Design, than to Post themselves on the Banks of the *Dyle*, to hinder the Confederates from passing the same, which was the very same Project that the Duke of *Vendome* had framed last Year; which made Him think fit likewise to continue his March all Night, as the only means to prevent the Enemy, and arriv'd at *Ferbank* with his Forces, very much Fatigued by the long March they had made, and the continual Rains for 24 Hours together. The *French* having notice of this Expeditious March, did not think

fit

fit to advance further than *Genap*, where they continued for some Time, both Armies keeping themselves within their respective Camps, for the rest of the Month of *June* and part of *July*; the Allies waiting for Prince *Eugenes* taking the Field, with an Army that was to be composed of the Troops of *Prussia* and *Hesse* some Regiments of the Elector *Palatine*, and some Imperialist's. The motion of this Body was retarded by several difficulties raised, concerning the March of the *Palatine* Forces, which the Duke of *Vendome* having Intelligence of, and concluding that the Allies would hardly venture to force him in the Passes and Defiles he had seiz'd on, immediately commanded a Detachment to March towards *Ghent* and *Bruges*, in order to surprize those Towns, which was accordingly executed on the 5th of *July* after this manner.

A Party of *French* Troops commanded by the Brigadiers *la Faille* and *Pasteur*, advanced before Break of Day to the first of those Places: Five or Six Soldiers went before, and upon the Opening of the Gates, the *French* pretended to the Watch, which consisted of Burghers, and was not more numerous, than those who amused them with Stories of Desertion, immediately after, another small Company of the same Kidney appear'd, and entertain'd the same Centinels, with the like Fictitious Relations, till Brigadier *la Faille* came in Person, who instantly appeared, and order'd the Guard at the Gates to lay down their Arms, and submit to the King of *Spain*. They obey'd his Orders without any Resistance, and that General after he had secured the Gates, and admitted his Troops, went directly to the *Town-House*, where he summoned the Burghers to meet. Upon their Convening, he Commanded a General Pardon to be Read, in which Assurances were given them of being Protected in their Antient Rights and Liberties.

As soon as the Town was taken, the *French* caused the Governor of the Citadel to be summoned to surrender; but the Officer who commanded therein, returned for Answer, *He would defend it to the last Extremity.* Hereupon the *French* form'd their approaches against it; and Major-General *Murray*, who was posted at *Marsenkirk* with Two *English*, and One *Spanish* Battalion, endeavour'd to throw a Reinforcement into the Castle, but was hinder'd in his Design, and obliged to retire. The Governor of the Citadel capitulated the next Day, as did the Town of *Bruges*, to a Detachment that arrived before it, without making the least Opposition, only some Ceremonies in the Matter were observed, and certain Conditions agreed upon respecting the Receiver of their Contributions, and his Comptroller. But the whole Air of the Capitulation was said by some that were Friends to the Duke of *Marlborough*, "to demonstrate that the Articles thereof were agreed upon long before by other Persons, than those that pretended to execute them, though some that were not implicite Believers of his Grace's Infallibility, reported the quite contrary, and did not stick to affirm, That Two such Places defenceless of themselves without Assistance from abroad, could not but submit to such a Number of Troops as came against them. Wherever the Fault lay, the Loss of these Towns gave, being to several Pasquinades at the *Hague*, said to be encourag'd by General *Slangenburgh*, wherein the Conduct of the Confederate Generals, especially his that bore the supreme Command, was highly censured

Upon Major-General *Murray*'s leaving the Town of *Ghent*, he retired to the *Saz*, where he found Messieurs *Tulleckeen*, *Quint*, *Steenberghen*, and *Neyveen*, Deputies of the States for the Affairs of *Flanders*, who seem'd concern'd at the Events which happen'd so contrary to the common Expectation. However,

T

ever, with these he concerted proper Methods to put the Frontiers in a Posture of Defence, and for securing such other Posts as seem'd most exposed. But whilst he and the Deputies were endeavouring to obstruct the Progress of the *French* in that Part of *Flanders*, from the Force and Intreigues of the Two Crowns. The Duke of *Marlborough* and Monsieur *d'Auverquerque* resolved to march towards their Grand Army, who had at that time invested *Audenarde*; in order to which they pass'd the Canal near *Brussels*, in Four Columns, their Right extending as far as *Moulin de Tombergh*, and their Left to *Anderlecht*. From this Camp, to prevent the ill Consequences of the former Misfortune, the General order'd Four Regiments for *Dendermonde*, and from thence they were to have proceeded further, but they came too late. At the same time the *French* passed the *Senne* at *Hall*, and *Tubise*, and were passing at the Mill of *Gosck* till late in the Evening, when the Confederates Right Wing, after a long March, came up within a League of them.

It was thought adviseable to attack them that Night, but early the next Morning his Grace gave Orders for the Army to form themselves into Battle Array, when the Enemy frustrated his Intentions by passing over the *Dender* with the utmost Expedition that very Night, and taking their Rout through the Town of *Ninove*, and over several Bridges, which were made near it for that purpose. So that the Detachment which was sent to fall upon their Rear-Guard came too late to find any thing but their small Baggage and the Forces which guarded it; the first of which became a Prey to the Conquerors after they had defeated the last.

This Enterprize being over, the Allies encamped at *Asche*, where Prince *Eugene* joined the Army, whose Presence very much contributed to those glorious Successes, which soon after attended the
Force

Forces under his, and his Grace's Command. Here the Army rested Two Days, and a Council of War was called. The March of the Baggage was regulated, and Pioneers sent before to clear the Ways, and put the Roads into such a Condition might facilitate their coming to Action. About this time the Duke of *Marlborough* was taken with fits of an intermitting Fever, but that Disease could not retard his Vigour, and it was not long but he saw himself in a Condition to perform the Duties of his Post In the mean time the *French* made a Motion to come to the intended Siege of *Audenarde*, with an Intent to take the Camp of *Lessines*, which if they had effected, that Town must of course have submitted to mercy, being absolutely cut off from receiving any Relief from the Confederates.

The *French* were so near this advantageous Post, that they thought themselves secure of it, and that, or some other hidden Cause, made them negligent of improving the present Crisis. But soon to their great Surprize, their Scouts brought them Notice, That the Troops of the Allies having marched all Night had prevented them in their Design, and were ready to enter into a Camp which they had mark'd out for their own The Measures that had been before concerted by the Confederate Generals, occasion'd so extraordinary and swift a March, that the whole Army had measured Fifteen Miles from Day-break to Eleven in the Morning of the same Day. Thus the *French* being disappointed in securing themselves *Lessines*, left the Road to that Place, and advanced by the Way of *Garve* to pass the *Scheld* here

This March of the Duke of *Marlborough* acquainted the *French* with his real Intention, and they knew him too well to suspect his Approach towards them, pretended any thing else but a Design to engage They therefore abandon'd the Siege of *Audenarde*, and made the best of their way

T 2   towards

towards their Lines. Whatever infatuated their Generals to vary thus in their Councils, and alter their Designs so often as they did, without being steady in any Resolve. I shall not pretend to determine it, it will be time enough to consider the Measures which they took in this Battle, after I have given the Description of it; but this is most evident that these their uncertain Proceedings gave the Confederates time to overtake their Armies before they were in a Condition to receive them.

Wednesday the 11th of *July*, N. S. was the Day appointed by Providence, in which the Troops of *France* lost both the Reputation of their Courage and their Military Judgment. All Things being ready in the Confederate Camp for an Engagement, and the Officers and Soldiers in General shewing an inexpressible Ardor to give Marks of their Resolution and Bravery, Major General *Cadogan* was detach'd with Eight Squadrons and Sixteen Battalions to *Audenarde*, to make Ways and Bridges there for the Passage of the Army over the River that runs near that Town. The Army follow'd in Four Columns about Eight of the Clock in the Morning and march'd in the same manner they had encamp'd before, directing their Rout to the Left. During the March, Advice was brought, That the Enemy's Army was still passing the River at *Gavre*, and that if they used Expedition, there were yet hopes of an Engagement. This Piece of News was so agreeable to the Army, that they all marched from the General Officers to the Private Men, with all possible Diligence, reciprocally encouraging one another to undergo the Difficulties of the Way, which would at length afford them an Opportunity of signalizing their Courage. So great was the Desire of the Soldiers for Action, that several, who were carried on Horses and Waggons before the Fight, dismounted when the Attack began, and
though

though Weak and Ill did very remarkable Service. At Two of the Clock the Front of the whole Army arrived at the Bridges, over which the Sixteen Battalions that march'd with General *Cadogan* were then passing.

Eight Squadrons, and Part of the former Detachment, with the Quarter-Masters and Major-General *Rantzau* at the Head of them, were posted behind a Rivulet that runs into the *Scheld*, and these Gentlemen took Notice that the *French* were partly marching, and partly drawn up in Order of Battle. The Troops that went forward, took their Road through the Village of *Heurne*, which is situated on the Banks of the *Scheld*, and has a High-way that runs through it, which extends it self along the River before-mentioned. Into this Post the *French* threw Seven Battalions; and the neighbouring Plains which confronted the little Village, were filled with the Troops of the Houshold, who were drawn up exactly opposite to the Eight Squadrons under Major-General *Rantzau*, no Obstacle but a small Rivulet dividing them: Behind the Village were Morasses, Woods, and Defiles, so that an Army had no other way conveniently to march, but through the High Road. This Disposition of the *French* made it uncertain whether their real Design was to hinder the Duke of *Marlborough*'s passing the *Scheld*, or to gain their own Lines between *Lisle* and *Tournay*, which they thought they might have done, not thinking that so considerable a Body as that of the Confederates could march Five Leagues in a close Country abounding in Passes and Defiles, have their Roads levelled, pass a great River, and made an Attack upon them the same Day. About Three in the Afternoon the *French* Cavalry began to disappear, directing their March towards their own Right. This Motion of the Horse gave Major General *Cadogan* an Opportunity of falling

upon

upon the 7 Battalions posted in the Village of *Heure*, who now had no other Aid at Hand than what their own Valour could befriend them with. That Officer order'd these to be charged with 12 Battalions of the 16 under his command, the other 4 being too far in the Rear: Brigadier *Sabin*, at the Head of his Brigade, began the Attack, and being well seconded by the rest, he utterly defeated them, taking 3 of the 7 Battalions entire, and making many of the Officers and private Men Prisoners, that belong'd to the other Four.

Immediately after, General *Rantzau*, at the Head of the 8 Squadrons, with the Quarter-Masters, passed the Rivulet, and enter'd into the Plain, where part of the *French* Horse had been drawn up between the Village of *Rose* and *Mullen*, a great many Squadrons of their Rear-Guard being still filing through that Plain. The 8 Squadrons, with the Quarter-Masters, being formed into Order of Battle, charg'd them with great Vigour, and drove them into the close Grounds, and the Highway which led into the March of their own Army. Here it was that the Electoral Prince of *Hannover*, who had obtained leave to make the Campagne in *Flanders*, and had arrived a few Days before, signalized himself, and acted Things worthy of his Birth, and those Illustrious Crowns his Family is entituled to. That Prince charged, with Sword in Hand, as a Voluntier, at the Head of his Father's Dragoons, commanded by Lieutenant-General *Bulau*. His Horse was shot under him, and Colonel *Luckey*, who headed the Squadron where he took Post, fighting like a Man of Honour, was killed in his presence; several other Voluntiers, of high Rank, distinguish'd themselves upon this Occasion, amongst whom was Lieutenant General *Schuylemberg*. These Gentlemen charged in the Van of the Horse, with equal Spirit and Gallantry, animating the private Men by their Example, till Fortune

declared

clared in their Favour. The *French* that were posted here, after they had behav'd themselves very valiantly, were put into confusion, and Colonel *Bartock*, who commanded them, having given sensible Proofs of his Courage and Conduct, was wounded and taken Prisoner, with the loss of several Officers, 12 Standards, and 2 Kettle-Drums.

The *French* Army, which seem'd to direct their March for *Taunnay*, observing the success of the Engagement at the Village of *Hearne*, and being sensible that the Confederates would soon attack them, (having for that purpose pass'd their Troops over the *Scheld*,) found themselves under a necessity to make a Stand, and drew their Forces up in order of Battle, before the Castle of *Broan*, having in their Front several Defiles, guarded with Enclosures of Hedges, Ditches, and Thickets. As the Confederate Troops came forward, the Duke of *Marlborough*, and Prince *Eugene* form'd the Right Wing, a little distant from the Castle, where the *French* drew up in Battalia, and after the discharge of a few Field-Pieces, the Action came on, and the Fire was most terrible, every Foot of Ground being disputed with the utmost Vigour and Obstinacy. But the Troops of the High Allies being encourag'd by the Presence and Example of the Generals, made their Way through all Obstacles, to Honour and Victory. They broke the Enemy every where, and obliged them, tho' with a great deal of Reluctance, to quit their Posts, which they had well defended.

The Left Wing, as yet, was little or nothing engaged, because of the Defiles, and the long Circuit they were to take, to be able to charge the Enemy; yet the Velt-Marshal, Monsieur *d'Auvenquerque*, who had been in a languishing Condition all the Winter long, was now mounted on Horse-back, and resolved to force the *French* to a Battle.

a Battle Neither the Fatigues of the many Campagnes he had made, the many Wounds he had received, nor his ill State of Health, could hinder him from shewing this, the last Proof of his great Courage He gave Orders to Major General *Week* to march with the Brigades of *Waffenaer* and *Oudenburgh*, which supported by the Cavalry under the command of the Count *de Tilly*, took Post in a small Plain, where they were rang'd into order of Battle. The *French* retired, and immediately shelter'd themselves under the Coverts of the Hedges, between *Broun* and *Lede*, towards the main Body of their Army, where the Fire was very hot. Hither came the Prince of *Nassau*, with Count *Oxenstern*, and 4 Brigades of Infantry, which charged the Enemy in Flank; and so about 6 in the Evening, the Right, Left, and Main Body, were all engag'd; soon after which, the *French* gave Ground every where, and in their Retreat met some Battalions of the Confederates, whose Earnestness to be forward in Fight, had carried them too far from their other Troops.

At last the Enemies finding themselves charg'd both in Front and Flank, and being unable to withstand the Efforts of their Antagonists Foot any longer the *King's-Houshold*, which had suffer'd very much retired in the utmost disorder, leaving many Prisoners behind them whom their Wounds, or the Croud, would not permit to retreat as fast as their Companions. The Dragoons favour'd them in this, and received several Discharges of the Confederate Foot so that they affirmed with a great deal of Justice That they sacrific'd themselves to save those Troops They would afterwards have made their Escape, but were intercepted by the Confederate Cavalry, and so cut to pieces, that out of 2 Regiments which were engag'd in this part of the Action, one half of their number were slain, and the rest surrendred them-elves Prisoners of War. Several other Regiments followed their Example, and secured themselves, accepting the like Terms

The Night which gives rest to all Men, put an end to the Slaughter, and sav'd the remainder of the French Troops: For if the Daylight had continued but 2 or 3 Hours longer, the Dukes of Burgundy and Berry must have given a much more dismal Account of the Campagne to their Grandfather. They were so sincere as to acknowledge, That several of their best Regiments were rendred unserviceable; that 2 very fine Battalions of Swiss, (viz.) Phiffer and Villars, underwent the same Fate; and that the Regiment of the Chevalier de Rohan, and the Queen's, were entirely destroy'd, and that of Burgundy in as bad a Condition.

Thus ended the Battle of Audenarde, which was concerted, enter'd into, and prosecuted with all the Judgment, Vigour, and consummate Prudence, that it was possible to exert on the Side of the Confederates; and 'tis hard to determine what Praise were due both to their Officers and Soldiers in general upon this account. To affirm what number of Men the French lost in this Battle, would be too presumptious, though it has been thought fit to affirm, in our publick Prints, whose Authority seems to be founded on a fair Computation, that it appear'd they left above 4000 Men dead upon the spot, and carried away, according to Letters from Ghent, above 5000 wounded, that above 8000 Prisoners remain'd in the power of the Victors, and among them 750 Officers, viz. 1 Lieutenant-General, 4 Major Generals, 5 Brigadiers, 14 Colonels, 6 Lieutenants, 96 Cornets, 186 *Gens d'Arms*, and 47 Quarter-Masters. The chief of these were the Chevalier *de Rohan*, the Duke *de St. Agnan*, the Duke *de Charost*, the Marquiss *de Byron*, and the Marquiss *de Russey* Those of the most considerable Rank that were kill'd, were the Sieur

U de

de Bertoch, and the Marquiss *de Ximenes*, Colonel of the Royal Regiment of *Rousillon*.

The Allies lost a Major-General, the Colonels *Adercas* and *Boisen*, Lieutenant-Colonel *Hop*, and 4[?] other Officers, with a 1000 private Men. The Brigadiers *Baudeken* and *Berner*, 4 Colonels, 16[?] other Officers, and near 2000 Men were wounded. Of the *English* Officers, Sir *John Matthews*, and Captain *Dean* of the Guards, were reckon'd among the slain; Major-General *Meredith* receiv'd a Wound in his Cheek, and Colonel *Groves*, and Colonel *Pennyfeather* were both dangerously wounded.

The Confederate Troops being return'd to their Camp, from pursuing the Enemy, who fled towards *Ghent*, rested for 2 Days, whilst the Duke of *Marlborough*, Prince *Eugene*, Monsieur *d'Auverque*, and the Deputies of the States-General, debated in a Council of War, what was necessary to be done, for the prosecution of the good Success wherewith God had been pleased to favour the Arms of the Allies. The result was, That the Army under the Duke of *Marlborough*, should immediately march towards *Menin*, pass the *Lys*, level the Lines between *Warneton* and *Ipres*, and hinder any Detachment from getting into the last of those Places. Prince *Eugene* was to march at the same Time towards *Brussels*, in order to assemble the Army which he was to command, to observe the Duke of *Berwick*, (who had drawn together a considerable Body, made up of Detachments from the *Rhine*, and other Places) and to hinder the *French* from retiring into *Brabant*, by the same Way they came.

According to these Resolutions, Count *Lottum*, General of the *Prussians*, march'd the 13th of J[?] at Night, with 30 Battalions, and 40 Squadrons, advanced towards the *French* Lines, after which the Army took the Road towards *Menin*, pass'd the *Lys*, near that Place, and encamp'd within a small
distance

...tance from the Town, whilst the Detachment ...Prussians demolished the French Lines, another ...sent to raise Contributions as far as Arras, ...Deputies of which not being able to agree ...the same, return'd back again. Upon this, ...Generals of the Allies had recourse to Milita-...Execution, and Two of the Suburbs of that ...wn were burn'd, and would have oblig'd the ...wn of Lens to undergo the same Fate, but that ...Inhabitants had so much Prudence, to give ...ostages for what was demanded of them. ...Other Detachments were likewise sent from ...Confederate Army, which did the same by ...ardy, as had been done by the Province of Ar-..., while those that were encamped near Menin, ...sied themselves with erecting vast Magazines ...that Place, and in providing Artillery, and all ...her Things necessary for carrying on some ...mportant Siege, which happen'd to be that of ...sle, after the Junction of Prince Eugene's Army ...ith the Duke of Marlborough. This the French had ...ot been wanting to foresee, but had likewise ...ade Provisions suitable to the Danger they ap-...re hended, and Monsieur Chamillard, the King's ...hief Minister, was order'd to repair thither, ...ith the Marshal de Boufflers, who was Gover-...our of that City, before it was invested; the ...ne to command the Besieged, and the Other ...chear up the Officers and Soldiers, with Promises ...f Preferment to such as should signalize them-...elves by their Fidelity, Patience and Courage in ...n Affair of so great moment. But the Money ...he former brought with him, was what chiefly ...nimated the Garrison, and inspired them with ...esolutions to defend the Place to the last Ex-...remity. Nor were these Precautions more than ...ecessary, for by this Time the Confederates were ...arching to attack the Place, which was actually ...vested on the 13th of August, by Prince Eugene,

while

while the Duke of *Marlborough* took upon h[im]
to cover the Siege, by pitching his Camp a[t]
Helchin, whence he had the conveniency to re[-]
inforce the Troops employ'd in that Enterprize
from Time to Time, or to march and fight th[e]
Enemy, if Occasion should require.

To recite the Particulars of this Memorab[le]
Siege, would take up more Time than my prese[nt]
Scheme will allow, wherefore I shall only a[c-]
quaint my Reader, That the Trenches were open[ed]
against the Town on the 22d of the same Mo[nth]
in which it was invested; and after various [At-]
tacks, wherein the Besiegers and Besieged had th[eir]
several Advantages, and as many fruitless Attem[pts]
to relieve it on the part of the *French*, someti[mes]
by pretending to offer Battle to the Confedera[tes]
at others, by using Stratagems to supply it w[ith]
Men and Ammunition, which was once effe[cted]
by the Chevalier *de Luxemburgh*, the City of L[ysle]
surrendred upon Articles on the 22d of *October* fo[l-]
lowing.

Not that History should be silent at a Transa[ction]
on that happen'd during the Prosecution of th[e]
Siege, which, tho' not executed by his Grace [in]
Person, highly redounds to his Grace's Honour,
being the result of his Foresight and Orders T[he]
Army before the Town as well as that which c[o-]
ver'd it, being in great Straits for want of A[m-]
munition and Provision, which were coming [to]
them from *Ostend*, and the Enemy having noti[ce]
of the great Convoy that was preparing for the[m]
at that Place, it was judg'd adviseable by the Du[ke]
of *Marlborough*, to send several Detachments [to]
cover the march of the Waggons According[ly]
General *Webb*, who was joined at *Tourhout*, by t[he]
Troops before-mention'd, on the 27th of *Septemb[er]*
received Advice, That Major *Savory*, of the Reg[i-]
ment of *Gethem*, had possess'd himself of the P[ost]
at *Oudenburgh*, whereupon he sent 600 Grenadie[rs]
und[er]

under the command of Colonel *Hamilton*, with that of *Foot*, commanded by Colonel *Wought*, the whole under the direction of Brigadier *Landsberg*, to reinforce that Post. The Day following at 8 in the Morning, all the Horse were order'd to *Hoogleed*, to wait the arrival of the Convoy there, except 50, who were sent the Night before, under the command of the Count *Lottum* to *Oudenburgh*, with Orders to the 2 Battalions, and 600 Grenadiers to Escorte, the Convoy to *Hocklaert*, and afterwards to retain the Foot at *Tourhout*. About Noon Count *Lottum* returned to *Tourhout*, with Advice, That in his way to *Jeteghem*, he met with an advanced Guard of the Enemy, which he push'd into the Plain, where he observed 16 Squadrons moun'ing in great haste, at the Alarm which their advanc'd Guard gave them; whereupon he thought it necessary to return to give the General an Account of it. Upon this Intelligence, all the Foot, consisting of 22 Battalions, Count *Lottum*, with his 150 Horse making the advanced Guard with the Quarter Masters and Grenadiers that were not detach'd, were order'd to march immediately to gain the Village of *Jeteghem*, by the Way of *Wynendale* They perceiv'd the Enemy in the opening of the Plain, whereupon the Quarter-masters and Grenadiers were drawn up in order of Battle. Major-General *Webb*, and Count *Woudenbourgh*, at the Head of the 150 Horse, advanced to *Reconnoitre* the Enemy, gave Orders, at the same Time, for the Foot to advance, and form themselves as fast as possible in the Plain. The 150 Horse were left at the Opening of the Plain, under the command of Count *Lottum*, to amuse the Enemy, and embarass the more, the Quarter-Masters and Grenadiers were posted in a low Coppice, on the side of the Plain, where the Enemy were expected to pass. As soon as the Troops pass'd out of the Defile, into the Plain, Major-General *Webb* drew

them

them up in Battalia, posting them in the Opening between the Wood of *Wynendale*, and the Coppice on the other side, where the Quarter-Masters and Grenadiers were posted. They had scarce got our Battalions into the Openings, when the Enemy began to cannonade us with 40 Pieces of Cannon, whereof 10 were of 3 Bores. Notwithstanding the great fire of the Enemy, the 150 Horse kept their Ground, which produced the desired effect, in giving the General Time to form his Foot in Two Lines. The Left Wing was extended beyond the low Coppice, as well to prevent the Enemy from passing that Way, as to cover our Flank. On our Right-Flank was posted in the Wood of *Wynendale*, the Regiment of *Hucksom*, and on our Flank on the Left, the Regiment of the Hereditary Prince of *Prussia*, commanded by Colonel *Rhader*, with Orders not to discover themselves, nor fire till they could take the Enemy in Flank; some Plotoons of Grenadiers, with the same Orders, were advanced 40 Paces upon the Right and Left, the Quarter-Masters were also posted in a Round on the Left, that crossed through the fore-mentioned law Coppice. The Enemy, after 3 Hours cannonading, advanced towards us on the Plain, in 12 Lines, whereof 6 were Foot, and 6 Horse: whereupon Count *Lottum* was order'd to retire, and post himself 300 Paces behind the Foot, which he did in very good order. The *French* continued to march strait up to us, with 40 Battalions, and 60 Squadrons, but the General perceiving they extended themselves to their Right on the Coppice, he sent Count *Nassau* to observe their Motion, who immediately order'd thither the Regiment of *Grumbkow*, commanded by Colonel *Beschfert*. Brigadier *Else* being come up with the last Regiment, was posted on the Right, in the Wood of *Wynendale*. About half a Quarter of an Hour before the Engagement began, the 2 Battalions, and 100 Grenarenadiers that had been detach'd, having Advice, that the Enemy advanced to attack us, rejoin'd just Time enough to form a Third Line. Some [minu]tes after, the Enemy began the Attack, mar[chi]ng withing 15 Paces of our Flank, on the Right, [wher]e the Battalions, who hid themselves, accor[ding] to the General's Orders, and who were not [fi]re till the *French* Flank came opposite to them, [gav]e them such a warm Fire, that their Left[w]ing gave into their Center, and the Regiment [of] the Hereditary Prince, who was posted on the [fla]nk of the Confederates Left, much about the [sam]e distance, did not miss the Opportunity of [th]eir disorder; but the *Swiss* Regiment of *Albemarle*, [u]nder the command of Colonel *Hirtgill*, advancing [u]pon their Horse, that were endeavouring to pe[n]etrate, engag'd them long enough, to give Time to the General, and Count *Nassau*, to bring up the Regiments of *Bemsdorf*, *Gauvam*, and *Lindeboom*, to supply the room of those that were pressed, which was done in a moment. However, the Enemy supported by so many Lines, made another Attempt to penetrate, but the Allies Battalions rather advanced than gave Way, tho' the General gave Orders against advancing, fearing left that might render the Fire of their Flanks useless. This Precaution had all the desired success; the Regiments, and Grenadiers making such a continual Fire, as forced the Enemies Two Wings upon their Center, and obliged the whole to retire in the greatest Confusion, notwithstanding all the Efforts their Officers could make, by Encouragement or Violence to keep them up, so that they only fired at a great distance on the Confederates Lines, which they returned, advancing by Plottoons, as to their Exercise, with all the Order imaginable. Major-General *Cadogan*, who came up some Time after the Action began, and to whom the Success of this Day was said to have been (tho' falsely) imputed,

through

through the Partiality of a certain very Great Man, offer'd to charge the Enemy, in their Disorder, with 2 Squadrons of Horse, the other 4 which he had sent for, not being arrived till near 7 at Night, but it was not thought consistent with common Prudence to charge the Enemy, who had brought up all their Horse, to favour their Retreat. The Battle lasted 2 Hours, and was very hot, in which the Allies had 912 Officers and Soldiers killed and wounded; but the Enemy, according to Assurances by Letters from *Ghent* and *Bruges*, and by report of Prisoners and Deserters, lost above 6000 Men, among whom were *Don Pantoja*, Nephew to Cardinal *Portocarero*, Monsieur *Grimaldi*, a Colonel, and Count *Copigni*. In the number of their wounded, were the Marquiss of *Caraccioli*, Colonel of Horse; the Marquiss *de Wemmel*, Brigadier, the Marquiss *de Aquaviva*, Colonel, and the Baron *de Lacren*, Brigadier, Son in Law to Count *Bergeick*, who died soon after of his Wounds.

They likewise made their Retreat in so much Confusion, that they left most of their Cannon in a Wood, which they did not carry off till the next Day, at 11 of the clock, after hearing that Convoy, which they would have intercepted, was passing *Reusselaer*, which, with the Victory, was very surprizing, because of several Detachments being made from the main Body of this little Army, the Victors had not above 6000 Men in the Action, when the Enemies, by their own Accounts, were no less than 24000.

This Action of *Wynendale* broke the Heart of the *French* Army; their Generals found to their costs, that their private Soldiers were perfectly dispirited, for after this, the Besieged, in *Lisle* made but a very faint Defence, and forgot the Valour they had exerted at the beginning of the Siege, from which it may properly be said, That the Reduction of that important Place was more

owing

owing to the Bravery of General *Webb*, who in pursuance of his Orders from the Duke of *Marlborough*, made this Glorious Stand, than the indefatigable Endeavours and Assaults of the Prince of *Savoy*.

It must be held for granted, indeed, that the *Webb*, by taking the Post of *Leffingben*, from a Detachment of *English*, that landed at *Ostend*, under the command of General *Earl*, and the unfortunate Expedition of the Earl of *Stairs*, into the Districts of *Furnes*, and *Dixmuyd*, made them some amends for that Disgrace, in retarding the Siege of the Citadel, which was very strong, and the Master-piece of the Great *Vauban*; though, after the Cessation of all Acts of Hostility between that and the Town, which was to expire 4 Days after its surrender, *viz*. on the 26th of *November*, according to the Articles of Capitulation, was continued till the 29th, during which Time, great Endeavours were used to persuade the Marshal *de Boufflers* to come to Terms with the Besiegers; and that at the earnest Desire of the Inhabitants, who were much afraid the *French* would not have so much regard for their Houses as the Allies had; the Negotiations for that purpose were broke off on the part of the Enemy, who finding their extravagant Proposals would have no manner of Impression, begun Hostilities with great Fury.

During the Cessation above mention'd, the Besiegers had cast up Intrenchments, and drawn a Parallel from one End of the *Esplanade*, or Place between the Town and Citadel to the other; they had also made several *Coupures* on the Walls near the Citadel, to the Left and Right, while the Prince of *Hesse-Cassel* fortified himself with a Detachment at *La Bassee* and the Duke of *Marlborough*, who had left his Camp at *Helchin* upon the Retreat of the *French*, who were casting up Intrenchments along

X the

the *Scheld* from *Tournay* to *Mortaigne*, continued a[t]
Rousselaer for the more easy Subsistance of his Army
But upon an Express from the States-Deputies tha[t]
the Elector of *Bavaria* was set down before *Bru[s]*
sels with 8 or 10000 Men, and made very furiou[s]
Attacks against it, as it must have needs surrender
ed without speedy Relief; his Grace and Princ[e]
Eugene, who had left a sufficient Force behind the[m]
to continue the Siege of the Citadel, which wa[s]
chiefly carried on by the Sap, recalled the Troop[s]
which were in the District of *Furnes*, and all th[e]
Detachments which were at *Lens* and *Le Bas[se]*
The same Day they receiv'd Advice, That th[e]
Dam which the Enemy had at *Gavers*, who boaste[d]
the Blockade of the Confederate Troops, whic[h]
they called their Entrenchments along the *Sche[ld]*
was not to be forced) was broke and carried awa[y]
by the Rapidity of the Stream. This was ver[y]
agreeable News, for had the *French* succeeded i[n]
their Design, their passing the *Scheld* would hav[e]
been attended with great Difficulties.

The Measures of the Confederates were concer
ted thus: That the Prince of *Savoy*'s Army shoul[d]
pass the River between *Escanaff* and *Hauseriff*, th[e]
Duke of *Marlborough* and Count *Tilly*, at *Kerkhoven*
and Count *Lottum* with the Earl of *Orkney*, betwee[n]
Gavre and *Aspeam*. Major Gen. *Cadogan* and Brigad[ier]
Evans, were sent before to lay the Pontoons ove[r]
the *Scheld*, who not only perform'd their Order[s]
but passed that River, and posted themselves an[d]
their Detachment on the other side, after havin[g]
put to flight a Body of Troops that lay entrench'[d]
near it. The Duke's Troops were therefore o[r]
der'd to march with all imaginable Diligence, an[d]
as they, likewise, pass'd the River, form'd them
selves into Order of Battle Prince *Eugene* hearin[g]
what happen'd, never staid to lay his Pontoon[s]
but forded directly over the River, and join'd h[is]
Grace at *Kirkhoven*, upon which Conjunction the
advance

advanced to *Berchem*, in order to dislodge the *French* from that Post; but Monsieur *Souteron*, who commanded them, fled away with the utmost Precipitation. The *Dutch* Cavalry under the Command of Count *Tilly* (Mounsieur *d'Auverquerque* was unfortunately dead before the Town of *Lisle* was taken) pursued them, and fell in the Fire of a Party of Grenadiers, who had lin'd the Hedges and Ditches, in order to secure the Retreat of the rest.

Here they lost a few Soldiers, and Major General *Baldwin* was shot through the Body, and the Earl of *Albemarle* and Count *Maurice* of *Nassau*, had their Horses kill'd under them From hence the Two Princes of *Marlborough* and *Savoy*, went to attack the *French* Troops on the Hills of *Audenarde*, under the Command of Monsieur *de Hautefort*, who made just as good, or a worse, Defence than the Detachment under Monsieur *Souteron*. But General *Lottum* met with a different Aspect from the Troops commanded by the Count *la Motte* The *Prussian* Commander pass'd the *Gavre*, and found the Enemy ready to receive him; but his Orders being to join the Duke of *Marlborough* with his Forces, filed towards the Troops of that General, without staying to try whether that was only an Amusement of the *French* Generals In the several Pursuits the Allies took Part of the Enemy's Baggage their Bread Waggons, several Colours, Standards, with Two or Three Pair of Kettle Drums, and kill'd and made Prisoners, about 1000 Men.

The whole Army being join'd, encamp'd on the Hills of *Audenarde* the Night after their passing the *Scheld*. On the next Day part of the Troops which Prince *Eugene* brought with him return'd to *Lisle*, and were follow'd by that Prince with the Remainder, and a Detachment of Eight Battalions and Thirty Squadrons, to push forward the remaining Part of the Siege of that Fortress, at the same time as Lieutenant General *Dompre* march'd with Forty Squadrons towards *Aloſt*, being order'd to encamp between that Place and *Aſche*, in order to relieve *Bruſſels* The Duke of *Marlborough* caus'd the main Body of the Army to follow him, and march to *Ombergh*, where he receiv'd Advice that the Elector of *Bavaria* was retired the Night before in great Precipitation.

But becauſe the Bravery of the Defendants, this City is highly worthy of mention, Hiſtory ought to take notice of the Particulars, which are theſe: The Elector of *Bavaria* knowing the Weakneſs of the Place, as ſoon as he came before it, ſent the following Summons. " His Electoral Highneſs
" knows, that the Commandant is not in a Condi-
" tion to defend himſelf with the few Troops he
" has; wherefore, if he obliges his Electoral High
" neſs to begin the Attack, he ſhall have no Ca-
" pitulation for himſelf or his Garriſon Let not
" the Commandant flatter himſelf that he can re-
" tire with his Garriſon to *Antwerp*, if he delays
" to ſurrender; for he is to know that he will ſoon
" ſend Troops to hinder his Retreat

To this the Governor anſwered.

MONSEIGNEUR,

" THE Commandant of *Bruſſels* is very un-
"   fortunate in not having the Honour to be
" known to your Electoral Highneſs. He dares
" aſſure you, That he will do all that a Man of
" Honour ought to do; that he is contented with
" his Garriſon: And that he has the Honour to be
" be with profound Reſpect,

MONSEIGNEUR,

Your Electoral Highneſs's moſt Humble Servant,

PASCAL
Nerled

Netled with this resolute Answer, the Elector
[began] at Nine at Night to attack the Counter-
[scarp] with great Fury, as well from the Batteries
[he] had caused to be erected for that purpose, as
[from] the Fire of his Troops who came upon the
[Assault] nine times, being as often repulsed, but at
[length] lodg'd themselves on the Glacis of it, be-
[tween] the Gates of *Louvain* and *Namur*. But about
[4] of the Clock the next Morning the Garrison
[made] a Sally from the Cover'd-way Sword in
[hand], with such Success that the Enemy were
[beaten] off, and forc'd out of their Works on the
[Counter]scarp, which were levelled. When after
[the] Defendants had again dispos'd all Things as
[well] as possible for resisting the Assailants, who re-
[ported], That they would not only Storm the Place
[again] in the Night, but also Fire into it with
[burning] hot Bullets to excite the Burghers to Sedi-
[ti]on; the Enemy's Army was observed to be in
Motion, and soon after to retire towards *Namur*
[with] such Precipitation on the Confederate Ar-
[my]'s Approach, that they left behind them Twelve
Cannon and Four Mortars, which fell into the
Hands of the besieged

The Siege of *Brussels* being thus rais'd, which
could not have held out 24 Hours longer, the
Duke made his Entry into it, where he was receiv'd
with great Acclamations of Joy, and complimented
by the States of *Brabant*, and the Magistrates of
the City upon their Deliverance, which they justly
ascrib'd, next to God, to the vigorous Resolution
of his Grace, and his expeditious March. He return'd the same Night to his Camp near *Alost*,
where his Troops rested the next Day And now
being informed, That the Garrison of *Aeth* had
surpriz'd St. *Guillim*, a Place between *Mons* and
Conde, and that the Enemy had sent some Troops
to retake that Post, Lieutenant-General *Dompre*
was sent with a strong Detachment to relieve it,
but

but heard in his way, that the Troops that were therein had surrender'd. He halted at *Atir*, and was order'd to bring from *Aeth* a great Convoy of Provisions and Ammunition design'd for *Lisle*.

In the mean time the Siege of that Citadel against which Hostilities had been begun on the 29th of *October*, was continued with all possible Vigour, and though it spun out into length upon its being carried on by the Sap, was so far advanc'd, that in the Absence of the Prince *Eugene* the Besiegers had lodg'd themselves on the Second Counterscarp, and begun on the First of *December* to raise Batteries thereon, till that Prince commanded again in Person, and prosecuting the Remainder of the same Work, that impregnable Fortress was oblig'd to capitulate on the 8th following, the Garrison being allow'd to march out with all the Marks of Honour, Six Pieces of Cannon, Four Mortars, and Two Cover'd Waggons, &c According to which Capitulation, they march'd out about 4000 strong, 1700 Dragoons which got into the Town with Ammunition being permitted to go out before, by Articles that were previous to its Surrender, which seem'd all to be very good Troops, but in very ill Cloaths. What remain for us to mention, is, that there were Ninety Pieces of Cannon, and a great many Iron ones, with 20000 weight of Powder found in the Citadel, as there had been 300 in the Town that fell into the Confederates Hands, likewise upon its Capitulation.

'Tis difficult to compute the Loss exactly on either side at this Siege; but if the Accounts of the Citizens of *Lisle* are to be depended upon, and they sure are the best acquainted with the Strength of the Garrison. The *French* were about 120[?] Men when the Allies first broke Ground before the Town, besides 3000 Burghers that did constant Duty with the Regular Troops. Of the Garrison the City, near 5000 retired into the Citadel, and its calculated, that about 2000 more were Sick and Wounded at the time of the Capitulation, that the *French* lost between 7 and 8000, upon reasonable Reckoning, and the Allies near 300.

The Siege of *Lisle* being over by the taking of the Citadel, the Confederate Army which encamp'd at *Berleghen* on the 10th of *December*, march'd the 11th from thence to *Melle*, where his Grace the Duke of *Marlborough* gave Orders for Bridges to be laid over the *Scheld*, for the Communication of the several Bodies which had already, pursuant to his Commands, invested *Ghent*. The same time the necessary Measures were concerted for the Siege, and chiefly as to the Forrage for the Subsistance of the Horses, and it was order'd that each Squadron should receive 180 Rations in a Day, and each Battalion 100. On the other hand, Prince *Eugene* pass'd the *Scheld* at *Ename* on the 18th, and came to the Camp at *Melle*, where a great Council of War was held on the remaining Operations of the Campaign, which had held longer than ever was known, and a General of each Nation, whereof the Army was composed, assisted therein, and according to the Resolution taken there, his Grace was to Command the Siege, and the Prince to cover it. All the Troops had taken their Posts before the Town on the 24th, when the Trenches were open'd, and the Works carried on with good success from St. *Peter*'s Gate towards Fort *Monterey*. The Day after this, the Count *de la Moth*, who had a Garrison almost as Numerous as the Besiegers offer'd to capitulate upon Terms which were rejected, but on the 6th, (viz. the 30th of *December*) to the great Surprize of the Allies, agreed to surrender the Place, which was accordingly done, though that Count had some time before received the following Letter from Monsieur *Chamillard* to

make

make as vigorous a Defence as was possible to [be] made.

SIR,

"THE preservation of *Ghent* is of so gre[at]
"importance, that you can never take to[o]
"many Precautions, in concert with the Baron
"*Capres*, Monsieur *de la Faye*, the Brigadiers, a[nd]
"other chief Officers, for a long and vigoro[us]
"Defence, in case the Enemy resolve to besieg[e]
"you in form. Notwithstanding the Place, i[n]
"it self, is not strong, yet it cannot be attack'[d]
"but by narrow difficult Places. You have [a]
"great number of Troops, which are more tha[n]
"sufficient to defend a Cover'd-Way, and sell de[ar]
"to the Allies the Conquest of that Place, if the[y]
"persist in their Design to make themselves M[as]-
"ters thereof. I cannot forbear to tell you, Th[at]
"to a great deal of Courage, and good Inclina-
"tion, it is necessary to add a great Calmness an[d]
"Sedateness of Mind, and Patience, in order t[o]
"make use of all the Difficulties which may di[s]-
"sturb the Enemies, and retard the Siege. D[o]
"not take upon your self alone, all the Motion[s]
"which are to be made, for there are severa[l]
"Officers who are capable to advise and assi[st]
"you. You know how much I interest my te[nder]
"in every Thing wherein you are personally con-
"cerned, tho' the Reasons of State oblige m[e]
"to explain my Thoughts to you on such Thing[s]
"which in my Opinion may contribute to a lon[g]
"Defence. I think, however, my self obliged [to]
"tell you, as relating to you alone. That aft[er]
"having had the Misfortune to command in [O]-
"stend, which the Enemy reduced in very fe[w]
"Days, and of having not succeeded in the rig[ht]
"of *Wynendale*, it is of the highest concern [to]
"your self, as well as to His Majesty, that [no]
Opp[ortunity]

Opportunity you have now, may give him so good an Opinion of you, as may obtain from His Majesty those Marks of Distinction, for which you have so long labour'd. I do not know whether you want any Majors-General of the King's Troops, but as all the Forces which are to be from *Ghent* to *Ypres*, with those in *Bruges* and *Newport*, and all the General Officers, and others, are to obey your Commands, you may signifie to those who are to command there this Winter what you shall think fit to be done, for the Service of His Majesty. According to the Repartition of the Winter-Quarters, which I send you with this Letter; you will find that several Regiments which were designed for *Ghent* and *Bruges*, are marched towards *Newport* and *Ypres*; for the first Disposition of the Troops was made in *view of the Winter-Quarters*, and not for *continuing* the Campagne, and *maintaining Sieges*. However, His Majesty has commanded me to let you know, That it is not fitting to change any Thing, as to the Garrison of *Ghent*. He is pleased to send Orders to Monsieur *de Puignion*, to leave in *Bruges* 14 Battalions, and 9 Squadrons, as Monsieur *Grimaldi* has desired it, but the rest of the Forces are forthwith to return towards the Frontiers of the Kingdom.

" If you are besieged, you must use all possible Means to protract the Siege, in so much that it may cost the Allies very dear, and dispute the Ground Inch by Inch, as Monsieur, the Marshal of *Boufflers* has done at *Lisle*. I know the difference between the Fortifications of *Lisle*, and those of *Ghent*; but there is in the latter a good Cover'd-Way, which is equally good every where, and after 6 Weeks Time, the Enemies were not entirely Masters of that of *Lisle*, tho' the Garrison of that Place was not so strong

"as yours. I write to Messieurs the Baron de
"Capres, and de la Faye, to desire them to act in
"concert with you, in every Thing that may
"contribute to the Good of the Service, and
"Content of the Burghers of Ghent, who deserve,
"and should have had, a happier Fate. I tell
"you nothing as to the preservation of the Troops
"you have, in my Opinion, a long Time, before
"you ought to think of their preservation, and I
"have reason to believe, that they will serve,
"with great Distinction, and Affection, under
"your command.

I am, most perfectly,

SIR,

Your most Humble, and

Most Affectionate Servant,

CHAMILLARD

The French Garrison was so very numerous, that they were marching out of the Place for several Hours, and the Consequences of the surrender of Ghent, was the quitting Bruges, Plassendale, and Leffingben, (the Duke of Vendosme having taken the Two last during the Siege of Lisle) and the Enemies retiring into their own Territories and the Duke of Marlborough, and Prince of Savoy, having setled the Winter Quarters, set out from Brussels on the 9th of January, for the Hague, where they arrived 3 Days after

Thus ended a Campagne, the most Glorious Active, and I may say, unparallell'd, if we consider its Length, the many Stratagems of War that were used in it; the Difficulties that were surmounted, and wonderful Period it was brought

that ever was read in History; nor were either of the Two Houses of Parliament then sitting neglectful of paying a just Deference to him, [who] was the Instrument of such great Successes to [our] Country, and the Grand Alliance, for the Commons, impatient of deferring their Thanks, till [his] return'd from abroad, the Duke being gone [from] the Hague again to Brussels, unanimously resolv'd, "That the Commons of Great Britain being truly sensible, not only of the Great and Eminent Services perform'd by the Duke of Marlborough, the last successful Campagne, so much to the Honour of Great Britain, and Advantage of all Europe, but also the indefatigable Zeal he persever'd in, for the Service of the Common Cause Abroad, while he might, with Reason, expect to be receiv'd with all the Marks of Honour and Satisfaction at Home, did, with a just regard to his Glorious Actions, return him the Thanks of the House, and order'd their Speaker, (Sir Richard Onslow) to transmit the same to his Grace." Which being done accordingly, the Duke was pleas'd to return for Answer:

Brussels, February 13. 1709.

SIR,

"I Am extremely sensible of the great Honour which the House of Commons have done me, in the Vote you have been pleased to transmit me by their Order: Nothing can give me more satisfaction, than to find the Services I endeavour'd to do the Queen and my Country, so acceptable to the House of Commons: And I beg the Favour of you to assure them, I shall never think any Pains or Perseverance too great, if I may, by God's Blessing, be instrumental in procuring a Safe and Honou-

" rable Peace, for Her Majesty, and my Fell[ow]
" Subjects.

I am, with Truth,

S I R,

Your most Faithful Humble Servant,

MARLBOROUGH.

The Duke of *Marlborough* being come to [St.] *James*'s, on the 1st of *March*, took his Seat in t[he] House of Lords the Day following, when t[he] Lord Chancellor return'd him the Thanks [of] that Illustrious and August Assembly, after t[he] manner.

My Lord Duke of Marlborough,

" I Have the Honour to be again comman[ded]
" by this House, to give your Grace th[e]
" most hearty and unanimous Thanks, for the gr[eat]
" and eminent Services you have perform'd t[he]
" last Campagne, particularly to Her Majesty, a[nd]
" Her Kingdoms, and, in general, to all [the]
" Allies.
" When I last obey'd the like Commands, I co[uld]
" not but infer from your Grace's former Succ[es-]
" ses, we had still most reasonable Expectan[ce]
" that you could not fail to improve them.
" I beg leave to congratulate your Grace, T[hat]
" the Observation then made has proved, as [in-]
" deed it was intended, perfectly true.
" I hope I shall not be thought to exceed [my]
" present Commission, if being thus led to c[on-]
" template the mighty Things your Grace [has]
" done for us, I cannot conclude without ackn[ow-]
" ledging, with all Gratitude, the Providence

" G

God, in raising you up to be an Instrument of so much Good, in so critical a Juncture, when it was so much wanted.

His Grace's ANSWER.

My LORDS,

I Hope you will do me the Justice to believe, "there are very few Things could give me "more satisfaction, than the favourable Approba-"tion of my Service by this House.
"And I beg leave to assure your Lordships, it "shall be the constant Endeavour of my Life to "deserve the Continuation of your good Opi-"nion.

We cannot embark the Duke of *Marlborough* to the *Hague* again, in order to make the Campagne for the Year 1709, without carrying the Reader backward, and observing, that before his Arrival from thence, the *French* induc'd to think of an Accommodation with the Allies, from their continued Successes, their own Scarcity of Money and Corn, and other concurring Circumstances, had made Overtures of Peace, a Copy of which, brought over by his Grace: But these being not thought sufficient to ground a Treaty thereupon, tho' the Allies were willing to consent to such Terms as were reasonable for the future Tranquility of *Europe*, the Lord *Somers*, who was then President of the Council, and suppos'd to know the Intentions of the Court, made a Motion, that an Address should be presented to the Queen,
"That Her Majesty would be pleased to take care "at the Conclusion of the War, that the *French* "King might be obliged to own Her Majesty's "Title, and the Protestant Succession; That Her
"Majesty's

"Majesty's Allies might be Guarantees of the
"same; and that the *Pretender* might be removed
"out of the *French* Dominions. Which Motion
was unanimously approved, and an Address presented accordingly.

In the House of Commons, likewise, Mr Secretary *Boyle*, to make the Conditions as advantagious to the Trading Part of *Great Britain*, as possible, represented, "That the *British* Nation, ha-
"ving been at a vast Expence of Blood and
"Treasure, for the Prosecution of this necessary
"War, it was but just, that they should reap
"some Benefit by the *Peace*. And the Town of
"*Dunkirk*, being a Nest of Pirates, that infested
"the Ocean, and did infinite Mischief to Trade,
"*be therefore moved*, That the *Demolishing of the*
"*Fortifications and Harbour*, should be insisted up-
"on in the ensuing Treaty of Peace, which was
"added as an Amendment to the Lords Address,
"who desired their Concurrence, as it, at its Pre-
"sentment, had that of the Queen.

Her Majesty having, in concert with Her Allies, who had sent Plenipotentiaries to the *Hague*, invested the Lord Viscount *Townshend*, with the Character of Her Ambassador Extraordinary for that purpose, to act with the Duke of *Marlborough*, at the Conferences that were to be held on that Subject. But before his Lordship's arrival there, or, indeed, his Nomination to that great Trust, Prince *Eugene* of *Savoy*, who had full power of the Emperor, for all Things relating to War and Peace, on the 8th of *April*, came to the *Hague*, where the Duke of *Marlborough* arrived the next Day. Those Princes had a long Conference with the Pensionary, and other Deputies of the States, wherein they debated the Proposals made on the part of *France*, which were not judged large enough to be the Foundation of a Treaty of Peace. According to that Resolution the Deputies of the

...tes returned an Answer to Monsieur *Roville*, who ...dispatch'd from *France*, to feel the Pulse of the ...ies, and had been there for some time, import... ...that his Overtures were not satisfactory, with... ...entring into any Particulars.

...pon this, that Minister sent a Gentleman to ...*illes* for new Instructions, who was sent back. ...15th, and arrived in *Holland* the 18th, when the ...ferences were renewed again. In short, these ...essages and Conferences had that Effect, that ...e Duke of *Marlborough* coming over soon upon ...to *England*, it was generally concluded he brought ...e fought Draught with him; and still the more, ...cause his Stay was very short, and that there ...s yet no Possibility of the Armies taking the ...ield, by reason of the Backwardness of the For- ...age.

...In the mean time the Marquis *de Torcy*, Prime ...Minister, and Secretary of State in *France*, coming ...o the *Hague*, the Peace was scarce doubted of, ...hough the States told the Marquis upon his Arri- ...al, that they could not allow any Conference ...without the Duke of *Marlborough*, who landed at ...the *Brill* the 7th at Night, and arrived the 18th in ...he Morning at the *Hague*. Whereupon he sent ...his Secretary to notify the same to the President ...of the States, and the Grand Pensionary. The ...ame Day the Marquis *de Torcy* went to my Lord ...Duke, and was about Two Hours with him, ...and the Lord *Townshend*. The 19th, the same Per- ...son was at his Grace's Levée, and both of them ...went to Prince *Eugene*'s Apartment, and the same ...Night had a Conference with the Grand Pensio- ...nary.

Prince *Eugene*, the Duke of *Marlborough*, and the Lord *Townshend*, having returned the Visit he had received from Monsieur *Torcy* on the 20th, that Marquiss presented to them the President *de Roville*, who had hitherto been with no other Ministers

than

than Monsieur *de Buys* and Monsieur *Vanderdussen*. The same Morning being appointed for a Conference, Messieur *de Torcy* and *Rouille* went thither and declared, That their Master consented to the Demolishing of *Dunkirk*, to abandon the Pretender, and other Articles insisted upon by the Court of *Great-Britain*, and likewise to renounce all Pretensions to the *Spanish* Monarchy; and lastly, to quit such Places as should be thought necessary for the Barrier demanded by the States, as *Furnes, Ipres, Menin, Tournay, Lisle, Conde, Maubeuge*, &c. They offer'd in regard to the Empire, to restore all Things as they were settled by the Treaty of *Ryswick* and to demolish the Fortifications. The Allies insisted on some other Articles, namely, on the Restitution of *Upper* and *Lower Alsace* to the Emperor, where the *French* Ministers declared, That they had no Power to make any further Concessions, broke up the Conferences, and went to the Pensionary to desire Passes to return Home. They sent again for the same, declaring they could not stay any longer; but this was only a Copy of their Countenance. For upon second Thoughts, and the Representation of a Neutral Minister, they consented to put off their Departure, and had another Conference. Monsieur *de Torcy* went alone the 21st to the Great Pensionary, to agree about that Conference which was held at Six in the Evening; and notwithstanding the *French* Ministers had declared the Day before, That they could not enlarge their Offer, they proposed to surrender *Strasburgh* in the same Condition it was at that present.

The Allies were not contented with these further Proposals, and another Conference was appointed for the 22d in the Morning, which proved likewise unsuccesful, upon which the *French* declared, That they were resolved to go away; and the better to perswade People that they were

Earnest, they took their Leave of Prince Eugene, the Duke of *Marlborough*, and the Ministers
of the Neutral Princes: But some of the latter
perswaded them to put off their Departure, and endeavour to bring these Negotiations to a happy Conclusion, which they readily consented to, and another Conference was held on the 23d, which lasted from Nine of the Clock till half an Hour past One in the Morning.

They begun to set down in Writing some Articles, and it was agreed to meet again at Six in the Evening, and Monsieur *de Torcy* promised to write to his Master about the Difference relating to *Alsace*. At this Meeting, they debated an important Article concerning the Security of the Execution of the Points agreed upon; but that Conference broke without Success, though it lasted till Eleven at Night. The Duke of *Marlborough*, Prince *Eugene*, and the Lord *Townshend*, did not continue there so long, but left the Deputies of the States to debate those Articles, being obliged to give a Visit to Count *Zinzendorf*, one of the Imperial Plenipotentiaries, who arrived that Afternoon.

On the 24th there was another Conference, which begun at Nine of the Clock, between the Deputies of the States and the *French* Ministers, and as soon as it was over, the former went to give an Account to the Imperial and *British* Plenipotentiaries, who having some important Affairs did not Assist at it

The same Day in the Evening, they met again and debated the Matter so long, that the Mail for *England* was dispatch'd away before the Conference concluded. They resumed therein, what related to the Security of the Performance of the Articles agreed upon, and chiefly as to the Evacuation of all the *Spanish* Dominions. The Allies demanded several Towns to be put into their Hands for that

Z purpose

purpose, and the *French* refused to give any, insisting, That the Ingagement the most Christian King enter'd into, to recal all his Troops from *Spain*, and his Promise to give no manner of Assistance to King *Philip*, directly or indirectly, was a sufficient Security; and that King *Philip* being thus forsaken by his Grandfather, would be obliged to quit *Spain*, and especially, because the *Spaniards* would then certainly declare for King *Charles*. This occasion'd warm Debates, but at last it was agreed That *France* should deliver some Place in the *Netherlands*, that were to be Part of the Barrier, before they enter'd upon the General Negotiations of Peace, by way of Preliminary.

On *Saturday* and *Sunday* there was no Conference with the *French* Ministers, but the Imperial and *British* Plenipotentiaries had several with the Great Pensionary and Deputies of the States, wherein they gave a full Account to Count *Zinzendorf*, of what had been transacted since the first Overture of those Negotiations, and they agreed upon the further Demands that were to be made on the Part of the Allies. This being agreed too, there was Conference held on *Monday* the 24th, following wherein Count *Zinzendorf* assisted for the first time, and they communicated their Demands to Messieurs *de Torcy* and *Rouille*, who desired some time to consider the same, and promised to return an Answer at Six in the Evening in a Conference which was to be held at the Great Pensionary's. This continued till Two the 28th in the Morning, and after many Disputes the Preliminaries were agreed upon. They appointed another Conference between Nine and Ten, when they examined again the said Articles, which were set down in Writing, and took Copies thereof; after which Monsieur *de Torcy* set out for *Versailles* to communicate the same to his most Christian Majesty, and engaged to procure the Ratification by the 15th of

Jun

They were pleas'd to tell the Duke of Marlborough and the Lord Townshend at the same time, that the French being sensible of the Advantage of Dunkirk, could hardly digest the Demolishing of that Fine Place, and the Spoiling of the Harbour which had cost much Treasure; and pretended that having bought that Town from King Charles the Second, it was very hard that Her Majesty should insist on the demolishing of it; and as they were debating the same, 'tis said the Prince of Savoy " told them with some Warmth, That he won-
" der'd they should spend so many Words about it,
" and that they ought rather to admire the Gene-
" rosity of a Princess, who having it in her Power
" to prescribe them harder Terms, and force them
" to deliver that, and what other Places she plea-
" sed, and revive other Pretentions of the Crown
" of England, gave an unparallel'd Example of Her
" Moderation.

The Duke of Morlborough demanded That the fatal Clause foisted in by a Jesuitical Trick into the 4th Article of the Treaty of Reswick, between the Empire and France, and which had been so very prejudicial to the Protestant Interest in Germany, should be in a particular manner made void: Whereupon Monsieur de Torcy answer'd with some concern, That *his Highness ought to apply himself on that Subject to another Court*, and indeed it is sufficiently known how that Affair was managed, and that a Cardinal's Cap was expected as a Reward, by the Minister who had the chief Hand in it.

The Ministers of some Princes of the Grand Alliance publickly expressed their Dissatisfaction upon their being excluded from the Conferences above-mention'd, but the Duke of Marlborough communicated to them the Reasons which did not allow their Pretentions, and they were so convincing, that the said Ministers, except one, were satisfied

there-

therewith. But now we are to come to the Preli[minary] Articles themselves, though we must do the French this Justice as to observe, before we pro[ceed] further, that Messieurs de Torcy and Rouille, di[d] not Sign them, and declined the same, having n[o] Instructions, as they said, to do it.

The Articles Preliminary to the Treaties [of] a GENERAL PEACE.

"I. A Good, firm, and lasting Peace, Confe[deracy], and perpetual Alliance an[d]
"Amity, shall be forthwith treated and establish'[d]
"between his Imperial Majesty, with all and eac[h]
"of his Imperial Majesty's Allies (principally th[e]
"Kingdom of Great-Britain, and the Lords th[e]
"States General of the United Provinces) on th[e]
"one part, and his Most Christian Majesty, wit[h]
"his Allies, on the other part. And seeing th[e]
"present Conjunctures have not permitted his Im[
"perial Majesty to take previously the Approba[
"tion and Consent of the Empire, upon all tha[t]
"relates to it, in several Articles contained i[n]
"these Preliminaries, his Imperial Majesty shal[l]
"endeavour to procure according to the Usag[e]
"establish'd in the Empire, as soon as possible, th[e]
"Consent and Ratification of the said Empire
"before the Execution of the Articles which par[
"ticularly concern the Empire.

"II. And to attain this good End speedily
"and to enjoy it as much as possible, from thi[s]
"time Preliminary Articles are agreed, to serv[e]
"for a Foundation of the Treaties of a Genera[l]
"Peace.

"III. First

"III. First, In Consideration, and in Consequence of the said good Peace, and sincere Union of all the Parties, *The Most Christian King shall, from this Time, acknowledge, publickly and authentickly, as also afterwards, in the Treaties of Peace to be made, King* Charles *the Third, in the Quality of King of* Spain, *the* Indies, Naples *and* Sicily, *and generally of all the Territories dependant, and comprehended under the Name of* The Monarchy of Spain, *in what Part of the World soever situate,* (except what is to be given to the Crown of *Portugal*, and the Duke of *Savoy*, pursuant to the Treaties between the High Allies, and the Barrier in the *Netherlands*, which the said King *Charles* the Third is to put into the Hands of the said Lords, the States-General of the *United Provinces*, agreeably to the Tenor of the Grand-Alliance, in the Year 1701, except also what shall be hereafter mention'd, touching the Upper-Quarter of *Gelderland*, and also except the Agreements yet to be made with the said King *Charles* the Third, without excepting any Thing more:) Together with all the Rights which the late King *Charles* the Second did possess, or ought to have possess'd, as well for himself, as his Heirs and Successors, according to the Will of *Philip* the Fourth, and the Compacts establish'd and receiv'd in the most Serene House of *Austria*.

"IV. And forasmuch as the Duke of *Anjou* is at present in possession of a great Part of the Kingdom of *Spain*, of the Coast of *Tuscany*, the *Indies*, Part of the *Netherlands*, 'tis reciprocally agreed, That for the sure Execution of the said Articles, and of the Treaties of Peace to be made, the said Treaties shall be finish'd within the Term of 2 Months, to begin from the First Day of the ensuing Month of *June*, if possible, during which Time, His Most Christian Majesty shall so order it, that the Kingdom of *Sicily* shall be

put

(174)

"put into the possession of His Catholick Maje
"sty Charles the Third. And the said Duke sha[ll]
"depart in full Safety and Freedom, out of th[e]
"Limits of the Kingdoms of Spain, with his Con[-]
"sort, the Princes, his Children, their Effect[s]
"and generally all Persons who are willing to fo[l-]
"low them. And if, before the said Term expir[es]
"the said Duke of Anjou do not consent to the Ex[-]
"ecution of the present Agreement, the Mo[st]
"Christian King, and the stipulating Princes an[d]
"States, shall, by concert, take proper Measure[s]
"that it may have entire Effect, and that all E[u-]
"rope may, by the full Performance of the sa[id]
"Treaties of Peace, speedily enjoy perfect Tran[-]
"quillity.

"V. To facilitate the Establishment of that Tran[-]
"quillity, His Most Christian Majesty shall, with[in]
"in the Term of the 2 Months, withdraw th[e]
"Troops and Officers he now has in Spain, and al[-]
"so those he has in the Kingdom of Sicily, a[s]
"well as in the other Countries and Territorie[s]
"depending on the said Monarchy in Europe, an[d]
"from the Indies, as soon as possible; promising[,]
"on the Faith and Honour of a King, not to send[,]
"henceforward, to the Duke of Anjou, (if he re[-]
"fuses to acquiesce with this) or to his Adhe[-]
"rents, any Succour, whether of Troops, Artil[-]
"lery, Ammunition, or Money, directly or in[-]
"directly.

"VI. *The Monarchy of* Spain *shall remain entire in*
"*the House of* Austria, *in the manner above-mention'd*
"*. None of its Parts shall ever be dismember'd; neither shall*
"*the said Monarchy, in Whole, or in Part, be united to*
"*that of* France; *nor shall one and the same King, or*
"*a Prince of the House of* France, *ever become Sove*
"*reign thereof, in any manner whatsoever, either by Will,*
"*Legacy, Succession, Marriage-Compact, Donation, Sale,*
"*Contract, or any other way whatever: No King who*
"*shall reign in* France, *shall ever reign in* Spain, *or*
"acquire

acquire within the Extent of the said Monarchy, any Towns, Forts, Places, or Countries in any Part of it, especially in the *Netherlands*, by virtue of any Donation, Sale, Exchange, Marriage-Compact, Inheritance, Legacy, Succession by Will, or in default of a Will, in whatever kind or manner soever, either for himself, or for the Princes, his Sons, or Brothers, or their Heirs or Descendants.

"VII. *Particularly, and especially*, France shall never become possess'd of *the* Spanish Indies, *nor send Ships thither to exercise Commerce, under any Pretext whatever.*

"VIII. His Most Christian Majesty being willing to give sure Proofs of the Intention he has to maintain a firm and lasting Peace, and to put an End to all Umbrage of his Designs, consents to deliver up to his Imperial Majesty, and the Empire, the City and Citadel of *Strasburgh*, in the Condition they are now in, with the Fort of *Kehl*, and its Dependencies and Appurtenances, situate on either side of the *Rhine*; without any demand of Cost or Expences, under what Pretext soever; with a Hundred Pieces of Brass Cannon of different Sizes, that is to say, Fifty Pieces, some Twenty four, some Twelve Pounders; and Fifty Pieces, some of Eight, some of Four Pound Ball, and Ammunition in proportion; to be re-establish'd in the Rank, Prerogatives and Privileges of an Imperial City, which it enjoy'd before it came under the Dominion of His Most Christian Majesty. Which said City of *Strasburgh*, and its Forts, shall be deliver'd up and evacuated immediately after the Ratifications of the Emperor and Empire shall be exchang'd at the *Hague*; and on the Appearance at the Gates of the said City and Forts of *Strasburgh*, of some Person authoriz'd by a full Power from His Imperial Majesty and the Em-

"pire, in the usual Form, to take possession o[f]
" them.
"IX. That the Town of Brisac, with its Terri[-]
" tory, shall be evacuated by His Most Christia[n]
" Majesty, and by him restor'd to His Imperia[l]
" Majesty, and the House of Austria; with all th[e]
" Cannon, Artillery, and Stores of War that sha[ll]
" be found in it, by the end of June at farthest
" to be henceforward enjoy'd by His Imperia[l]
" Majesty, as his own Property, so as His Impe[-]
" rial Majesty has enjoy'd, and ought to have en[-]
" joy'd it, in execution of the Treaty of Peace
" concluded at Reswick, with the Cannon, Arti[l-]
" lery, and warlike Stores now in it.
"X. His Most Christian Majesty shall from
" henceforward possess Alsace, in the literal Sens[e]
" of the Treaty of Munster; so that he shall con[-]
" tent himself with the Right of Prefecture ove[r]
" the Ten Imperial Towns of the said Alsace[,]
" yet without extending the said Right to th[e]
" prejudice of the Prerogatives and Rights belong[-]
" ing to them in common with other free Town[s]
" of the Empire; and he shall enjoy his said
" Right, together with the Prerogatives, Reve[-]
" nues and Demesnes, in such manner as his sai[d]
" Majesty ought to have enjoy'd them from the
" Time of the Conclusion of the said Treaty,
" putting the Fortifications of the said Town[s]
" into the same Condition they were in at tha[t]
" Time, excepting the Town of Landau, the Pos[-]
" session and Property of which shall belong fo[r]
" ever to His Imperial Majesty, and the Empire
" with power to demolish the said Place, if th[e]
" Emperor and Empire shall think fit.
"XI. In Consequence of the said Treaty o[f]
" Munster, his said Most Christian Majesty shall
" within the Time agreed, cause to be demolish'd
" at his own Expence, the fortify'd Places he ha[d]
" at present on the Rhine, between Basil and Ph[i-]
" lipsburgh

(177)

...burg, namely, *Hunningben*, *New-Brisac*, and *Fort-Lewis*, with all the Works belonging to the said Fort, on each side of the *Rhine*, so that they may never be rebuilt hereafter.

"XII. That the Town and Castle of *Rhynfels*, with their Dependencies, shall be possess'd by the Landgrave of *Hesse-Cassel*, till it shall be agreed otherwise.

"XIII. The Queen of *Great-Britain*, and the Lords, the States-General, affirming, That the Clause inserted in the Fourth Article of the Treaty of *Reswick*, relating to Religion, is contrary to the Tenour of the Peace of *Munster*, and consequently ought to be repeal'd; 'tis thought fit that this Affair shall be refer'd to the Negotiation of the General Peace.

"XIV. As to *Great-Britain*, His Most Christian Majesty shall, from this Time, and in the Negotiation of the Treaties of Peace to be made, acknowledge the Queen of *Great-Britain* in that Quality.

"XV. His said Majesty shall also acknowledge the Succession of the Crown of *Great-Britain* in the *Protestant-Line*, as 'tis setled by Acts of the Parliament of *Great Britain*.

"XVI. The Most Christian King shall deliver up to the Crown of *Great-Britain*, what *France* possesses in the Island of *Newfoundland*; and on the part of the Queen of *Great-Britain*, as well as on the part of His Most Christian Majesty, all the Countries, Islands, Forts and Colonies, which have been possess'd by the Arms of either Side, during the present War, in what Part soever of the *Indies* situate, shall be mutually restor'd.

"XVII. His said Majesty promises to cause all the Fortifications of the Town of Dunkirk, its Harbour and Rysbanks, with what belongs thereto, to be raz'd at his Expence, without exception; so that one half of the said Fortifications shall be raz'd, and one half of

" the Harbour fill'd up within the space of Two Month
" and the other half of the Fortifications shall be raz'[d]
" as well as the other half of the Harbour filled up in t[he]
" space of Two Months more, to the satisfaction of t[he]
" Queen of Great-Britain, and of the Lords the Stat[es]
" General of the United-Provinces: Nor shall it [be]
" permitted ever to rebuild the Fortifications, or make t[he]
" Harbour navigable again, directly or indirectly.

" XVIII. The Person who pretends to be Ki[ng]
" of Great Britain, having desir'd to depart t[he]
" Kingdom of France, to prevent the Dema[nds]
" which the Queen of Great-Britain, and the B[ri]
" tish Nation have made, He shall retire into su[ch]
" Country, and in such manner, as by the ne[xt]
" ensuing Treaty of a general Peace shall be agre[ed]
" as to the means of his retiring.

" XIX. In the principal Negotiation of the Tre[a]
" ties to be made, care shall be taken to settle [a]
" Treaty of Commerce with Great-Britain.

" XX. As to the King of Portugal, His M[ost]
" Christian Majesty shall consent, that he shall e[n]
" joy all the Advantages stipulated in his favo[ur]
" by the Treaties made between him and his [Al]
" lies.

" XXI. His Majesty shall acknowledge the K[ing]
" of Prussia in that Quality, and promise not [to]
" disturb him in the possession of the Principal[ity]
" of Neufchatel, and of the County of Valeng[in].

" XXII. And as to the Lords, the States-Gener[al]
" His Majesty shall yield, and make over to the[m]
" in the most express Terms that shall be jud[ged]
" proper, the Place of Furnes, with its Distri[ct]
" (the Fort of Knocque being therein include[d]
" Menin, with its Verge, Ipres, with its Castella[ny]
" and Dependencies; which from henceforwa[rd]
" shall be Bailleu, or Belle, Warneton, Comines, W[er]
" wick, Poperingen, and what depends on the P[la]
" ces above-mention'd, (the Town and Caste[lla]
" ny of Cassel, remaining to His Most Chris[tian]
" Majes[ty]

(179)

Majesty *Lisle*, with its Castellany, (the Town and Government of *Douay* to be excepted) *Conde* and *Maubeuge*, with all their Dependencies; the whole in such Condition as the said Places are at present, and particularly with the Cannon, Artillery, and Stores of War therein; to serve with the rest of the *Spanish-Netherlands*, for the Barrier of the said Lords, the States General, upon which they may agree with the said King *Charles*, according to the Tenour of the Grand Alliance, as well with regard to the Garrisons which the said Lords, the States General shall maintain therein, as to all other Things in the *Spanish-Netherlands*, and particularly as to their having the Property and Sovereignty of the Upper-Quarter of *Gelderland*, according to the 52d Article of the Treaty of *Munster*, in the Year 1648, as from Time to Time they shall think fit. But 'tis understood, that if there is a general Magazine in *Tournay*, the Quantity and Quality of the Artillery and Ammunition to be left in the said Place, shall be agreed.

"XXIII. His Most Christian Majesty shall also deliver up all the Towns, Forts, and Places which he shall have possess'd himself of in the *Spanish Netherlands*, in the Condition they are now in, with their Cannon, Artillery, and Warlike Stores. But 'tis understood, that if since the Troops of the Most Christian King enter'd *Namur*, any Magazine has been erected, or Stores of Artillery and Ammunition laid up in that Town and Castle, more than for their defence, they shall be remov'd by the Officers of His Most Christian Majesty, in concert with those of the States-General, at the Time of the Evacuation; which shall not, on this account, be retarded, but shall be done within the Time that shall be limited, the whole on this express Condition, That the *Roman Catho-*

A a 2

"lick Religion shall be maintain'd in all t[he]
"said Places to be deliver'd up, and in the
"Dependencies, in the same manner as 'tis no[w]
"establish'd there; except that the Garrisons [of]
"the States may exercise their own Religion, [as]
"well in the Places yielded and made over for e[n]
"larging the Barrier, as in the Places of the Sp[a]
"nish-Netherlands, that are to be restor'd.

"XXIV. And to the end that this Agreeme[nt]
"may have its full effect, His Most Christia[n]
"Majesty promises not to cause to be remov['d]
"from this Time, any Cannon, Artillery, or A[m]
"munition, out of the Towns and Forts whi[ch]
"are to be restor'd and yielded up, by virt[ue]
"of these Articles.

"XXV. His Majesty shall grant to the sa[id]
"Lords, the States-General, in relation to the[ir]
"Commerce, what is stipulated by the Trea[ty]
"of Ryswick, the Tarif, (or Book of Rates) [of]
"1664, the suppression of the Tarifs made sinc[e]
"the Revocation of the Edicts, Declarations, an[d]
"Arrests posterior to them, contrary to the sa[id]
"Tarif of 1664, and also the Abolition of th[e]
"Tarif made between France, and the said Lord[s]
"the States-General, the 29th of May, 1699; [so]
"that, with respect to them, the Tarif of th[e]
"Year 1664. only shall be of force: And a[ll]
"Dutch Vessels trading in the Ports of France sha[ll]
"be exempted from paying the Tonnage Du[ty]
"of 50 Sols per Ton.

"XXVI. At the signing of the Treaties of Peac[e]
"His Majesty shall acknowledge the Ninth Elect[o]
"rate, erected in favour of his Electoral Highne[ss]
"of Hannover.

"XXVII. The Duke of Savoy shall be re insta[t]
"ted in the possession of the Dutchy of Savo[y]
"the County of Nice, and of all the other Plac[es]
"and Countries hereditarily belonging to hi[m]
"and of which his said Majesty shall have possess[ed]
"himse[lf]

himself by his Arms, during the Course of the present War, without any Reservation; His Majesty consenting besides, that his Royal Highness shall enjoy all the Countries, Territories and Places, which have been yielded and made over to him by the Emperor and his Allies.

"XXVIII. That the King make over to the Duke of *Savoy* the Property and Sovereignty of the Towns of *Exilles*, *Fenestrelles*, and *Chaumont*, now possess'd by the Arms of his Royal Highness, together with the Valley of *Pragelas*; as also whatever lies on this side the *Genevre*, and other Mountains; so that from hence-forward the said Mountains may serve for a Barrier and Limits between the Kingdom of *France*, and the Principality of *Piemont*.

"XXIX As to the late Electors of *Cologne* and *Bavaria*, their Demands and Pretensions shall be refer'd to the Negotiation of the Treaties of Peace: And the Dispositions and Decrees of his Imperial Majesty, and the Empire, made and issued during this War, shall be maintain'd, with respect to his Electoral Highness Palatine, who shall remain in possession of the *Upper Palatinate*, the County of *Cham*, and the Rank and Dignity with which he has been invested by his Imperial Majesty; as also with respect to what has been done in favour of the Imperial Town of *Donawert*, and to several other Dispositions of that nature. And for what relates to the Garrisons which on the part of the Lords the States-General, may be plac'd in the Town of *Huy*, the Citadel of *Liege*, and the Town of *Bon*, they shall remain there, till an Agreement otherwise be made with his Imperial Majesty, and the Empire.

"XXX. And for removing all DOUBTS touching the Execution of the said Articles, and
" furthering

"furthering the Execution of them, upon which
"depends the Re-establishment of the general
"Tranquillity, and of reciprocal Confidence and
"Amity between the Parties:

"XXXI. 'Tis agreed, That the farther De-
"mands, which the Emperor, the Queen of *Great*
"*Britain*, and the said Lords the States-General
"may make in the Negotiation of the general
"Peace, as well as the most Christian King, shall
"not interrupt the Cessation of Arms, which
"will be mention'd in a subsequent Article.

"XXXII. As for the Empire, the four Associ-
"ated Circles, the King of *Portugal*, the King of
"*Prussia*, the Duke of *Savoy*, and other Allies, they
"shall be free to make in the said general Con-
"gress such Demands (besides what is above grant-
"ed to them) as they shall think convenient

"XXXIII The general Negotiation shall be fi-
"nish'd, if possible, within two Months, as is a-
"foresaid.

"XXXIV. And to the end the said Negotiation
"may be the better terminated within the space
"of the said two Months; and that upon the Ex-
"ecution of the said Articles, the Peace may im-
"mediately be made, 'tis agreed that there shall
"be a Cessation of Arms between the Armies of
"all the Parties who are at War, to commence e-
"very where, as soon as the Conclusion of the
"said Articles shall come to the knowledge of the
"said Parties at present in War.

"XXXV. The most Christian King, to give
"proofs of his Desire and Inclination to put a spee-
"dy End to this Bloody War, promises, immedi-
"ately after the Conclusion and Ratification of the
"said Articles, to evacuate, as is abovesaid, in the
"*Netherlands*, the Towns of *Namur*, *Mons* and
"*Charleroy*, before the 15th of *June* next; *Luxem-
"burgh*, *Conde*, *Tournay*, and *Maubeuge*, within
"fifteen days after, and before the 15th of *July*
"th

the Towns of *Newport*, *Furnes*, with Fort *Kuen* and *Ipres*; and before the Expiration of those two Months, to raze and fill up (as is above stipulated) the Fortifications and Harbour of *Dunkirk*; the delivering up of *Strasburgh*, and the Fort of *Kehl* being refer'd to the Stipulation of the eight Article.

" XXXVI. His most Christian Majesty promises likewise, from the time of the said Conclusion, and before the Expiration of the two Months after it, to execute all that has been formerly stipulated, with respect to the other Allies.

" XXXVII. And in case the King of *France* executes all that is above-mention'd, and that the whole Monarchy of *Spain* be deliver'd up, and yielded to King *Charles* III. as is stipulated by these Articles, within the limited Term; 'tis agreed, That the Cessation of Arms, between the Parties in War, shall continue till the Conclusion and Ratification of the Treaties of Peace which are to be made.

" XXXVIII. All this shall serve for the Basis and Foundation of the Treaties of Peace to be made, which shall be drawn up in the most ample Forms that have usually been observ'd in Treaties of Peace, with respect to Cessions, Successions, Renunciations, Dependencies, and Appendages, Evacuation of Cannon, Artillery, and Stores of War, Galleys, Crews serving in Galleys, without Cost and Charges, and the like Things.

" XXXIX. The Ratification of the Preliminary Articles, above specify'd, shall be furnish'd and exchang'd, on the part of the most Christian King, the Queen of *Great-Britain*, and the Lords the *States-General*, before the 15th of *June* next; on the part of the Emperor, by the 1st of *July* following; and of the Empire as soon

" as

"as possible: And upon the Delivery of the sa[id]
"Ratifications of the Queen of *Great-Britain*, an[d]
"the Lords the States General, the Execution [of]
"what is stipulated touching the Evacuation [of]
"the Places which his most Christian Majesty [is]
"to restore and yield up in the *Netherlands*, as al[so]
"touching the Demolition of the Town of *Du[n]-
"kirk*, and the filling up of its Harbour, and [e]-
"very thing granted to the said Potentates, sha[ll]
"be immediately be set about, and perform'd ou[t]
"of hand: The like Execution shall take pla[ce]
"with respect to what is stipulated in favour [of]
"the Emperor, and King *Charles* III. after his Im[-]
"perial Majesty's Ratification, and all that relat[es]
"to the Empire shall be executed, after the Ra[ti]-
"fication of the said Empire shall be exchang'[d.]
"As to the other Allies, the Articles that conce[rn]
"them shall be executed, after they have acquiesc[ed]
"with, sign'd, and ratify'd the said Articles.

"XL. And to hasten the Conclusion of the Tre[a]-
"ties of a general Peace, 'tis agreed, that on t[he]
"15th of *June* next, the Congress shall begin [in]
"this Place of the *Hague*: And all Kings, Prince[s]
"and States in the Alliance, and others, shall [be]
"invited to send hither their Ministers Plenip[o]-
"tentiaries. And to prevent all Difficulties a[nd]
"Disputes about the Ceremonial, and to forwa[rd]
"as much as possible the Conclusion of the Gen[e]-
"ral Peace, those of the said Ministers who sha[ll]
"have the Character of Ambassadors, shall not d[e]-
"clare it, till the Day of signing the Treaties [of]
"the said Peace.

"Done, concluded, and sign'd, by the Ple[ni]-
"potentiaries of his said Imperial Majesty, of h[er]
"Majesty the Queen of *Great Britain*, and of t[he]
"Lords the States-General of the *United Provin[ces]*
"with the Ministers Plenipotentiaries of his m[ost]
"Christian Majesty, in the *Hague*, the 28th [of]
"*May*, 1709.

Eug[ene]

...e of *Savoy*.	The Prince and Duke	*Welderen.*
...*Lewis*, Count	of *Marlborough*.	
...*de Sintzendorf*.	*Townshend*.	

A. Heinsius.
Bonima.
Baron de
Reed Van.
Rensvvoude.
Goslinga.
Iserstein.
Wichers.
Wil. Buys.
Van Dussen.

But the Marquiss *de Torcy*, tho' he had promis'd the *French* Kings Ratification of the foregoing Articles, either had not Interest enough with that Prince to do it, or was backward in perswading Him to it; for on the 2d of *June*, to keep his Word with Prince *Eugene*, to whom he had agreed this Departure, to signifie his Masters Sentiments upon the first Opportunity, He sent Him the following Letter.

SIR,

"According to my promise, That you should
" know the 4th Instant at the farthest, tho
Kings Resolutions about the Projects of Peace,
concluded at the *Hague*, I give my self the Honour
to tell you, That His Majesty having examined
the same, finds it impossible for Him to accept
it, and therefore has sent Orders to the President
de Rouille, to notifie the same to the Potentates
engag'd in this War. It is to be hoped, that
more favourable Times will present, for establishing a Peace so necessary to all *Europe*, and
consequently so much desired by every Body.

" In

"In the mean time, I have no occasion to be so
"ry for my Journey, seeing it has procured m[e]
"the Honour of your Acquaintance, and that [I]
"know by my self, that your Reputation whi[ch]
"fills the World, is so justly due to you, bei[ng]
"founded on true Merit.

Versailles, June 1707.

I am SIR,

Your Highnesses most Obedie[nt]

and most humble Servant,

TORCY.

The President *de Rouilles* Dispatches were to th[e] same Effect, who, sometime after the Receipt o[f] them, had a Conference with the Great Pensiona[r]y, and the Deputies of the States, wherein he acquainted them, that his Master could not ratifi[e] some Articles agreed to, and concluded with Monsieur *de Torcy* on the 28th of *May*. He offer'd several Reasons, which had been alledged in forme[r] Conferences, endeavouring to perswade them, tha[t] these Terms were so very hard, that it was not expected his Master could comply therewith, and s[o] the Conferences ended. Thereupon, the Confe[]derates held one among themselves, and agreed t[o] signifie to that *French* Minister to depart in Twen[]ty Four Hours

But he made a Visit next Day, which was th[e] 6th of *June* to the Duke of *Marlborough,* and th[e] another Conference was held that Night, nothin[g] material was Transacted: Only the Allies decla[]red to Monsieur *Rouille,* that they could no[t] Rece[de] from any one of the Articles agreed to, and if h[is] Master did not think fit to comply therewith, th[e] Allies would not think themselves bound by th[e] said Articles, or restrain their Pretensions to th[e]
Content

Contents thereof, after the 15th Instant, the Time allowed by the same Articles. The *French* King according to the Report of his Minister excepted in particular against Five Articles, (*viz.*) As to the 10th, he agreed to the same as far as it concern'd the Possession of *Alsace*, according to the Literal Sense of the Treaty of *Munster*, but insisted, that *Landau* should be restored to Him; and as an Equivalent offered Old *Brisac*, both which Places were yielded up to *France* by the said Treaty of *Munster*. The next Exceptions were about the 11th Article of the said Preliminaries, and the *French* Court would not consent to the Demolishing of *Huningen*, New *Brisac*, and *Fort Lewis*. The 28th Article relating to the Place yielded to the Duke of *Savoy*, was likewise excepted against, and refer'd to a further Discussion and Elucidation, to say nothing of the Barrier between *France* and *Piedmont*, which they were not pleased with. He disliked also the whole 29th Article, whereby the Proceedings of the Emperor against the Electors of *Bavaria* and *Cologn* were approved, but would have the same refer'd to the Negotiations of a General Peace, with this Proviso; that the Upper *Palatinate* and the Dignity thereunto annexed, should not be confirm'd to the Elector *Palatine*. He would have also the Interests of the Electors of *Cologn* and *Bavaria* settled in the Preliminaries. The *French* King would also have the Conditions of the 37th Article more easy; whereby there were but Two Months allow'd for the Delivering up the *Spanish* Monarchy, as thinking that Time somewhat too short, and would have it enlarged; but consented to recal his own Troops from thence, according to the Tenour of it. But the quitting of the *Spanish* Dominions to the House of *Austria*, was what stuck most with him; for Monsieur *de Rouille*, a little before his Departure, being press'd to declare, if he had any Orders tending to Peace, only return'd for Answer,

that, if the Allies would content themselves wi[th]
the Fifth Article of the Preliminaries, in relati[on]
to *Spain*, without insisting on the others that bo[re]
Reference to the Delivering up of that Monarch[y]
He thought His Majesty would be induced to d[e]
part from the other Exceptions relating to *Alsa[ce]*
the Duke of *Savoy*, &c. But the recovery of t[he]
Spanish Monarchy from the *French*, being the on[ly]
means to restore the Ballance of *Europe*, the M[i]
nisters of the Potentates in War against Him, d[id]
not think fit to depart from any one of the Articl[es]
they had agreed upon to secure the Evacuatio[n]
thereof, and so Monsieur *de Rouille* took his leave.

All the Ministers of the Allies were desired there[]
upon, to meet in a Congress on the Part of t[he]
States, wherein the Great Pensionary gave the[m]
a full Account of the Steps that had been made i[n]
the Negotiations, especially since the *French* Kin[g]
had refused to agree to the Preliminaries, and th[e]
President of the secret Affairs, spoke on that Sub
ject with a great deal of Warmth, desiring the sai[d]
Ministers to give an Account to their respectiv[e]
Masters of those unfair Proceedings of *France*, an[d]
exhort them to redouble their Efforts against an E
nemy, who could never be brought to Reason bu[t]
by Force. Count *Zinzendorf* took this Opportunit[y]
to tell the Deputies of the States, that the Emper
our, the Empire, and King *Charles* the III. woul[d]
doubtless express their Satisfaction for the grea[t]
Firmness and Constancy their High Mightynesse[s]
had manifested in the Course of these Negotiati
ons. The Duke of *Marlborough* gave the sam[e]
Assurances on the Part of the Queen of *Great*
Britain, as did also the rest of the Ministers on th[e]
Part of their several Principals. In a word, al[l]
signified to the Great Pensionary, how much every
Individual Allie was obliged to Him, and satisfye[d]
with the Prudence and Integrity, which he had ex[]
press'd in the Negotiations: Which contrary t[o]

expectation of the Enemy, proved a new Co[n]-[tes]t for the Grand Alliance, and an Argument [to] convince the Princes concerned in it, that the [War] was to be Prosecuted till *France* was reduced [to the] Necessity of submitting to any Terms they [shou]ld think fit to prescribe.

The Allies in general, being much Exasperated [again]st *France*, for eluding the Hopes of Peace, [wh]ich She so much wanted, and seem'd so pressing [in] to seek for: The Princes of *Marlborough* and [*Eugene*], went immediately to *Lisle*, to make the ne[ces]sary Dispositions for opening the Campagne, [an]d to endeavour that Way, to bring the Enemy [to] Reason. The Confederates thereupon, that [w]ere before Assembled at *Courtray* and *Menin*, form[e]d the Army on the 21st of *June* near the last Place [(a]nd indeed the backwardness of the Season would [no]t well allow it sooner) from whence they march'd [th]e 22d towards *Lisle*, encamping between *Linselle*, [*Tourcom*] and *Rabaix*. The 23d the Right Wing un[de]r Prince *Eugene* of *Savoy*, passed the lower *Deule*, [an]d at the same time the Left, under the Duke of *Marlborough* passed the *Marck*, and the Army En[c]amped in the Plain of *Lisle*. on both sides the Up[p]er *Deule*, and Orders were sent for the Artillery to [c]ome from *Menin* to *Lisle*, with an Express to Lieu[te]nant General *Dompre*, who was left with a Flying [C]amp near *Aloft* to join the Army with all speed [O]n the 24th the Quarter-Masters General went [o]ut with 1200 Horse to view the Ground between [th]e Army and the Enemies, and the Situation of [th]eir Camp, and observed that they were strongly [p]osted between *Pont a Vendin*, *Cambrian*, and *Beauvi*[gn]ian, that they were perfecting their Intrenchments [w]ith all imaginable Application, and that their [l]eft and Right were covered by *Morasses*, and [th]eir Front by some Villages which they had forti[fi]ed. On the 25th Lieutenant General *Dopff*, went [o]ut with another Detachment, to get a more exact
Knowledge

Knowledge of their Posture, and upon his rep[ort] join'd to that of Lieutenant General *Cadogan*; the[re] was a Council of War held on the 26th to take t[he] proper Measures for Attacking the Enemy, b[ut] the General did not think fit to go upon that ente[r]prize, by reason of the advantagious Situation [of] their Camp, and the difficulty of the Ground b[e]tween the Enemy and their own Camp, and cam[e] to a resolution of Besieging *Tournay*.

This resolution was kept very Private, and th[ey] Decamped the 26th at Night, from the Banks [of] the *Deule*, without beat of Drum or Sound of Tru[m]pet, the Baggage being sent away to *Lisle*, and t[he] whole Army thinking they were Marching to A[t]tack the Enemy, when they were very much su[r]priz'd, at their being caus'd suddenly to turn on th[e] Left towards *Tournay*, which was soon after Inve[st]ed with such Dispatch that the *French* could n[ot] have any Notice of the Design, or Time to p[ut] any Reinforcements therein, but on the contra[ry] suffer'd themselves to be impos'd on so far, as t[o] draw several Battalions out of the Garrison, [to] strengthen their Army against an Attack. The Garrison of *Tournay* according to the best account consisted of 12 Battalions, and 5 Regiments [of] Dragoons, and the Marquis *de Sourville* Lieutena[nt] General, who was Wounded in the Siege of *L[isle]* was Commandant, Monsieur *Megrigni*, who as fir[st] Engineer, had the Directions of the Fortification of the Citadel was Governour of it, and the chi[ef] Stength of the Works in general, consisted in th[e] Mines that were made under them; so that ther[e] would be great occasion for Sapping; for whic[h] Service, Miners were sent for from *Lisle*, and othe[r] from *Maestricht*, and with them Monsieur *du Me[...]* who was Director of the Great Attack again[st] the Town of *Lisle*.

The first Thing the Duke did, while the Line[s] of Circumvallation were making, was to send De[...]
tachment[s]

ments to surprize *Zest-Amand*, a Place on the
, which might be of great use to the Besie-
at that Time, and likewise *Mortaign*, a Post
the *Scarpe* falls into the *Scheld*, both which
soon taken possession of, the Enemy ritiring
their approach. On the Side of the Enemy,
Governour of the Place sent out a Party of
to fetch in the large Cattle out of the Neigh-
hood, upon the Confederates arrival, but that
was cut off, and made Prisoners, except 9
Dragoons, and 4 Officers, who made their
cape to *Conde*. The said large Cattle, to the
mber of 700 were by his Grace's particular Di-
ions, restor'd to the Peasants. At the same
ime the *French* General being sensible of his Mi-
ke, in weakning the Garrison, order'd 7 or 800
Horse from *Mons*, to advance to *Timogres*, hoping
get into the Town, by the great Road that rea-
hes from *Audenarde* to it; but 6 Squadrons, and 6
attalions being sent over to the *Hainault* Side of
Schelde, to reinforce the Posts there, and to se-
re some Intervals and Passages, the Enemy found
emselves obliged to retire, without attempting
y Thing.

Another Party of *French* Soldiers, of greater
rength than the former, hover'd also about the
amp, to endeavour to throw themselves into
Place, but such Means were taken to prevent
em, that they could not effect it, tho', by the
eport of Officers, taken in Peasants Habits, the
hevalier *de Luxemburgh*, who was successful in re-
forcing *Lisle*, was employ'd by the Marshal *de*
illars, for that purpose, and was in motion near
aiencsennes, with 12 Squadrons of Horse Not but
us General incommoded the Besiegers in another
anner, and having found it impracticable to
rengthen the Garrison of *Tournay*, weaken'd the
onfederates, by attacking the Post of *Warneton*,
herein the Allies had a Lieutenant-Colonel, a
Major,

Major, and 700 Men made Prisoners, before Lieutenant-General *Wills*, with 2500 Grenadiers, a[nd] 30 Squadrons, could come up to their assistance.

The Trenches were open'd on the 7th, and c[ar]ried on by 3 several Attacks, the Principal of whi[ch] was commanded by General *Lottum*, the 2d [by] General *Fagel*, and the 3d by General *Schulemberg*[; and] as there was nothing wanting in the Besieg[ers] to expedite the Conquest of this important Tow[n,] so the Besieged, on their Part, gave undeniab[le] Tokens of their Skill in Affairs of War; but [as] nothing could resist the Victorious Forces of t[he] Allies, who contemn'd all Dangers, and were n[ot] to be discourag'd at the greatest Difficulties, [so] the Enemy was forc'd to give way to the Super[i]ority of their Opponents Valour, (whereby t[he] *English* distinguish'd themselves in a particular ma[n]ner) after they had in vain contended for the R[e]ward of Heroical Actions, not only in sight [of] their Commanders, but in subterranean Conflic[ts,] the practice of which was, before this Siege, a[l]most unknown.

In a Word, after several fruitless Sallies, spring[-]ing several Mines, and an incessant Fire from t[he] Town, when the *French* saw Preparations made f[or] a Storm, fearing to be taken Sword in Hand, th[ey] hoisted a white Flag at General *Schuylemburgh*'s A[t]tack, and desired to capitulate for the Town, whi[ch] was granted upon this *Proviso*, That the Duke [of] *Marlborough* would consent to it; who, with Prin[ce] *Eugene* cover'd the Siege, and observ'd the Arm[y] under the Marshal *de Villars*. Their Highness, a[c]cordingly, gave their consent, and sign'd the A[r]ticles: Those which concern'd the Garrison, co[n]taining in substance, "That the *Lisle-Gate* shou[ld] " be deliver'd up the 30th in the Morning, a[nd] " the Garrison retire into the Citadel the 31[st,] " at which Time the Town was to be deliver'd [up.] " That the sick and wounded, which were i[n]
" Conditi[on

(193)

Condition to be removed, should go to *Valenciennes*, or *Doway*, at their own charge, Six Days after the signing of the Capitulation; but a List was to be taken, and they to be subject to the Capitulation for the *Citadel*, those which were unable to march out, being allowed to stay in the Town till their recovery, &c.

Accordingly the Town was deliver'd up, tho' the *French* knowing the Importance of it, had done all that was in the power of Art to make it strong, and in the place of the ancient Castle, had built a Citadel, (that yet remain'd to be taken) which was look'd as the most exquisite Piece of Fortification. In short, they had made so many Works for the Defence of it, that they esteem'd it impregnable, as is to be seen by the following Inscription upon One of the *Half-Moons*, which is printed in the *History of the French-Academy*, by Mr. *Pelisson*, of the *Hague* Edition, 1688.

Ludovicus Decimus Quartus
Incertum Bello, an Pace major:
Omnibus Copiis, Consiliis, Animo, Celeritate, Fortunâ,
Anno M. DC. LXVII. Nerviorum Urbem,
Quatriduo ceperat;
Eandem, ne unquam postea caperetur,
Inter cætera Munimenta, hoc quoque
Diebus vix octo,
Ab Areâ & Fundamentis
Ipse Instans Operi,
Victricibus Militum Manibus
Extruxit,
Anno Domini, M. DC. LXXI.

In English thus.

LEWIS the Fourteenth,
Whether he was greater in War or Peace is uncertain,

C c   With

With those Forces, Counsels, Presence of Mind,
and Happy Success,
Which he had taken the City of *Tournay*, in the Year
MDCLXVII.
After a Siege of Four Days.
Has, amongst other Fortifications, that it might
be no more taken,
Built this Citadel
From the Ground, and its very First Foundations
Whilst he in Person carried on the Work,
By the Victorious Hands of his Soldiers.
In the Year of our Lord MDCLXXI.

But notwithstanding all this, it was forced to submit to the Glorious Arms of the Allies, in less than 3 Days, after open Trenches, and that, as it were, in sight of a numerous Army, under a daring Commander who made no Attempt to relieve it, and the Conquest was still so much the more advantagious, by how much the Loss of the Allies was very inconsiderable, in reference to the Strength and Importance of the Place.

After the surrender of the Town, the Allies set themselves vigorously at work, to carry on their Approaches towards the Attack of the Citadel, but Monsieur *de Sourville*, who found by one of the *Articles*, that the Garrison was therein intended to be made Prisoners of War, if they continued obstinate in defending it, proposed to the Besiegers to appoint a Person to treat with another under the same Character from him: Whereupon the Princes of *Marlborough* and *Savoy*, commissioned the Sieur *de Lalo*, Brigadier in the *British* Troops, and the *French* Governour, the Marquiss *de Ravignan*, a Major General in his, who having conferr'd together, drew up Seven Articles, in which it was condition'd to deliver up the Place on the 5th of *September*, and in case Monsieur *de Ravignan* brought the Ratification of them from the *French* Court,

...te was to be given up to the Allies the Day af-
...; but this, and the rest, with *Proviso*, The King's
...my should not oblige the 30 Battalions, and 10
...adrons, which amounted to 18000 Men, and
...e employ'd in the Siege, to break up from be-
...e the Place.

These Articles were sent to *Versailles*, for His
...jesty's Approbation; But that Monarch gave
...fresh Instance of his unsincere Dealing, and ma-
...fested to the World, That the Proposal for deli-
...ring up the Citadel, was but an Artifice to gain
...ime. The *French* King would not ratifie these
...rticles, but upon Condition there should be a
...essation of Arms in general, (there being one
...tween the Garrison and Besiegers during the
...bove-mentioned Time) in the *Netherlands*, till the
...th of *September*, which the Allies rejected, and
...rried on the Siege with all possible Vigour. As
...r their Part, the *French* continued on the other
...ide of the *Scarpe*, intrenching themselves up to
...eir Noses, while the Confederate-Army routed
...eir Detachments every Day, and brought in
...any Prisoners into their Camp.

But to return to the Besieged, who did all that
...en could do, under a very brave Commander;
...ey disputed every Inch of Ground, and made se-
...eral Sallies, and sprung abundance of Mines,
...t to no other End, than to make the Assailants
...ore obstinate in their Attacks, wherefore after
...ey had been forced to quit the greatest part of
...eir Works, and had born the Fatigues of Action,
...th above and below Ground, Day and Night,
...thout ceasing, from the 8th of *August* to the
...ist, they made an Offer to surrender upon Con-
...itions to be permitted to go out of the Cita
...el, with all the Marks of Honour, 12 Pieces of
...annon, and 6 Mortars, and 4 Covered-Waggons,
...t it being thought fit to have the Garrison Pri-
...ners of War, as well for the Honour of the Con

C c 2 federate

federates Arms, as in return for the French King
having refused to agree to the former Capitulation; they were told, They must yield to thos[e]
Conditions, or if they stood a general Assault, b[e]
put to the Sword. Tho' the Duke of Marlboroug[h]
was pleas'd afterwards to allow, "That all the O[f-]
" ficers and Soldiers should retain their Sword[s]
" and Baggage, and leaving their Colours an[d]
" Arms behind them, be permitted to return t[o]
" France, upon Condition, that they should no[t]
" serve until they were actually exchanged again[st]
" the like number of Officers and Soldiers of th[e]
" Allies, among whom, those taken at Warnet[on]
" were to be immediately sent back as part of th[e]
" exchange. They accordingly march'd out o[n]
the 5th of September, and were conducted to Cond[é]

The Grand Army decamped as soon as a Gat[e]
of the Citadel was deliver'd to the Besiegers, whic[h]
was 2 Days before the surrender of the whole; th[e]
Hereditary Prince of Hesse being detach'd befor[e]
break of Day, to force the Enemies Lines.

That Prince, accordingly, got over the Trouille
and the Enemy forsook their Redoubts, and reti[-]
red towards St. Guislam, so that the Horse whic[h]
he commanded, could not possibly overtake them[.]
In the mean Time, the Army under the Duke o[f]
Marlborough, came with its Right to Fontoburgh, an[d]
the Left to Hion, while the Prince of Savoy encam[-]
ped at St. Denus, their main Design seeming t[o]
be against Mons. But on the 7th the Duke receiv['d]
Advice about Noon, That the French were upon [a]
full March to attack the Body of Troops, unde[r]
the command of the Prince of Hesse; whereupo[n]
Orders were given for the Army to decamp, an[d]
leave their Baggage behind, and their Tents stand[-]
ing They halted on the Hills of Belian, wher[e]
the said Prince of Hesse had his Quarters, and ha[-]
ving received Advice, That the Enemy had no[t]
passed the Defiles of Wasme, but that they wer[e]
encampe[d]

…mped at *Quievrain*, and the said Defiles, the…
…continued in that Camp the following Night, in order of Battle.

…ow the Duke of *Marlborough* being informed, … the Garrison of *Mons* consisted only of Nine … *Spanish*, and Two *Bavarian* Battalions, besides … Dragoons of *Pasteur*, conjectured, That the … Design of the Enemy, in these Motions, was … oblige him to draw all his Forces into the Plain, … een *Belian* and *Framieres*, that they might have … Opportunity of throwing Re-inforcements into …, sent some Troops towards St. *Guislain*, to … vent the same. On the 8th nothing material … pened, and the Generals spent the whole Day … viewing the Ground between the Two Armies. … t Morning the Enemy made a Motion, as if … y would march towards *Bossu*, but his Grace be- … advanced with some other Generals, to take a … row View of their Army, soon perceived that … Motion of their Left was only a *Feint* to cover … March of their Right, which filed off at the … e Time; whereupon, being unwilling to lose … Moment's Time, he order'd his Army to march … his Left, by which Motion, the Two Armies … me so near to each other, that both were cano- … ded till the Evening.

The *French* were posted in the Woods of *Great* … *gues*, and the Allies on the Edge of the same … oods, from *Larox-fosse*, *Blaregnies*, and *Bieron*, be- … een the Wood of *Sart*, and *Sansart*, being drawn … in order of Battle, upon Three Lines. The … nemy were drawn up in sight of the Allies, be- … een the said Woods, and it was in that Place that … ey cannonaded each other. Both Armies con- … inued in order of Battle on the 9th, all Night, … well as the following Day, when the *French* be- … an to entrench themselves, upon which the Ge- … erals, and Field-Deputies, held a Council of War, … Result of which was, That Orders were immediately

mediately sent to the Troops that were on their march from *Tournay*, to decamp from *Havre*, and join the Grand Army with all speed. On the 11th, in the Morning, about half an Hour past 7, the Confederates cannonaded the Enemy with great Fury, while the Troops moved to attack them, upon which ensued a most terrible and bloody Battle, the first Intimation of which came by Letter to Mr. Secretary *Boyle*, from the Duke of *Marlborough*, in the following Words.

SIR,

"AS soon as I had dispatch'd my Letter to
" you, on *Saturday*, from *Havre*, we were
" alarm'd with the Enemies marching to attack
" the Prince of *Hesse*, upon which the whole Ar-
" my was immediatly put in motion; but it was
" next Day, at Noon, before all the Troops could
" come up. In the Morning they sent out a De-
" tachment of 400 Horse to observe our March,
" which the Head of the Prince of *Hesse*'s Troops
" attack'd, and took the Colonel who commanded
" them, with the Lieutenant Colonel, and seve-
" ral other Officers, and about 50 Prisoners. Up-
" on notice of our Armies lying on this side the
" *Haisne*, the Enemy stretched out their Line from
" *Quievrain*, to the Right, which they continued
" to do the next Day, and Yesterday they pos-
" sess'd themselves of the Wood of *Dour* and *Blan-
" gies*, where they immediately began to entrench.
" This Motion of the Enemy kept our Army for
" 2 Nights under Arms, and in the Evening, as
" soon as the 21 Battalions and 4 Squadrons we
" were expecting from *Tournay*, were come within
" reach, it was resolved to attack them, and the
" necessary Dispositions being made, we accor-
" dingly began at 8 this Morning. The Fight
" was maintained with great Obstinacy, till near

12 a Clock before we could force their Entrenchments, and drive them out of the Wood into the Plain, where their Horse was all drawn up; and Ours advancing upon Them, the whole Army engaged, and fought with great Fury, till 3 in the Afternoon; when the Enemy's Horse began to give Way, and to retire towards *Maubeuge* and *Valenciennes*, and Part of Them towards *Condé*. We pursued Them to the Defile of *Bavay*, with great Slaughter; all our Troops behaving Themselves with the greatest Courage. We are now encamped on the Field of Battle. You may believe the Loss must have been very great on both Sides. We have a good Number of Officers Prisoners; but as I send this by Lieutenant-Colonel *Graham*, who carries a Letter to the Queen, I must refer you to my Next for further Particulars. In the mean Time I heartily congratulate you upon this great Success, and am truly

SIR,

Your Most Faithful Humble Servant,

MARLBOROUGH.

" I had almost forgot to tell you, that we took *Guislain* Yesterday in the Evening, Sword in Hand, and made the Garrison of Two hundred Men Prisoners of War.

This being but a cursory Account of the Victory, it will not be improper to refer the Reader to the Lieutenant-Colonel's Relation before mentioned, which was to this Effect. " Our Army being " joined by the Troops which were expected from " *Tournay*, stood with their Front to the Woods of " *Blangies*, *Sart* and *Sansart*; the imperial Troops
" on

" on the Right, the Forces of the States on
" Left, and the Subjects of *Great Britain* in
" Centre. The Enemy was posted in Bod
" entrench'd within those Woods, and drawn
" on the opposite side of them in Two Lines, th
" Lines being also Entrenched. At Eight in
" Morning the Cannon began to Fire on the
" nemy, and the Left of the Prince of *Sav*
" Army joined the Right of the Duke of *Marl*
" rough. A little before Nine the Signal was
" ven for the Charge, which was made with
" utmost Bravery; after an obstinate Dispute
" *British* Troops forced into the Enemy's Entren
" ments, and the Right of the Duke of *Mar*
" rough's Army marched through the Woods w
" great Difficulty, forcing the Enemy to retire
" they advanced. When we had pierc'd q
" through, Our Foot with that of Prince *Eug*
" began to form themselves on the Plain after
" ing much divided by Fighting through
" Thickness of the Wood: The Duke of *Mar*
" rough commanded an Halt as soon as they ca
" into the Plain, and rode to observe what
" passed on his Left, where the Troops of
" States attack'd the Enemy in a Plain betw
" the Woods of *Sart* and *Sanfart*. The Army
" the States had pierced the first Entrenchme
" with great Slaughter on their Side, as well a
" that of the Enemy, and had marched on to
" Second; but (that being guarded by *Fr*
" Troops) were forced to retire to their first I
" The Duke of *Marlborough* observing the g
" Loss which the *Dutch* Troops had suffered,
" dered Lieutenant-General *Withers* to march
" the Body under his immediate Direction to
" stain them, but upon further Deliberation,
" Notice that the Lieutenant-General had
" attack'd, and was actually engaged with
" them, and that all things went well on
' Ri

Right; the Duke thought fit rather to press on the Advantages then, than to hazard a new Motion towards the Left in the Heat of the Action; soon after the Enemy's Left began to retire towards Attick, and draw off their Cannon from the Plain before Bleron, their Foot also began to break in the Centre: Whereupon the Duke of Marlborough commanded the Earl of Orkney to attack the Enemy in their Re-trenchments on the Plains of Bleron, with Directions, if he succeeded there to Post himself in those Re-trenchments, and cover our Horse as they may file off through the Woods into the Plain, in Order to charge the Cavalry of the Enemy, which were drawn up. This was executed with great Resolution and Success; but before the Horse of the Allies were all march'd into the Plain, and while they were forming Themselves into Order of Battle, the French Horse retired by the Way of Bavay; and the Right of their Foot which were Entrenched on the Plains at Bleron march'd off with great Precipitation between the Source of the River Honneau, and the Wood Sansart. The Duke of Marlborough detach'd General Bulau to pursue the Enemy. Their Army now giving way from One Wing to the other, great Numbers of Prisoners and wounded Men fell into our Hands. The Fight was very obstinate and bloody, and continued till Twelve at Noon before we had forced the Enemy into the Plain; we pursued them to the Defile of Bavay, where was made a very great Slaughter, and when Lieutenant-Colonel Graham was dispatch'd, the Duke of Marlborough was encamped in the Field of Battle.

The foregoing Gentleman being an Aid de Camp His Grace, and having been more immediately ploy'd in those Parts of the Army where Her jesty's Forces were concerned, could not be

D d   particular

particular in what paſſed among the other Troop[s]
of the Allies, tho' ſubſequent Accounts tell u[s]
that ſeveral Squadrons of Prince *Eugene*'s Army un[-]
der the Command of General *Vink* ſurrounded ſe[-]
veral Battalions of the Enemy's Right, after th[e]
Earl of *Orkney* had poſſeſs'd Himſelf of the Re[-]
trenchments on the Plain of *Bleron*, and ſummone[d]
them to ſurrender Priſoners of War; but the *Fre[nch]*
being cover'd by a Moraſs, made their Retre[at]
along the Edge of a Wood. Three *Daniſh* Regi[-]
ments of Cavalry falling at the ſame Time amon[g]
the Fugitives made terrible Slaughter among the[m]
till having gained a ſecond Wood they foun[d]
means to eſcape. Eighteen Squadrons being de[-]
tach'd to endeavour to diſperſe them in thei[r]
March towards *Quievrain*, met their whole Le[ft]
Wing on the ſide of the little River *Quaiſneau*; con[-]
ſiſting of about 100 Squadrons, commanded b[y]
Mareſchal *de Boufflers* in Perſon; and perceivin[g]
only at firſt the Enemy's Rear, poſted at a Corne[r]
of a Wood, the Dragoons made up to them, an[d]
drove them without Reſiſtance; but Colone[l]
la Lippe and a Cornet advancing too far, were ta[-]
ken, without being perceived by their own Me[n.]
The Wood being forced, the 18 Squadrons advan[-]
ced into the Plain; but perceiving before the[m]
the Enemy's whole Left Wing in their Columns[,]
One of which retreated in good Order, the othe[r]
Two in ſome Confuſion; they made a ſhort Halt[,]
and were ſomewhat ſurpriz'd to ſee the Enemy fac[e]
about, and draw up in Order of Battle: Howe[-]
ver, this ſmall Body of the Confederate's Horſ[e]
kept their Ground, and Poſted Themſelves upon [a]
riſing Ground, with the Wood of *Elonge* on thei[r]
Right, expecting to be attacked; but they imme[-]
diately perceived that the *French* made a Stand with[h]
no other Deſign than to paſs a Rivulet that was i[n]
their Way to a Defile leading to *Bavay*, which the[y]
gained before the Allies, who purſued them ful[l]
Gallop

llop, could come up with Them However, the latter followed the Chace as far as the Village of Quivrain; where the French having Posted a Brigade of Foot, and at the same Time, some of their Squadrons Posting Themselves on an advantagious Ground near the River Hasneau, the Confederates thought fit to give over the Pursuit, and the Enemy pass'd it, and march'd unmolested to Bavay: The rest of their broken Army retired, as before in the Duke's Letter, in great Confusion, some towards Maubeuge, and Valenciennes, and others to Condé, leaving the Allies in Possession of the Field of Battle, 16 of their Cannon, 20 Colours, 8 Standards, other indisputable Marks of Victory; not to mention abundance of Prisoners, among whom were 301 Officers. Some of these were taken in the Action, Others in the Pursuit, and the far greater Number the next Morning in Bavay, and other neighbouring Places, either Weariness or their Wounds not permitting them to follow the Gross of their Army, which having that Night passed the Rivulet of Renelle, encamped with their Right at Quesnoy, extending their Left towards Valenciennes.

When the Battle was over the Confederate Generals at sight of the advantagious Posts from which they had driven the Enemy, were amaz'd to see what Difficulties they had surmounted; for indeed all the Troops, Officers, and Soldiers on the Part of the Enemy had shewn in this obstinate Action, as great Resolution, Intrepidity and Firmness, as were even known in these latter Times, or stand recorded in ancient Story, and either spirited by their Intrenchments, or animated by the Shame of the former Defeats defended themselves with unexpected Bravery, from Half an Hour past 8 in the Morning, till Half an Hour past 2 in the Afternoon. It is true indeed, they were forc'd to give Way to the superior Courage and good Fortune, of the Allies, whose Generals, Prince *Eugene*, the Duke of *Marlborough* Count *Tilly*, and the Prince of *Nassau*, were during the whole Fight, continually at the Head of the Troops in the hottest of the Fire Monsieur *Gslinga*, One of the Field Deputies did also animate the Soldiers by his Example, and was so near Danger, that he had a Horse shot under him, and one of his Attendants wounded. Great Numbers likewise fell on the Side of the Allies, who publickly own'd that they had above Eighteen thousand Men, either kill'd or wounded. Among the first were several Officers of Distinction, particularly General Count *Lottum*, General *Tettau* of the *Prussians*; Count *Oxenstiern*, Lieutenant General, the Lord *Tullibardine* Eldest Son to the Duke of *Athol*, and Colonel of a Regiment of Foot in the Service of the States. Among the Wounded were Prince *Eugene* of *Savoy*, slightly on the Head as was also Brigadier *May* in the same Place, Lieutenant Generals, *Spar*, *Wackerbaert*, and *Hamilter*, the first mortally, Brigadier *Croonstrom* Count *Oxenstiern* Adjutant, dangerously; and Monsieur *Duts*. Adjutant to the Prince of *Friezland*. His Highness Himself had 2 Horses kill'd under Him, but He escaped unhurt; as did also the Duke of *Argyle*, tho' he received several Musquet-shot thro his Clothes, and Perriwig. To be more particular as to the *British* Troops, Brigadier *Lalo*, a *French* Refugee, in great Esteem with the Generals, Sir *Thomas Pendergrass*, Colonel of a Regiment of Foot, Colonel *Rivet* of the Guard, Colonel *Campone*, Lieutenent-Colonel *Arundel*, and Lieutenant-General *Berkel*, were reckoned among the Slain. Lieutenant-General *Webb* in the Beginning of the Action, receiv'd a very dangerous Wound by a Musquet-ball that lodged it self near the Groin Lieutenant-Colonel *Rumsey*, Major *Lashley*, and Major *Row*, died of their Wounds: But Lieutenant-tenant-Colonel *Farmer*, Major *Chivers*, and many of the Inferior Rank survived theirs.

The *French* were very industrious in lessening and concealing their Loss from the Publick, but some private Accounts from their Army own'd, that they had about 54 Officers killed on the Spot and 1068 Wounded; besides 301 taken Prisoners, and the Number of their private Men Killed, Wounded, or taken, was modestly computed at 15000. Among their Slain, were Messieurs *de Courfillon*, *de Chamerault*, *Palavicini*, *de Lautree*, *de Greberges*, *de Moret*, and *Sheldon*, Lieutenant Generals, Count *de Beusl*, Messieurs *de Roulrau*, *de Rochebonne*, and *de Tournefort*; Major Generals, Count *de Agennes*, Messieurs *de Coafquin*, and *de Stokenbergh*; Brigadiers, the Duke of St. *Agnan*; and Messieurs *de Schawestern*, *de Jalis*, *de Seignelay*, The Chevalier *de Croy*, *de Teligonde*, *de Molezun*, *Fitzgerald*, *de Bapintia*, St. *Laurent*, and the Duke of *Charoft*; among the Wounded was the Marshal *de Villars* himself, who in the heat of the Battle receiving a Shot in his Knee, was obliged to leave the Command of the Army, to the Marshal *de Boufflers*; the Duke *de Guiche*, the Chevalier *de St. Forts*; Messieurs *de Conflans*, *de Beaufremont*, *de Savigne*, *de Craufat*, *de Mornefiers*, *de Opride*, *de Refuge*, *de Albergotti*, the Prince *de Lambaffe*, and *de Monbufon*; Messieurs *de Brillac*, *de Toutnemine*; *de Renty*, *de Berville*, *de Autel*, and *de St. Hillaire*. Upon the whole matter, those who judged impartially were of Opinion, that all things consider'd the Allies gained, indeed, a very remarkable and glorious Victory, but paid so dear for it, that some said, *Two such Victories more would have undone them*; and on the other Hand, there were not wanting those that affirm'd, that tho' the *French* were beaten from their fortifyed Camp, and lost the Field of Battle, yet they retrieved their former Reputation. But then their not attempting afterwards

to

to relieve *Mons*, as it expos'd their Impotence, so did it make appear, that their Loss was much greater than they pretended

The Action at *Blaregnies* being over, the Victorious Army was order'd to Encamp a little beyond the Battle, which was cover'd with the Bodies of Men Dead, Dying and Wounded; and on the 12th of *September* (N. S.) they return'd to their old Camp at *Belians*, Prince *Eugene* taking his Quarters in the Village of *Quarignan*, the Duke of *Marlborough* his in the Abby of *Belian*, and Count *Tilly* his in the Village of Port *Quesoy*. The same Day the Allies were busie in Burying their Dead and removing their Wounded Men, and there having been a great many of the *French* Officers and Soldiers left Wounded on the Field of Battle and in the Adjacent Houses, the Duke of *Marlborough* gave notice to the Marshal *de Villars* and *Boufflers*, that he would permit them to send a Number of Waggons to fetch them off, and Order Lieutenant General *Cadogan*, with 200 Horse to meet at *Bavay*, such General Officers as they should send with a like Number to settle the Manner, and take the Paroles of Honour of Officers that they carried off, with the Number of the Private Soldiers, to be afterwards accounted for upon an Exchange Accordingly they sent the Chevalier *de Luxemburgh*, with whom, General *Cadogan* concerted every Thing: Two Days being allowed the Enemy for Burying their Dead, and bringing off their Wounded according to their desire.

The 15th of *September* (N S.) being appointed as a Day of Thanksgiving to Almighty God, for the late wonderful Victory, was observed very devoutly thro' the whole Confederate Army, and the Evening concluded with Salvoes of Artillery and Musquets, and other Military Rejoycings; and it is observeable, that upon the first News of this Battle, and a fond Report that the *French* had the Advantage

vantage, they likewise put on the same Countenance for it, at *Charleroy*, *Namur*, and other Places; but they were soon undeceived, and their Joy appall'd On the 16th Eighteen Battalions that had suffer'd most in the Action, were order'd to go and Recruit themselves, and their Room was soon after supplied by Twenty Four Battalions, drawn out of the Garrisons, Twenty of which were *Dutch*, the other Four *British*.

The Confederate Generals having resolved to lay Siege to the Important Town of *Mons*, the Capital City of *Hainault*, and the late residence of the Elector of *Bavaria*, Lieutenant General *Cadogan* went on the 18th to *Brussels*, to hasten the March of the Artillery and Ammunition Waggons designed for that Enterprize. A great Number of Horses were sent from the Army to bring up the same to the Camp, and on the 19th the Duke of *Marlborough* remov'd his Quarters to the Castle of *Havre*, to be nearer *Mons*, where the Count *de Bergheyck*, who was the Chief Manager of King *Philips* Affairs in the *Netherlands*, was at the Time of its being Invested, and from whence, He had given some Hints of his Masters willingness to enter into a Treaty of Peace, in the following Letter sometime before the Battle as may be seen by the Date. It was directed to his Grace after this manner.

My LORD,

"I do my self the Honour to send to your Highness by a Drummer, a Letter which the
" Duke of *Alba* and I have, by Order from the
" King my Master, written to your Highness,
" 'Tis with the greatest Pleasure, My LORD,
" that I take this Opportunity to assure Your
" Highness, for my having for you all the Respect
" and Deference that is possible, and I take the
" Liberty

"Liberty to desire Your Highness to give me
"leave to add to the Letter which we both write,
"that if Her Majesty the Queen of *Great-Britain*
"should by the means of your Highnesses good
"Offices, think it for the Interests of the Nation
"to have regard to it; I am provided with Power
"from the King my Master, to explain my self
"more particularly, to such Person, and in such
"Place as your Highness will be pleased to No-
"minate, upon whatever may be most to the
"Satisfaction of Her Majesty, and for the Interest
"of the Nation; as also to the peculiar Satisfacti-
"on of your Highness. I have the Honour to be
"with all the most profound respect,

My LORD,

Your Highnesses most Humble

and most Obedient Servant

The Count de BERGHEYCK.

His Grace did not think fit at the Time of receiving it, to have any private Conference with
that Minister; but as the latter happen'd to be in
the Town as above mention'd, he was on the 21st
of *September*, permitted to have an Interview with
his Grace, who granted him Passports for several
Ladies, and several Persons of Distinction that went
out of *Mons* before the Siege was Formed. The
Duke likewise receiv'd a Letter from the States-
General, the Day before this Interview, in Answer
to one of his, that gave them notice of the Battle of *Blaregnies*, the Day after it was Fought,
which ran thus,

SIR,

(209)

SIR,

"WE have receiv'd the Letter of your Highness, dated the 12th Instant, and we return you Thanks for your obliging Congratulation, on the compleat Victory, obtained by the Arms of the Allies, the Day before, after the most hard and obstinate Fight that ever was heard of. Our Deputies have acquainted us with the Particulars of the whole Action, and have not forgotten to let us know how much your Highness has contributed to the gaining of that Victory, and what is due to your Valour. If Glory attends the Greatness of Difficulties and Dangers surmounted, that which you have acquired, on this great Occasion, must exceed all others; and this Day alone is sufficient to render your Name immortal, tho' it was already so by your preceding Victories. We congratulate you hereupon with all our Hearts, and praise the Lord of Hosts for that Glorious Success. We hope that the Enemy being, at last, sensible, that all their Forces assembled together, their Entrenchments, nor any Advantage of Ground, are not capable to withstand the Conduct, and incomparable Valour of the Generals, and the Intrepidity, and Unparallell'd Bravery of the Troops of the Allies, will think of giving satisfaction to all, in order to settle a General Peace. We pray God to bless more and more your Enterprizes, and are, with the greatest Esteem and Sincerity, SIR,

Your Highness's most Affectionate to do you Service,
The States-General of the United-Provinces
of the Netherlands.

..., September
..., 1709

(Signed)

G. HOEUFF,

And by their Order,   J. FAGEL.

All Things being ready for the Siege, and th[e] 30 Battalions, and 30 Squadrons, which were t[o] carry it on under the command of his Highnes[s] the Stadtholder of *East-Friezland*, being arrived i[n] the Camp before the Town: He gave Order[s] pursuant to his Instructions from the Duke [of] *Marlborough*, for dreining the Innundations betwee[n] *Conde* and *Mons*, which was so happily effected, th[at] the Watters fell 6 Foot on one side, by the 25t[h] when the Trenches were open'd, at Night, at t[he] Attack of *Bertamont*, with all success imaginabl[e] and with little Loss. Another Attack was lik[e] wise carried on at the Gate of *Havre*, from whic[h] there was a Sally the next Day, with 300 Me[n] who killed and wounded about 60 Men of Brig[a] dier General *Hill*'s Regiment; but that Regime[nt] being supported by that of Prince *Albert*, the Ene[] mies were oblig'd to retire. Its remarkable, in th[e] Siege, That the Allies made no Lines of Circumv[al] lation, which added to the natural Strength of t[he] Place, as well as its Fortifications and Garriso[n] made it wonderful that the Besieged should be[at] the *Chamade*, on the 20th of *October* following[;] when in the last War, the Town had withstood th[e] Attempts of a *Royal-Army*, commanded by th[e] *French* King in Person, for a much longer Tim[e.] To pass by other Particulars, which shew'd t[he] *French* quite dispirited by their late Defeat, let [it] suffice, That after Hostages were exchang'd, a[nd] those on the part of the Enemy, sent to the Prin[ce] of *Savoy*'s Quarters, Articles of Capitulation we[re] sign'd on the 21st, which was the next Day fo[l] lowing, by that Prince, the Duke of *Marlboroug[h]* and the Deputies of the *States-General*, on O[ne] Part, and General *Grimaldi*, Governour of t[he] Town, on the Other; immediately after whic[h] 500 Men, of the Forces of the Allies, took p[os] session of the Gate of *Nimi*.

The Reduction of this important Place, after the Memorable and Bloody Battle of *Blaregnies*, as a plain Demonstration, That the Confederates gained in it something more substantial than the Name of a Victory, since the Enemy, who had hazarded an Engagement to prevent the Siege of it, made not the least motion to relieve it: Notwithstanding the Assurances given by the Marshal *Boufflers*, to the *French* King, That His Majesty should not lose an Inch of Ground by that Action; and his boasting of marching towards the Allies Army, if His Majesty's Service required it. On the 23d of *October* the Garrison marched out with all the Marks of Honour allow'd them by the Articles, leaving, as Hostages with the Allies, the Count *Bergeyck*, and Monsieur *Brouckhoven*, for satisfying the Debts contracted in the Place, and in the Province of *Hainault*, as also for such Debts as were contracted the Year before in *Ghent*, &c when the said City was in the possession of *France*. But as they were allow'd no Cannon by the Capitulation, so out of Compliment to the Besieged, the Confederate Generals granted them 2 Pieces of Cannon, and 1 Mortar. The whole did not exceed 1909 Men, the rest being either sick or wounded, and a great number of *Walloons*, and others, having staid in the Town, to list themselves in the Service of the Allies. After this, Count *D'hona*, who was appointed to command in *Mons*, march'd into it with a Detachment of Troops, which were to be in Garrison during the Winter.

Of the *British* Troops employ'd in this Siege, Brigadier-General *Hill* receiv'd a Hurt in his Side, Colonel *Clayton* was dangerously wounded in the Eye, and Colonel *Foxton*, and Major *Mortimer* kill'd, with several other inferior Officers, and Soldiers, as were several other of different Nations, the whole Loss amounting on their Side to 1700 Men. Nor did the *French* lose a less number, the

Garrison being 4500 when they sat down before it.

The Season being so far advanced, as not to admit of any farther Enterprize, the Winter-Quarters were setled; and the 26th, the Army pass'd the Haisne, came to Thieuries, and there continued the 27th, which Day was celebrated as One of Thanksgiving to Almighty God, for the taking of Mons, with so little Loss. On the 28th the Army separated, to march to their respective Winter-Quarters; 2 Days after which, the Duke of Marlborough, who had written to the States General, upon the Reduction of the foregoing Place, receiv'd the following Letter.

SIR,

"Altho' we were already informed by our
"Deputies, of the taking of Mons, and
"the Reduction of the Province of Haynault, the
"Letter whereby your Highness congratulates
"on that happy Success, has not been, for all that
"less acceptable to us. We look upon this Con-
"quest, as one of the Fruits of the last Victory
"and of your Labours; and we rejoice the more
"at it, because, (besides its own importance)
"it must convince all the World, That the Ad-
"vantage, as well as the Glory of the last Battle
"remain on the Side of the Allies. We congra-
"tulate, with all our Heart, Your Highness there-
"upon. If the Season permitted to go as far
"as your good Will, we might surely promise
"our selves, That the Valour of Your High-
"ness would procure us new Advantages before
"the End of the Campagne: But seeing the
"Season of the Year does not allow of any far-
"ther Action, this must be refer'd to next Spring
"unless the Enemy prefer Peace to War, upon
"mo-

"more equitable Conditions, than they have hi-
"therto express'd.

"We are, with much Esteem,

SIR,

Your Highness's most Affectionate to do you service,

The States General of the United-
Provinces of the Netherlands.

His Grace, after the Repartition of the Winter Quarters, set out from *Brussels*, on the First of
November, for the *Hague*, where he arrived 2 Days
after, as did Prince *Eugene*, on the 7th of the same
Month. On the 12th their Highnesses had a long
Conference with several Deputies of the States,
wherein Prince *Eugene*, who spoke first, represented, among other Things, "That tho' there
"was reason to hope, That the Glorious Victo-
"ry, and other great Advantages obtained the
"Last Campagne, would induce the Enemy to
"comply next Winter with such Terms as might
"secure a Good and Lasting Peace, to prevent
"the Continuation of the War, and save the
"great Charges they must be at, to bring the
"Army into the Field, the next Campagne, yet
"as this was still uncertain, there was an abso-
"lute Necessity, to take in Time, and without
"any delay, the necessary Measures, for being
"early in the Field, the next Spring, in order
"to act with more Vigour than ever. That, a-
"bove all Things, it was necessary to make suf-
"ficient Magazines of Forrage, Corn, Meal, and
"other Things requisite, in the most convenient
"Frontier Places, that the Troops might be as-
"sembled, subsisted, and put into a Condition to
"act, even before there was Grass upon the
"Ground;

"Ground; and that a sufficient number of Wag-
"gons be provided, for transporting to the Ar-
"my, Bread, and other Necessaries; the Troops
"having been more than once in great Straits,
"the Last Campagne, and having, for some Days,
"been without Bread, for want of Waggons, of
"which the Field-Deputies, of their High Migh-
"tinesses had been Witnesses: That Magazines
"were indispensably necessary, to prevent the E-
"nemies being in the Field before them in the
"Spring, and to take such advantagious Posts, as
"might enable the Allies to penetrate into the
"French Territories, without being put to the ne-
"cessity of hazarding a Battle, and attacking them
"in their strong Entrenchments. That it was also
"necessary to have double the number of Wag-
"gons they had before, for transporting Bread,
"and other useful Things, from the Frontier-
"Places, to the Army; because, otherwise, they
"could not advance at any distance from the
"said Frontiers, and penetrate into the Domini-
"ons of *France*, how fair an Opportunity soever
"they had for it, and less still at present than
"before, because the Enemies Territories afforded
"no Provisions to subsist an Army. That there-
"fore he earnestly recommended these Two Ar-
"ticles of *Magazines* and *Waggons*, as Two Things,
"without which they could not promise to them-
"selves to obtain the Advantages that might be ex-
"pected from the next Campagne, in case they
"were oblig'd to continue the War: *Concluding*, with
"desiring them, That the Contracts for furnish-
"ing the *Imperial* and *Palatine* Troops with Bread
"and Forrage, might be performed and exe-
"cuted without delay, for preventing all Incon-
"veniencies and Disorders.

The Duke of *Marlborough* spoke next, on the same Heads, and recommended, with the utmost Earnestness, the Articles relating to the MAGA-
ZINES

ZINES and WAGGONS, adding, "That being to go for *England*, he left there General *Cadogan*, who was impower'd to settle with the Council of State, the Contracts for the Subsistance of the *Imperial* and *Palatine* Troops, and other Affairs, which were to be regulated in concert between *Great-Britain*, and the *States*.

His Grace represented, afterwards, "The absolute necessity of Recruiting and Re-establishing the Forces with all speed, and renewing the Capitulations with such Troops, which, without a new Agreement, could not continue their Service, concluding, That it was also highly necessary, to regulate also, in Time, the Rout of the *Hessian* Troops, that were marching into their own Country, that they might return, without any delay, as soon as Occasion should require.

This Conference having been reported to the *States-General*, their *High-Mightinesses* resolved to concur in every Thing that was or should be proposed, for making the utmost Efforts the next Campagne, in order to bring the War to the desired Conclusion.

The Confederate-Ministers had several other Conferences together, wherein it was warmly insisted on the Part of *Great-Britain*, and *Holland*, That since the Empire made such great Demands upon *France*, (as the Restoration of the Three Bishopricks of *Metz*, *Toul*, and *Verdun*, and all *Alsace*, and *Franche-Comte*) its Members ought to furnish their full Quota's, towards this necessary War. To which Prince *Eugene* answer'd, "That the Emperor thought the Thing so reasonable, that he " would readily take any Measures, in concert " with His Allies, to compel the respective States " and Princes of the Empire to the punctual Performance of their Duty and Engagements, it " being well known to all the World, That His
" Imperial

" Imperial Majesty was not wanting in setting
" them an Example, since he furnished sever[al]
" Thousands of Men, and considerable Sums [of]
" Money, more than his Quota. They also co[n]
sulted together, about proper Means to extingui[sh]
the War in the North, or at least to prevent i[ts]
spreading into the Empire, and any ways affect[ing]
the Grand-Alliance.

As soon as the Campagne in the *Netherlands* w[as]
at an end, the *French* Court, as has been hint[ed]
before, in Count *Bergeyck*'s Letter, thought fit [to]
make new Advances, towards the setting aga[in]
on Foot, a Negotiation of Peace. In order, [to]
this, Seignior *Foscarini*, the *Venetian* Ambassado[r]
who, about this Time, came to *Holland*, took [a]
Turn *incognito* to *Amsterdam*, to feel the Pulse [of]
the Burgo-Masters of that City. On the oth[er]
Hand, Monsieur *Petkum*, Resident of the Duke [of]
Holstein, at the *Hague*, who had been under ha[nd]
employ'd, the Winter before, in the Negotiatio[n]
then in agitation, and had since continued to ho[ld]
a Correspondence with the Marquiss *de Tor*[cy]
made some new Overtures on the Part of *Fran*[ce]
and desired Passes for their Commissioners to co[me]
to the *Hague*, which having been taken into Co[n]
sideration by the *Imperial, British,* and *Dutch M*[ini]
sters, and the Report of their Conferences co[m]
municated to the *States-General,* their *High-Migh*
nesses refused the Passes, but consented, That Mo[n]
sieur *de Petkum* should go to the *French Court*, pursua[nt]
to their Desire, to know what further Offers th[ey]
had to make. According that Minister set out f[or]
Paris about the middle of *November*, as did, not m[a]
ny Days after, the Duke of *Marlborough* for *Lond*[on]
and Prince *Eugene* for *Vienna*. I should follow t[he]
First of these Princes to the Court and Parliame[nt]
of *Great-Britain*, but Negotiations of Peace bei[ng]
now upon the *Anvil*, between the High Allies, a[nd]
the common Enemy of *Christendom*, it will be ve[ry]

...ch to our purpose, for a while, to go along with ...Pettecum, to obtain a faithful Relation of what ...the Consequence of his Journey.

That Gentleman was receiv'd at the French Court ...more respect than is usually paid to a Mini- ...of such an inferior Rank, as a common Resi- ...t, and with an affected Parade and Ostentation, ...make their famish'd and murmuring People be- ...e, that Peace was at hand; not without some ...Insinuations, That the Allies themselves had ...him to make Proposals towards it, tho' 'tis cer- ...he had no such Power or Direction from them ...er he had for some Days confer'd with the Mar- ...is de Torcy, and the other French Ministers, and ...eiv'd a Present for the Trouble and Charge of ...Journey, he was dismiss'd to the Hague with the ...owing Answer in writing.

ednesday, November 27, at 4 of the Clock in the Afternoon.

MOnsieur Pettecum returning to the Hague, "is desired to acquaint Monsieur the Pen- ...onary, that it would be impossible for the King ...o execute the 37th Article of the Preliminaries, ...ven altho' His Majesty might resolve to sign ...he same.

"That without entring upon the Observations ...at may be made on the Expressions and Form ...f the other Articles, it is evident that they ...were proposed by the Allies, 6 Months ago, ...pon no other View, than for preventing, by ...Suspension of Arms, the Events of the Cam- ...gne, which was then ready to begin; for it ...ing possible, that the Operations of War ...ight change the Dispositions that appeared ...en towards a near Conclusion of the Peace, ...rudence required to prevent the same.

F f "That

" That, that Reason is now over, and does n[ot]
" subsist at this Time, because the Winter Seaso[n]
" does naturally establish a suspension of Arm[s]
" without any Agreement in Writing.

" That therefore, without speaking any mo[re]
" of Preliminary Articles, the three Months [of]
" this Winter might be employed for treating D[e]
" finitely of Peace.

" That suppressing the Form of those Article[s]
" the King would preserve the substance there[of]
" and that they should Treat on the Part of [his]
" Majesty, and that of the Allies on the Found[a]
" tion of the Conditions, to which the King w[as]
" pleased to consent for the Satisfaction of the E[m]
" peror, the Empire, *England, Holland,* and th[e]
" Allies; tho' his said Majesty had declared, t[hat]
" those Conditions should be void and of no [ef]
" fect, if they were not accepted during the [time]
" of the Conference held at the *Hague.*

" That his said Majesty is ready to resume [the]
" Negotiations on the same Foot, name Pleni[po]
" tentiaries in order thereunto, and send them [to]
" such a Place as shall be agreed upon, to be [there]
" to confer with the Allies on the 1st Day of J[a]
" *nuary* next.

" If it be consented to enter upon Negotiatio[ns]
" the *Sieur Petticum* might forthwith return for [sett]
" ling the Passes, and other Formalities, for [the]
" Place and manner of Meeting

" These Proposals from *France* having been R[ead]
" and Examin'd by Persons deputed for that P[ur]
" pose the States General came to the follow[ing]
" Resolution.

" The *Sieur Van Welderen,* and other Deputie[s of]
" their High Mightynesses for Foreign Aff[airs]
" having according to their Commission of the
" Instant, Examined the Answer brought f[rom]
" *France* by the *Sieur* Resident *Pettecum,* which
" has delivered in Writing, such as it was C[om]
" " munic[ated]

municated to Him, by the *Sieur Marquiss de Torcy* Secretary of State.

" The said Deputies have reported to the Assembly, That having seriously weighed and considered the Contents of the Answer aforesaid; it has immediately appeared to them, that in the said Answer they entirely recede and depart from the Foundations that have been hitherto laid, and on which the Negotiations for grounding those of a general Peace, were begun, and have been hitherto continued; for it is evident, that the Negotiations were at first begun, to adjust and settle certain Preliminary Articles, which when agreed upon, might serve for a Foundation, to enter upon the Negotiations of a General Peace; from which Negotiations, People could not expect any good Success, and therefore would not be induced to begin the same, till certain Preliminary Points were adjusted and agreed upon for the Foundation thereof. That it was upon those Grounds, that the President *de Rouelle*, in the first Place, and the Marquiss *de Torcy* after Him, being come hither, Preliminary Articles were adjusted with them, which Preliminaries were Signed the 28th of *May*, this present Year by the Plenipotentiaries of His Imperial Majesty, those of Her Majesty the Queen of *Great-Britain*, and those of their High Mightynesses, and which were immediately Ratifyed on the part of Her said Majesty of *Great-Britain*, and of this State.

" That His most Christian Majesty having not thought fit to approve the said Preliminaries, by Reason, only of the 37th Article thereof, and the Negotiations breaking off thereupon; yet upon new Inducements, and advances made on his Part, the said Negotiations were resum'd by Letters, for endeavouring to remove the Difficulties about the 37th Article aforesaid, by an
" Equivalent

" Equivalent, or any other Expedient, which h[as]
" been the only Subject of the New Negotiatio[ns]
" that have enfued thereupon. Affurances bein[g]
" given in the mean time on the part of *Fran[ce]*
" That their King approved all the other Article[s]
" and would ratifie the fame as foon as they cou[ld]
" agree upon the 37th Article aforefaid: Th[at]
" this was the only Subject of the Journey of t[he]
" *Sieur Pettecum*; for feeing this Point could n[ot]
" be agreed upon by Letters, they made on t[he]
" Part of *France*, repeated Inftances, that the fa[id]
" *Sieur Pettecum* might go thither, to fee, wheth[er]
" his Prefence at the *French* Court, might help t[o]
" wards finding an Expedient, for overcomi[ng]
" and removing the Difficulties about the 3o[th]
" Article aforefaid: But feeing by the Anfw[er]
" they have returned, that they recede entire[ly]
" from the Preliminaries aforefaid, that the fam[e]
" are wholly fubverted, and that they talk of e[n]
" tering upon Negotiations of Peace, witho[ut]
" making any further mention of Preliminarie[s]
" whereby the Foundation that was laid at fir[ft]
" is rejected and fubverted, as well as the Aim a[nd]
" Defign that was Built thereupon, *viz.* That th[ey]
" might be affured on the fide of the Allies of ce[r]
" tain Points, before they enter'd upon any form[al]
" Negotiations of Peace, and of the due Exec[u]
" tion of the faid Points, during the faid Negot[i]
" ations, and before the Conclufion of the Peac[e]
" which two points and Articles being rece[ded]
" from by the faid Anfwer, the faid Deputies a[re]
" therefore of Opinion. That it ought to be [in]
" fifted on this fide, on the Foundations that ha[ve]
" been laid in Concert, and with the Approba[ti]
" on of the Allies; and that it ought to be decl[a]
" red with the like Concert, That for the Reafo[ns]
" aforefaid, the Anfwer brought by the *Sieur P*[*et*]
" *tecum*, is not Satisfactory; and that the faid Pr[e]
" liminary Articles ought to be infifted upon, [
" whi[ch

"which Articles there being no Difficulties raised on
" the part of *France*, but only upon the 37th, and
" your High Mightynesses and your Allies, having
" been of Opinion, that an Expedient might be-
" sought for, to the satisfaction of all Parties, they
" persist still in the said Sentiment.

" And it being taken into Consideration there-
" upon, That altho' all the Lords Deputies of the
" respective Provinces, are unanimously of Opi-
" nion, that upon the good and fundamental Rea-
" sons alledged, their Advice and Sentiments
" ought to be followed in all its Parts; yet it is
" thought, it will be of a greater Force and Effi-
" cacy, if it be Corroborated by an Unanimous Re-
" solution of all the Members of the Union.
" Therefore it is thought fit, and resolved, That
" notice hereof shall be given by Letters to the
" Lords-States of the respective Provinces, and
" that it shall be represented to them. That the
" *Sieur Pettecum*, who at the Desire, and the repeat-
" ed instances of *France*, was permitted with the
" Consent and Knowledge of the Allies, to go
" for *France*, to see if any expedient could be found
" out for removing the Difficulties about the 37th
" Article of the Preliminaries, is, contrary to all
" expectation, returned, not only without bring-
" ing any such expedient with him, but with an
" Answer, in which, there is not the least mention
" made of the Proposals that were made here some
" time ago, and in which, they recede entirely
" from the Foundations, which were agreed to
" with a Common Consent, as it has been said be-
" fore, and with a Proposal to enter into a formal
" Negotiation of Peace, without settling and ad-
" justing any thing before hand: A Proposal which
" in all times before, has been judged dangerous
" and not to be admitted by the Allies, and is con-
" trary to the Declaration, which has been always
" made on the part of *France*, after the adjusting

of

" of the Preliminaries, and even by the laſt Let-
" ters; viz. That all the Preliminary Articles
" ſhould remain firm as they were ſettled, only
" with ſuch alterations in the Terms of the Exe-
" cution, which the Courſe of Time had render'd
" neceſſary, except only the 37th Article: That
" from this Way of proceeding nothing can be
" concluded, but, that the Enemy is not ſincerely
" diſpoſed to agree to a good and ſafe Peace, and
" that little regard is to be had to the aſſurances of
" their good Intention and Inclination in that Re-
" ſpect, ſeeing the Effects agree ſo little with their
" Words; but rather that all is concerted and de-
" ſigned to ſow if poſſible, Miſtruſts and Jealouſies
" between the Allies and this State, while they
" are reſolved to continue the War, as it appears
" by all the Publick Advices, and otherwiſe, and
" muſt be neceſſarily concluded from the Prepa-
" rations they make every where, with greater
" Zeal and Application than before.—

" That it follows neceſſarily from thence, that Pru-
" dence and Precaution require, that they ſhould
" not be on the Part of the Allies, miſled by ge-
" neral Aſſurances and Proteſtations, made by
" the Enemy of their Inclinations to Peace, and
" by any faint Appearance tending that way, nor
" ſuffer themſelves to be diverted from the neceſſa-
" ry Care that is to be taken of all that is requiſite
" for carrying on and proſecuting this War, in
" Hopes of the further Favour and Aſſiſtance of
" God. But that in the preſent Conjuncture,
" more than ever; the reſpective Members of
" the Union go Hand in Hand with Unanimi-
" ty, Courage and Conſtancy, for making the
" neceſſary Preparations for proſecuting a War,
" in which God has in ſo wonderful a Manner bleſ-
" ſed the Arms of the Allies with great and marvel-
" lous Succeſſes, and bringing the ſame to a good
" End and Concluſion, and not let ſlip out of their
                                              " Hands,

(223)

"Hands, and lose the Conquests and Advantages
"that have been obtain'd with so many Dangers,
"and at the Expence of so much Blood and Trea-
"sure. That above all things it will be necessary
"that the utmost Efforts be made without the
"least Delay or loss of Time, to get in a readiness
"all that is requisite for beginning early the next
"Campagne, before the Enemy are in a Condition
"to take the Field, and pushing on the same
"with Vigour. That therefore the Lords-States
"of the Respective Provinces shall be desired
"(where they have not given a full Consent to
"the general Petition and State of the War spee-
"dily to consent to the Petition for erecting Ma-
"gazines of Forage, recruiting of Forces, extraor-
"dinary Armaments by Sea, and other Charges,
"and to finish actually, and in Time, the Sums
"they have consented to, that the High Allies
"seeing the Unanimity, Zeal, Sincerity, and
"Courage of the State, for preserving and pro-
"moting the Good of the Common Cause, may
"be encouraged and induced, not only to do the
"like on their Part, but also, according to their
"Power to make greater Efforts; and that the
"Exhortations which Your High Mightinesses
"will think fit to make to them, may make a
"greater Impression, and be more favourably re-
"ceived: And likewise, that the Enemy seeing
"the Firmness, Constancy, Unanimity, and Re-
"solution of the State, and their High Allies for
"continuing the War, and prosecuting the same
"even with more Vigour than before, may be
"brought to shew no longer with *Words* but by
"*Deeds* their Inclination to Peace. And so those
"Efforts to be made, and Preparations for the
"next Campagne will have a good Effect if the
"Enemy can be brought thereby to more reaso-
"nable Thoughts, and will be unavoidably neces-
"sary if they prefer War before Peace: That Their
"High

" High Mightinesses know very well, that the Ex-
" pences of War are very burthensome; but they
" consider that this War, which was begun for pre-
" serving so dear and precious Pledges as those of
" Liberty and Religion, ought not, after so many
" Successes, to be ended and concluded, before the
" said Liberty and Religion are through the Bles-
" sing of God, settled upon a safe and lasting
" Foundation, and rather the more, because it
" appears that the War is no less burthensome to
" the Enemy, who begun, and have continued the
" same, only for gratifying their Ambition.
" That moreover it shall be represented to the
" High Allies in the most earnest and effectual
" Manner, that seeing it appears by the Answer
" brought by the Seiur *Pettecum*, that the Com-
" mon Enemy has not any Inclination to Peace,
" and that they are resolved to continue the
" War, making great Preparations, to make
" the next Year extraordinary Efforts, it will
" be unavoidably and absolutely necessary, that
" the High Allies in general, and every One
" in Particular, exert themselves in an extra-
" ordinary Manner, and make, in Time, the
" necessary Preparations for prosecuting with Vi-
" gour and Hopes of Success in the next Cam-
" pagne, the Advantages obtain'd in the former:
" That every Body knows the great Efforts the
" States have made since the beginning of this War:
" How great Charges they have, out of Zeal for
" the publick Cause, taken upon themselves; and
" how they have upon that Consideration, from
" Year to Year augmented the same: That ne-
" vertheless, Their High Mightinesses are willing
" and ready according to the Utmost of Their
" Power to continue the same; and still to exert all
" that depends on Them for prosecuting and pro-
" moting the Common Good; but, that they
" promise Themselves, and expect that the High
' Allies

"Allies, and every One of Them in particular, in Promotion to their Power; will not only continue to contribute what they have hitherto furnished for this Common War; but will also augment their Forces for the next Campagne, especially such amongst the said Allies, who are most able to do it, because it appears plainly from the Preparations of the Enemy, that their Intentions is, as they divulge it every where, to take the Field, and act with more numerous Forces the next Campagne, than in the last; and consequently it will be absolutely necessary, on the Part of the Allies, to bring greater Armies into the Field for prosecuting the War with Hopes of Success, and bringing the Enemy to such a Condition as shall be thought necessary by the Allies, for their Safety and Security: That therefore the High Allies aforesaid, shall be desired and exhorted, to take in Time, the necessary Measures for carrying on the War with Vigour the next Campagne; and hold in a Readiness all that is requisite for beginning the Operations of the War early in the Spring; and chiefly that every one according to his Ability, may augment his Forces The Sieur *Van Welderen*, and other Deputies of their High Mightinesses for Foreign Affairs, are for that Purpose appointed to confer with the Ministers of the High Allies residing here, and report what shall be done in the said Conferences

"And for the End and Purpose aforesaid, Letters shall be written to the Emperor, the Diet of the Empire at *Ratisbonne*, the confederated Circles, as also the Electors and Princes of the Empire, and likewise to Her Majesty of *Great Britain* and the Duke of *Savoy*. And their Majesties the Emperor, and the Queen of *Great Britain* shall be desired, that Prince *Eugene* of *Savoy*, and

G g "the

" the Prince and Duke of *Marlborough*, may
" come hither early in the Spring before the End
" of *February*, to confer about the Operations of
" War, and concert, in Time, the necessary
" Measures for the Campagne.

To return to the Duke of *Marlborough* whom we are now to find in *England*, He was no sooner arrived, but attended by a Deputation of the House of Commons, who in Pursuance of a Vote for that Purpose, waited upon him to give him their Thanks

In answer to which His Grace was pleas'd to reply.

IT is a very great Honour and Satisfaction to me, that the House of Commons is pleased to take so much Notice of my Endeavours to serve the Queen and my Country. I cannot but be just to all the Officers and Soldiers, who have served with me, unless I take this Occasion to assure you, that their Zeal and Affection for the Service, is equal to the Courage and Bravery they have shewn during the whole War.

The Lord Chancellor likewise congratulated His Grace upon his first taking his Place in the House of Lords, in their Name to this Effect.
" That he was commanded by their Lordships to
" give His Grace the Thanks of that House for
" His continued Services to Her Majesty and the
" Publick, during the last Campagne. Of which
" nothing could be greater said than what Her
" Majesty (Who always speaks with the utmost
" Certainty and Exactness) had declared from the
" Throne, that *It had been at least as Glorious as any which had preceeded It*. But that this Repetition of the Thanks of that August Assembly, had this Advantage of the former, that it must be look'd upon as added, and standing on the Foun-
" dations

" dations already laid in the Records of that House,
" for the preserving his Memory fresh to all future
" Times. So that His Grace had also the Satisfac-
" tion of seeing the Everlasting Monument of His
" Glory rise every Year much higher. That God
" might continue, in a wonderful Manner to pre-
" serve so invaluable a Life, that he might not on-
" ly add to that Structure, but finish all with the
" Beauties and Ornaments of an Honourable and
" Lasting Peace.

To this His Grace made Answer.

My LORDS,

*I Look upon it as the greatest Mark of Honour I could re-
ceive, that Your Lordships are pleased to take Notice
of my Endeavours to serve the Queen and my Country. I
beg Leave to do Justice to all the Officers and Soldiers,
who have served with me. It is not possible for Men to
shew more Zeal for Her Majesty's Service, or greater
Bravery than they have done.*

What further related to that Duke, during his Stay in England, was that the House of Commons upon a Motion made by Sir *Gilbert Heathcote*, who has lately taken upon him to be more than ordinarily solicitous about State Affairs, made an Address to the Queen in concert with the Lords, to send him instantly over to *Holland*. The Purport of it is fully explain'd in the following Words.

Most Gracious SOVEREIGN,

"WE Your Majesty's most Dutiful and Loyal "Subjects, the Lords Spiritual and Temporal, and Commons, in Parliament Assembled, having Reason to believe that the Negotiation of Peace will suddenly be renewed in *Holland*, and being justly apprehensive of the crafty and insinuating Designs of our Enemies to create Divisions among our Allies, or by amusing them with deceitful Expectations of Peace, to retard their Preparations for War, do think our selves bound in Duty, most humbly to represent to Your Majesty, of how great Importance we conceive it is to the Interest of the Common Cause, that the Duke of *Marlborough* should be abroad at this Juncture.

"We cannot but take this Opportunity to express our Sense of the great and unparallell'd Services of the Duke of *Marlborough*'s, and with all imaginable Duty to applaud Your Majesty's great Wisdom, in having Honour'd the same Person with the great Character of General and Plenipotentiary; who in Our humble Opinion, is most capable of discharging Two such important Trusts.

"We therefore make Our Humble Request to Your Majesty, that You would be pleased to order the Duke of *Marlborough* immediate Departure for *Holland*, where his Presence will be equally necessary to assist in the Negotiations of Peace, and to hasten the Preparations for an early Campagne; which will most effectually disappoint the Artifices of our Enemies, and procure a safe and honourable Peace for Your Majesty and Your Allies.

The

The foregoing Address was a Subject of Speculation to many People, especially such as were zealous for the Prerogatives of the Crown, and Asserters of the Queen's undoubted Rights of making Peace and War; some did not stick to affirm that is was of a Peice with a certain Transaction the Year before, wherein Her Majesty was desired not to make Peace without the Demolishing of *Dunkirk* &c. and the Surrender of the whole Monarchy of *Spain*; however it was thought adviseable on the Part of the Soverign at this Time, to acquiesce under, and comply with the Sentiments of Her Subjects, and give them the following Most Gracious Answer.

My Lords and Gentlemen,

I Am so sensible of the Necessity of the Duke of Marlborough's *Presence in* Holland, *at this Critical Juncture, that I have already given the necessary Directions for his immediate Departure, and I am very glad to find by this Address, that you concur with Me in a just Sense of the Duke of* Marlborough's *eminent Services.*

Accordingly the Duke set out for *Harwich* the next Day in his Way to *Holland*; but because the principal Motive of his Journey, was to assist on the Part of *Great Britain* at new Conferences that were then in Agitation, it will be highly material to speak of what happen'd thereupon before his arrival at the *Hague*, which the *Reader* is desired to take the ensuing Method.

Upon the vigorous Resolutions taken by the 2 maritime Powers for the Prosecution of the War, the Court of *France* thought fit to make further Overtures of Peace: In Order to which the Marquiss

quiss *de Torcy* did, on the 2d of *January*, 1710 N. S. send a Project to Monsieur *Pettecum*, con sisting of Five Articles which imported.

I. That immediately after the Signing of Peace the *French* King would acknowledge King *Charles* as King of the whole Monarchy of *Spain*; and not only withdraw all the Succours he had given his Grand-son, but also not send him any Assistance for the future, and forbid his Subjects to List among his Troops; as also consent, that no Part of the Monarchy of *Spain* should ever be United to *France*.

II. That as for the Emperor and Empire, the *French* King would restore the Town and Citadel of *Strasburgh*, and the Town of *Brisac*, content himself with the Possession of *Alsace*, according to the literal Sense of the Treaty of *Munster*, leave the Empire the Town of *Landau*; raze the Fortifications he had caused to be built on the Rhine, from *Basil* to *Philipsburgh*; and acknowledge both the King of *Prussia* and Elector of *Hannover*.

III. That as to *England*, he would acknowledge QUEEN ANNE, and the Succession in the Protestant Line, restore *New-found-land*, and agree to a mutual Restitution of all that had been taken in the West-*Indies* on both Sides; demolish the Fortifications of *Dunkirk*, and ruin the Harbour thereof; and consent to the *Pretender*'s leaving *France*.

IV. That; as to the States-General, he would yeild to them for a Barrier all the Places specify'd in the 22d Article of the Preliminaries; and confirm'd what he had offer'd to them in Respect to their Trade. And,

V. A

V. As for the Duke of *Savoy*, that he was willing to grant the Demands made for him by the Allies: and that he likewise demanded that the Electors of [Cologn] and *Bavaria* should be restor'd to their Estates and Dignities.

This Project being rejected by the Confederates, the *French* resolved to make further Overtures, and dispatch'd a Courier of the Cabinet to the *Hague*, with a Letter from the Marquiss *de Torcy* to Monsieur *Pettecum*, which contained in Substance, that the *French* King consented, that the Preliminaries that were concerted the Year before should be the Foundation of the future Treaty, and had appointed the Mareschal *de Uxelles*, and the Abbot *de Polignac*, his Plenipotentiaries to that [treat with] the Allies of an Equivalent for the 39th Article, relating to the Evacuation of *Spain*, and that the said Ministers should be ready to meet those of the Allies at *Antwerp*, or any other Place, if the Allies would but send them the necessary Passes. Monsieur *Pettecum* having communicated this to the States, they in a Conference with the Minister of *Great Britain*, and the Emperor's Plenipotentiary agreed that he should return for Answer; " That " the said Declaration of the *French* Court being in " uncertain and ambiguous Terms, the Allies re- " quired that the *French* King should declare, in " plain and express Words, that he consented " to all the Preliminaries, except the 37th Ar- " ticle; which done, they would send Passes to " his Ministers to treat of an Equivalent for the " said Article.

Another *French* Courier being returned to the *Hague* with a satisfactory Answer, Passes were dispatched for Plenipotentiaries of that Nation, who came

came to *Antwerp*, on the 9th of *March*, 17$\frac{2}{10}$, and after they had defired Monfieur *Pettecum* might meet them there, which was not granted by the *Dutch* went on board a Yatch, prepared for them at *Moordyke*, where Meffieurs *Buys* and *Vanderduffen*, the States-Deputies foon after met them, and had a Conference with them. The next Day they had another, which lafted feveral Hours, and then the States Deputies fet out for the *Hague*, and the *French* Plenipotentiaries went for *Gertruydenburgh*, the Place appointed for their Refidence, and the holding of future Conferences, the *French* having fhewn an Unwillingnefs to treat at *Antwerp*, which had been at firft pitch'd upon; or in any other Town belonging to the *Spanifh Netherlands*, undoubtedly out of Compliment to King *Philip*. By this Time the Duke of *Marlborough* was come to the *Hague*, with whom Meffieurs *Buys* and *Vanderduffen*, as likewife with the Lord *Townfhend*, and Count *Zinzendorf*, held a Conference in the Prefence of the Great Penfionary, and the Deputies of the States, and to whom they communicated what had pafs'd between them and the *French* Plenipotentiaries, which was, " that the Perfons laft menti
" oned, had, in the Conferences held with them,
" endeavour'd, in the Firft Place, to perfuade
" them, That it was the Intereft of the Allies to
" make a feparate Peace with *France*, exclufive of
" *Spain*; and that to render the fame effectual,
" and remove the Umbrages the Allies feem'd to
" have taken, That the King of *France* might
" underhand affift his Grandfon; His *Moft Chri*
" *ftian Majefty* was willing to enter into the moft
" folemn Engagements to the contrary, and give
" Cautionary Towns for the Performance of that
" Promife. That the Deputies of the State an
" fwered, That thefe Offers of *France* were not
" fufficient; and that the Allies having chiefly

under-

undertaken the War for restoring the Monarchy of *Spain*, to the House of *Austria*, they could not treat with the *French* King, (who had placed his Grandson on the Throne of that Monarchy) without stipulating that he should relinquish the same; adding, That the High Allies would be very much surpriz'd to hear, That after the pressing Instances the *French* had made for these Conferences, their Plenipotentiaries were come to offer what had been already rejected, and would doubtless take it as an Evidence that their Court was not sincere, and sought only to amuse the Allies. That Messieurs *d'Uxelles*, and *de Polignac* pretended, That they did not know that any such Thing had been offer'd; but they were told, That though Ministers might be allow'd sometimes to dissemble, yet this was not a fit Time, to make use of that Privilege, and that they ought plainly to speak their Minds. That those Gentlemen pretended, That their Sincerity ought not to be question'd; and then enlarg'd on the sincere Inclination their Master had for Peace; but concluded, That His Majesty could never be so prevail'd upon to enter into a War against His Grandson, or take any other violent Measures against him. That they enlarged on the Affection of the *Spaniards* for that Prince; and at last declared openly, That they saw no other Expedient for procuring the *Spanish Monarchy* to King *Charles*, than to give a Share of it to King *Philip*; concluding, That if the Allies would consent to give him *Naples* and *Sicily*, King *Philip* might be induced to resign the rest to the Arch Duke: They represented, That this was the only way for preventing a further Effusion of Christian Blood, and which would save the Allies abundance of Trouble, and secure to the House of *Austria*

H h " the

" the Monarchy of *Spain*; whereas the Fate of
" Arms being uncertain, it might still happen,
" that the Allies might be oblig'd to make Peace
" upon other Terms. That the Deputies confuted
" these Reasons, without any great difficulty; and
" having represented that such a Partition was con-
" trary to the Treaties the Allies had amongst
" themselves, and to the whole Tenour of the
" Preliminaries, which the *French* themselves ac-
" knowledged for the Foundation of the Treaty
" they declared in express Terms, That they were
" sent to hear what equivalent they had to pro-
" pose for the 37th Article of the Preliminaries
" which they excepted against; but not to de-
" bate upon any other Point. Whereupon they
parted. The same Day, to prevent any Jealousie
among the other Ministers of the Allies, the Deputies of the States likewise communicated to the
Prussian Plenipotentiaries what had been transacted
at *Moerdyke*, and the next Day the same was in
more solemn manner communicated to all the
Ministers of the Allies, who were desired at the
same Time, to use their Interest with their respective Masters, that their Troops might be in
readiness to begin the Campagne as early as possible,
as the most effectual Means to force the common
Enemy to accept such Conditions, as might secure a safe and lasting Peace.

On the 18th of *March*, N. S an Express from
the *French* Plenipotentiaries arriv'd at the *Hague*
and the next Day acquainted the Grand Pensionary,
That they had received an Answer from the Court
to their last Dispatches, and desir'd either that
they might be permitted to come to the *Hague*, or
that the States-Deputies might again confer with
them at *Gertruydenburgh* The First being denied
and the Latter granted, Messieurs *Buys* and *Van-*
derdussen

[...]ssen set out the 20th for *Gertruydenbergh*, where [...] the 21st and 22d, they had several Conferences with the Ministers of *France*, who again proposed a Separate Treaty, exclusive of *Spain*; offering, as before, all manner of Security, That the [Most] *Christian King* should not assist His Grand[son]. Which being rejected, they proposed several Schemes of a Partition of the *Spanish Monarchy*. They mention'd, in the First Place, *Naples* and [Sicily] for King *Philip*; afterwards, That, if this Partition was not liked, the Allies would leave him in possession of the Kingdom of *Arragon*; and, lastly, That if this was not approved, that [the Prince] would content himself with *Sicily*, *Sardinia*, and the *Spanish* Places on the Coast of *Tuscany*. The *Dutch-Deputies* having told the *French Plenipotentiaries*, That they were surpriz'd to hear of no [E]quivalent for the 37th Article, as their Court had promised, and on which consideration alone the present Negotiation was agreed on by the Allies; That they had no power to treat of any Partition. They took their Leave of them, who [sen]t an Express to *Versailles* for further Instructions; and not many Days after, gave notice of his [Ret]urn. Hereupon new Conferences were held [on] the 8th and 9th, wherein the Ministers, on [the] Part of *France*, insisted on a Partition of the [Spa]nish Dominions, according to the Schemes they had before proposed; but seem'd, however, to de[par]t from what they had said in relation to *Sicily* [an]d *Sardinia*, pretending that 'twas by way of Conversation, and adher'd to the Article of *Naples*, [an]d the Places on the Coast of *Tuscany*, or else [the] Kingdom of *Arragon*, which occasion'd great [D]ebates between them and the Deputies of the [S]tates. The *French Ministers* mention'd afterwards [the] Articles of Security for the performance of [w]hat should be stipulated in the Preliminaries.

and proposed what they expected from the Alli[es]
for themselves; but would not explain their Mea[-]
ning on the Security to be given by *France* [to]
the Allies, for the performance of the Prelim[i-]
naries.

The Deputies of the States were very much di[s-]
satisfied with the Plenipotentiaries of *France*, an[d]
told them in express Terms, *That the Allies we[re]
tired with this way of Treating, and therefore expe[cted]
a full and clear Declaration of* France *on the Matte[rs]
already debated, or else would break off all manner [of]
Conference with them.* Whereupon Monsieur d'Uxell[es]
Abbot of *Polignac*, desired Time to send anothe[r]
Courier to *Versailles* for further Instructions, add[-]
ing, *That the final Resolution of their Master depende[d]
on that of the Court of* Madrid, *which was expe[cted]
about that Time at the* French Court.

This dilatory and shuffling way of Treating
(of which Messieurs the Deputies made thei[r]
Report of on the 10th of *April*) confirm'd th[e]
general Opinion, That the *French* had not a re[al]
Intention to come to a Peace, even by way [of]
Partition, and that they had no other Design i[n]
these Conferences, than either to divide or amu[se]
the Allies. In both which they were equally di[s-]
appointed For Prince *Eugene* being come to th[e]
Hague on the 12th, and having concerted with th[e]
Duke of *Marlborough*, and the Deputies of th[e]
States, what was to be done in the followin[g]
Campagne, for the early Opening whereof grea[t]
Magazines of dry Forrage and other Necessarie[s]
had been provided, those Two Princes set ou[t]
on the 15th for *Tournay*, near which Place th[e]
Confederate Troops quarter'd on the *Maeze*
Brabant, and *Flanders*, were order'd to rendez[-]
vous.

It was by many expected, that the early Success of those Armies, in passing the Lines on the 21st, and investing *Douay*, would have accelerated the slow Paces of the Negotiators at *Gertruydenberg*. But Messieurs *Buys* and *Vanderdussen* being again return'd thither on the 24th of the same Month at the desire of the Plenipotentiaries from *France*, had the same Day a Conference with them, in which they desir'd to know, on the Part of the Allies, *Whether, by their last Courier, they had any further Instructions on the Grand Affair, for which they were come into those Provinces?* The *French* Ministers answered, *That they had no other Proposals to make, but what they had already offer'd, and told to them; and that they expected the Answer of the Allies on their said Proposals.*

This Declaration occasion'd some warm Debates amongst them, and the Deputies complained of the Insincerity of the *French* Court; telling them, in express Terms, "That the Ministers of *France* having so often, and so positively declared, by Letters, and otherwise, that their Plenipotentiaries were to propose an Expedient for the XXXVIIth Article, the Allies could not but be surprized, that after so many Conferences, they should hear nothing from them, but a Proposal for a Partition of the *Spanish Monarchy*, and so the Conference broke up without any success.

The next Morning the Deputies above-mention'd, went to take their Leave of the *French Plenipotentiaries*, and insinuated to them, in general Terms, That the Armies being actually in the Field, and there being no Stops made in the past Conferences, towards procuring a General Peace, for which they

they were set on Foot; they thought it was to no purpose to continue them: Whereupon it was alledg'd, on their Part, That they had made several Proposals and Overtures, which, in their Opinion, might have conduc'd to the Attainment of a General-Peace, and that they wonder'd the Allies had made none on their Part, since they were not satisfied with those of *France*. After which they desired the *Dutch-Deputies*, to give them their Answer, or Declaration in Writing, that they might transmit it to their Court but this being denied. the Deputies return'd to the *Hague*, and those that had their Commissions from *France*, dispatch'd the Marshal *d'Uxelles*, his Secretary to *Versailles*.

Many were still of Opinion, that the passing of the Lines, and the Siege of *Douay*, would have obliged the *French* Court to alter their Stile; which was not all together improbable; for it was then strongly reported, That in the Council that was held upon the first Advice of the Allies, taking the Lines, there appeared a great Division among the Princes of the Blood: Some insisting upon the necessity of Peace, to preserve *France* from entire Ruin, and others with as great Vehemence standing up in Defence of a contrary Opinion, That it was better to venture the Fate of another Campagne, than agree to such Ignominious Terms as were demanded by the Allies.

Upon the Report made at the *Hague*, by Messieurs *Buys* and *Vanderdussen* of the last fruitless Conferences, the Imperial Minister thought fit to declare, *That the Emperor his Master could not consent to any Partition of the* Spanish *Dominions*, and therefore proposed, *That the* French *Plenipotentiaries should be admitt'd*: But others were of different Sentiments affirming

firming that since those Ministers had sent an Express to their Court, it was but reasonable to expect his Return, and see whether the late Progress of the Confederate Arms, had caus'd an Alteration in the Measures of that Court. It was not long before the Allies were satisfyed in that matter: for the Express being return'd on the 3d of *May*, the *French* Ministers wrote the next Day, the following Letter to Monsieur *Pettecum*.

Gertruydenburgh, May 4th,

" We could wish our Conferences had produced
" a Peace, but as we have no Order to make any
" other Proposition than those we have already
" made, we patiently expect that the Deputies
" will come hither to declare themselves more o-
" penly than their Manner has been hitherto, or
" to give us our Dismission, or at least, the great
" Pensionary will be pleas'd to send us an Order
" to be gone.

This being communicated to the States-General, and by the Pensionary to the Imperial and British Ministers, it was thought fit to do it in the same manner to all the Ministers of the Allies, who met thereupon on the 9th of *May*, and unanimously resolved that Monsieur *Pettecum* should be desired to Write to the *French* Plenipotentiaries, *That seeing they had nothing further to propose, and that the Allies had nothing more to say than what they had said before, it was to no purpose to continue insignificant Conferences, but that he should avoid to speak any thing of* Dismission *or Order to Depart*, Which was accordingly done by that Resident after this manner,

MESSIEURS,

MESSIEURS,

"HAving received the Letter which your Excellencies did me the Honour to write to Me, the 4th of this Month, I have communicated it to those who are entrusted with the Affair. Report has been made of that Letter, not only to the State, but likewise to the Ministers of the Allies, to whom, had already been Communicated, all that the Deputies related to have passed in the last Conference; And seeing your Excellencies declare in your Letter, That you have no Order to make any other Proposition than those which have been made, and that on the part of the Allies, all has been said, that could be said, I am Commissioned to make known to Your Excellencies, That 'tis thought unnecessary for the Deputies to repair again to Gertruydenburgh to continue useless Conferences. M. Buys and Vanderdussen have desired Me to make their Compliments to your Excellencies, and to assure you, that they think themselves much obliged for all the Civilities they have received. For my own part, I hope that the Departure of your Excellencies will not deprive Me of the Honour of your Favours.

I am,

Hague, May the 5th, 1710.

With profound Respect, &c.

The next Day the Plenipotentiaries of *France* sent Monsieur *Pettecum* the following Answer.

SIR,   *Geertruydenbergh, May* 10.

WE have received the Letter which you took the Trouble to write to us the 9th of this Month, by the Direction of the great Pensionary, and of the State, as well as of all the Ministers of the Allies; in which you tell us, that they will give no farther Answer to any of our Propositions, nor confer with us. We are extraordinarily concern'd to see, that notwithstanding all the Advances the King, our Master, has made for procuring Peace, they so obstinately refuse it. Since those Gentlemen have thought fit to break off the Negotiations, we are preparing to depart; and we desire you to thank Messieurs *Buys* and *Vanderdussen* for their Civilities. We shall always retain a thankful Remembrance of them, and desiring you to assure them of our Gratitude, we remain, &c.

Sign'd,   UXELLES.
                               POLIGNAC.

After this Declaration it was generally believ'd that the *French* Plenipotentiaries would have set out for *Paris*, the rather, because they had begun to pack up their Baggage: But it seems this Political Farce was not yet to be unravell'd; for having on the 14th of *May* received another Courier from *Versailles*, they gave Notice of it on the 20th following to the Resident of *Holstein*, desiring at the same Time that the States would once more send their Deputies to *Geertruydenbergh*. These new Conferences met with some Difficulties, Count *Zinzendorf*, the Imperial Minister, insisting upon his being admitted in them; but his Demand was over-ruled, (by reason other Ministers of the Allies, particularly the *British*, might with equal Justice have claimed the same Privilege,) and Messieurs *Buys* and *Vanderdussen* went on the 23d for the Place assigned for another Conference, the Report of which was made on the 26th following

to the Great Pensionary, in the Presence of the Imper[ial]
and *British* Ministers, signifying, 'That after many P[ro]
' testations of the most Christian King's Sincere Inc[li]
' nation to Peace, the *French* Plenipotentiaries had to[ld]
' them, that upon that Consideration his most Christi[an]
' Majesty had been prevail'd upon to recede fro[m]
' the former Demand he had made of *Naples, Sici[ly]*
' *Sardinia*, and the Places on the Coasts of *Tuscany*, a[nd]
' therefore was willing that *Naples* should rema[in]
' to the House of *Austria*; and that King Phi[lip]
' should content himself with *Sicily, Sardinia*, a[nd]
' the Places on the Coast of *Tuscany*. The Deputi[es]
' added, that they had thought fit thereupon, wit[h]
' out granting any Part of the Proposals, to ask t[he]
' said Plenipotentiaries what Security they had [to]
' propose to the Allies for the Evacuation of *Spa[in]*
' and the *Indies*, by the Duke of *Anjou* to Ki[ng]
' *Charles*, supposing that these Proposals of a Partiti[on]
' should be accepted? But that they had decline[d]
' to give them any Satisfactory Answer: Wher[e]
' upon the said Deputies had told them, that th[e]
' Allies being daily more and more convinc'd tha[t]
' the *French* Court kept up these Conferences no[t]
' out of a Sincere Desire of Peace, but only to e[n]
' courage their Subjects to bear the Burthen of the Wa[r]
' more patiently, they should find themselves oblig[ed]
' to break off all further Conferences with them, fo[r]
' removing all Occasions of Jealousie amongst them[
' selves: And the *French* made great Protestations o[f]
' the Sincerity of their Master, and said they woul[d]
' send another Express to their Court with an Accou[nt]
' of these Conferences.

The *Dutch* Deputies having made the like Repo[rt]
to the States of *Holland* and *West-Friesland*, thei[r]
High-Mightinesses took no Formal Resolutio[n]
thereupon, and thought fit to put it off to anothe[r]
Meeting, to give Time to the *French* Plenipotenti[a]
ries to receive Instruction from their Court, whic[h]
they did on the 6th of *June*, and immediately writ [a]
Lette[r]

... (with one enclosed to the Great Pensionary) Mr. *Patricum*, for Messieurs *Buys* and *Vanderdussen* ... return once more to *Geertruydenbergh*. Thereupon the Imperial Plenipotentiary renew'd his former ... tension to assist at the Conferences; and being ... denied, and his Orders from *Vienna* to insist in ... Demands being positive, he sent an Express to ... *Eugene* for his Highness's Opinion, who advis'd him to follow the Example of the *British* Minister, whose Mistress, tho' She contributed more ... the War than any other of the Allies, was yet well satisfied of the Wisdom and Integrity of the ... General, as to trust them with that Preliminary Negotiation of Peace. The Result of this ... Conference, which was complied with, and ... on the 15th and 16th of the same Month, was, ... the Ministry of *France* declared, ' That the King, their Master, was so sincerely inclined to Peace, that in order to procure the same, he receded from the Demand made in the last Conference of the *Spanish* Places on the Coast of *Tuscany*, and would content himself with *Sicily* and *Sardinia* for King *Philip*: That his most Christian Majesty would use all possible Means to perswade his Grandson to consent to that Partition; but that this required Time, and that if that Prince would not acquiesce in that Proposal, the most Christian King, tho' he could not consent to declare War against his Grandson, would however furnish a Sum of Money towards the Charge of the War to be continued against him, till he had surrender'd *Spain* and the *West Indies* to the House of *Austria*. This Declaration of the *French* Plenipotentiaries being likewise reported to the Great Pensionary, in the Presence of the Imperial and *British* Ministers occasion'd Two or Three Conferences between them, and render'd it almost beyond a Doubt, that the *French* had no other Design than either to amuse the Allies, or to decoy them to a Separate Peace,

exclusive

exclusive of *Spain*; where, notwithstanding their Promises, they might underhand assist King *Philip*, and carry on the War with such visible Advantages, as might in the End tire out, if not quite exhaust the Principal Members of the Grand Alliance. The Imperial Embassador was still of Opinion, that since the *French* Ministers did not propose an Equivalent (or Expedient) for the 37th Article of the Preliminaries, they ought to be dismiss'd, and therefore moved, that the Resident of *Holstein*, who, as he pretended, went on the 21st of *June* to *Geertruydenbergh* for some Private Affairs, should be desired to signifie to them, that the Allies would not consent to any further Conferences. But it was thought more advisable that Mr. *Pettecum* should make the following Declaration on the Part of the Allies, ' That the
' last Proposal made by the *French*, (*viz.*) of con-
' tributing a Sum of Money for the Charges of the
' War, to oblige the Duke of *Anjou* to quit the Mo-
' narchy of *Spain*, and content himself with *Sicily*
' and *Sardinia*, if he would not do it voluntarily,
' was not acceptable to the Allies upon several Ac-
' counts, and namely, because this would produce
' but a *Separate*, and not a *General*, Peace, which
' was the End the Allies proposed to themselves.
' Secondly, That the Allies insisted to have *Spain*
' and the *Indies* deliver'd up according to the Preli-
' minaries. And, Thirdly, That this Foundation
' being laid and agreed upon, the Allies would con-
' sent to continue the Conference on the other Arti-
' cles.

The *French* being somewhat dilatory in returning an Answer to this Home Declaration, Messieurs *Buys* and *Vanderdussen* were directed to send an Express to *Geertruydenbergh* to press them to explain themselves speedily upon that Subject, which return'd with an Answer, importing, *That by Virtue of their Power and Instructions, they were always in a condition to explain the Sentiments of the King, their*

their *Master*, and therefore desired that the said Deputies would confer once more with them. This Answer was taken into Consideration by Count *Zinzendorf*, and the Lord *Townsend*, who met afterwards at the Great Pensionary's, and after a long Debate resolv'd to comply with it, with this Instruction to the *Dutch* Deputies, That they should insist upon a Plain and Positive Answer to the Articles delivered to the said Plenipotentiaries by *Monsieur* Pettecum. Messieurs *Buys* and *Vanderdussen* accordingly had a Conference with the *French* Plenipotentiaries on the 13th of *July*, that lasted about Four Hours, tho' to as little Purpose as the former; for the *Dutch* Deputies resolving not to recede from the Declaration made on the Part of the Allies by the Resident of *Holstein*, the *French* said they had no further Instructions, but would send another Express to their Master for a Final Answer, which they would communicate upon the Return of the Courier, for whose Journey Fifteen Days were allowed. Monsieur *Vanderdussen* being as it were ascertain'd of the Insincerity of the *French* by these Proceedings, could not forbear making some warm Expostulations about it, to which the Abbot *de Polignac* replied in very high Terms; not without reproaching the *Dutch* with Ingratitude to the Crown of *France*, which had been their main Support upon their first shaking off their Obedience to *Spain*; whereupon this Conference, which proved to be the last, broke off unkindly. Thus far the Accounts on the Side of the Grand Alliance; but as I undertook to be Impartial in my first Introduction to these Memoirs, so it is but Just that I should also relate what the *French* said for themselves in this Unsuccessful Negotiation, which cannot be done better than in the Contents of the following Letter from their Ministers to the Great Pensionary, which being artfully written, deserves the Reader's Perusal.

Geertruy-

Geertruydenbergh, July 20th, 1710.

SIR,

'YOU know that we have agreed to whatever Messieurs the Deputies have propos'd to us, and it cannot be said that we have varied upon any Point whatsoever, much less that we have retracted the Offers we had made by Order of the King our Master, with Intention to procure a Peace so necessary to all *Europe*.

' Messieurs the Deputies have taken the Matter otherwise You have not forgotten what has pass'd between them and us from the Beginning of the Negociation. Give us Leave, Sir, to lay before you the Proposals newly invented, unjust, and impossible to be executed, which those Gentlemen made to us in the last Conference for a Final Answer to ours. They told us

' That the Resolution of their Masters, and their Allies, was to reject absolutely all Offers of Money on the Part of the King to assist them to maintain the War in *Spain*, whatever the same might be, and whatever Security his Majesty would give for the Payment.

' That the Republick and Her Allies pretended to oblige the King, our Master, to make War singly against the King, his Grandson, to compel him to renounce his Crown, and that without Uniting their Forces to those of his Majesty, they would have that Monarch dispossess'd of *Spain* and the *Indies* within the Term of Two Months.

' That this Term expiring, without the Catholick King's being actually driven from the Throne, the Truce to be agreed upon between the Allies and the King, our Master, should cease ; and that they would resume their Arms against his Majesty, tho' he should have perform'd all the other Conditions contain'd in the Preliminary Articles. ' That

'That before the signing of those Preliminaries they were willing, upon the Condition above-mentioned, to explain themselves positively as to the Partition which they would consent to leave to the King of *Spain*, and that they would likewise facilitate an Agreement upon the further Demands to be made.

'Lastly, That they might be willing to permit as a Favour, that the Troops they have in *Portugal* and *Spain* should act jointly in concert with those of *France*, during the Space of Two Months, to facilitate the Conquest of *Spain* and the *Indies*, which his Majesty should be oblig'd to make in Favour of the Arch duke: But that immediately, upon the Expiration of that Term, those Troops of the Allies should cease so to act, and that the Truce should break off.

'We represented to Messieurs the Deputies, that these Propositions were contradictory, as well to those they had all along made to us, as to the 4th and 5th Articles of the Preliminaries, whereto the 37th Article, which it was our Business to regulate, belonged, as to the Manner of securing to the Allies *Spain* and the *Indies*.

'They Answer'd, that the Concession of a Partition, on which they would explain themselves afterwards, and which they have not yet declared, gave them a Right to insist now upon more than the 4th and 5th Articles import.

'We replied to this with an unanswerable Argument, by demanding of them, whether in all our Conferences a Partition had not been the Matter in Question? And whether upon that Foundation they had ever required any Thing else of us, than the taking of Measures in concert, and the Union of Forces?

'Messieurs the Deputies did not deny it, for they could not; but they said, that if they had propos'd the taking of Measures by concert, and the Union of Forces, they would do it no more; that they
had

' had Orders to declare it in the Name of the Allies
' and to tell us that they pretended in a Word, whe-
' ther the Partition were accepted, or whether it
' were not, to receive from the Hands of the King,
' our Master, the Monarchy of *Spain* and the *Indies*,
' leaving to him alone the employing of such Means,
' either of Perswasion, or of Compulsion, as he
' should judge most Effectual, to put the Arch-duke
' into the actual Possession of his Dominions within
' the Space of Two Months.

' So formal a disclaiming of all the past Proceed-
' ings, and of all the Demands made on the Part
' of the Allies, as also the rejecting whatever was
' possible to be done on our Part, sufficiently discover'd
' Sir, a form'd Design to break off all Negotiation.

' 'Twas endless to allow us the Term of Fifteen
' Days for the procuring the Answer of the King, our
' Master, to these Demands, altogether New, and
' till now unheard-of, the Performance of which
' is out of our Power.

' His Majesty has long since intimated, That for
' the Sake of a Definitive and Secure Peace he
' would yield to such Conditions as he himself could
' execute; but he will never promise what he
' knows impossible for him to perform. If by the
' Injustice and Obstinacy of his Enemies he be de-
' prived of all Hope of obtaining Peace, then trust-
' ing in the Protection of God, who is able, when
' he pleases, to humble those whom unhop'd for
' Prosperity elevates, and who make no Account of
' the Publick Calamities, and Effusion of Christian
' Blood, he will leave it to the Judgment of all *Eu-*
' *rope*, even to the Judgment of the People of *England*
' and *Holland* to distinguish who are the true Authors
' of the Continuance of so Bloody a War.

' On one Hand, they will see the Advances which
' the King, our Master, has made, the Consent he
' has given to the hardest Proposals, and the En-
' gagements into which his Majesty yielded to enter

for

'for removing all Diffidence, and forwarding the
' Peace. On the other Hand, they may observe a
' continual Affectation to speak obscurely. That there
' might be always Room to form Pretensions beyond
' the Conditions agreed upon, insomuch that we had
' no sooner yielded to one Demand, and such as
' seem'd to be the utmost that could be ask'd, but it
' was receded from to substitute another more ex-
' orbitant in its Place. They will likewise perceive
' a Variation wholly regulated, either by the
' Events of War, or by the Facilities which the
' King, our Master, shew'd for Peace. It ap-
' pears by the Letters written to us by Messieurs
' the Deputies that they themselves do not deny
' this.

' Last Year the *Dutch*, and their Allies, look'd
' upon it as an Injury, that Men should think them
' capable of demanding of the King to unite his
' Forces, to those of the Confederacy, to oblige the
' King, his Grandson, to quit the Crown. They
' appeal'd even to the Preliminaries, which speak
' only of taking Measures by Concert. They have
' since made no Difficulty to insist peremptorily up-
' on it.

' They would now have his Majesty undertake it
' singly; and they have the Assurance to say, That
' if they would have formerly contented themselves
' with less, their Interest, which they now better
' understand, induces them not to be content with it
' any longer. Such a Declaration, Sir, is a formal
' Rupture of all Negotiation, and what the Chief of
' the Allies wish for.

' Should we continue longer at *Geertruydenbergh*,
' should we spend whole Years in *Holland*, our Stay
' would be to no Purpose, seeing those who Govern
' the Republick are perswaded, that 'tis their Inte-
' rest to make the Peace depend upon an impossible
' Condition. We do not offer to perswade them to
' prolong a Negotiation which they have a Mind

K k ' to

'to break; and in short, whatever Desire the King, our Master, has to procure Quiet to his People, it will be less grievous to them to support the War, an End of which they know his Majesty would purchase by so great Sacrifices against the same Enemies, with whom he has been Fighting these Ten Years, than to have them add the King his Grandson to those Enemies, and imprudently undertake to Conquer *Spain* and the *Indies* in Two Months, in a certain Assurance when that Term is expired, to find his Enemies strengthned by the Places he must yield to them, and by Consequence in a Condition to turn against himself the new Arms he should put into their Hands.

'This, Sir, is the positive Answer which the King has order'd us to make to you upon the new Propositions of Messieurs the Deputies. We do it, at the End of Six Days, instead of Fifteen, which they had allowed us as a Favour. This Dispatch may serve at least to satisfie you that we do not seek to amuse you; and that if we have frequently desired Conferences, 'twas not to multiply them to no Purpose, but to omit nothing that might conduce to Peace.

'We pass over in Silence the Proceedings towards us in Contempt of our Character. We say nothing to you of the injurious Libels, full of Falshood and Calumny, which have been suffer'd to be Printed and Dispersed during our Stay, with Design to inflame the Minds of those whom we were labouring to reconcile. We do not even complain, that in Breach of the Publick Faith, and in Contempt of our so oft repeated Complaints, all the Letters which we have receiv'd, or written, have been opened: From which, however, this Advantage results to us, that the Pretext made use of to palliate those Indignities was discovered to be ill grounded. None can reproach us with having at-

tempted

'tempted any of the least Practices, contrary to the
'Laws of Nations, which were violated towards us,
'and 'tis palpable, that by hindring any from ma-
'king Visits to us in our *Kind of Prison*, the Thing
'most feared was our discovering such Truths as
'were industriously concealed.

'We desire you will please, Sir, to return an
'Answer by our Express, whom we have order'd to
'wait for it; or if you will not Answer, to give a
'Certificate of your Receipt of this Letter. We are
'most entirely,

SIR,

Your most Humble,

and most Obedient Servant,

UXELLES.
POLIGNAC.

This Letter having been communicated to the States, produc'd a Resolution, that the Two Deputies engag'd in the foregoing Conferences should give the *French* Ministers to understand in Writing, that they having rejected the Propositions made to them on the Part of the Allies, and thereby broken off the Negotiations, nothing more remain'd than to acquiesce therewith, without entring into any Debates upon the Contents of their Letter, notwithstanding it might with much Facility and Reason be refuted, as well with Respect to Things as Words. Not but they thought fit afterwards that the said Letter should be answer'd at large, and made Publick, as a Matter that concern'd the whole Alliance, which Answer being in the Form of a Memorial, and too long to be here inserted, is purposely here omitted.

Pursuant

Pursuant to their Mightinesses Resolution, Messieurs *Buys* and *Vanderdussen* return'd a short Answer, importing, That seeing the *French* Court would not give a sufficient Security for the delivering up *Spain*, it was to no Purpose to continue the Conferences. Whereupon the *French* Plenipotentiaries left *Geertruydenbergh* to return Home. It was observ'd, that about this Time the Accounts from *France* spoke of Peace with some Indifference, either in Hopes of a Diversion in the North; or which at that Distance seem'd more probable, in a fond Expectation that the Heats and Animosities raised in *England* by Dr. *Sacheverell*'s Trial would occasion a favourable Turn of Affairs in that Court.

By this Time the Confederate Army, under the Command of the Duke of *Marlborough* and Prince *Eugene*, had made a considerable Progress, a Detail of which may not be improper to succeed the foregoing Negotiations. Those Two Princes being arriv'd at *Tournay*, after they had before sent Orders to the Earl of *Albemarle*, Governour of that Place, to make himself Master of *Mortaigne*, held a Council of War, the Result of which was, That all the Troops which had their Winter Quarters in *Flanders*, *Brabant*, and other Places, and were then Assembled and Encamp'd in the Neighbourhood of *Tournay*, should provide themselves with Bread and Forrage for a secret Expedition. On the 20th of *April* the Army began their March towards the Enemies Lines in Two Columns, which was so well contrived, and so sudden, that notwithstanding the great Preparations which the *French* had made for Fortifying and Defending their Lines, the Chevalier *de Luxembergh* being for that Purpose Encamp'd with about 4000 Men near St. *Amand*, and the Mareschal *de Montesquiou* (or *d' Artagnan*) having Assembled about Forty Battallions and Sixty Squadrons near *Lens* and *Bethune*, yet the next Day, about Six of the Clock in the Morning, the Prince of *Wartembergh*

rough and Lieutenant-General *Cadogan*, with a Detachment of Fifteen Battallions and Fifty Squadrons from the Duke of *Marlborough*'s Column, enter'd those Lines at *Pont a Vendin*, without any Opposition; the few Troops that guarded that Post being surpriz'd, and retiring at the Approach of the Confederates, without firing one Shot. Upon this unexpected Success the whole Army pass'd the Lines, the Right at *Pont a Vendin*, and the Left at *Courieres*, which struck such a Pannick Fear into the Enemies Troops Assembled near *Lens*, that they likewise made a speedy Retreat, partly towards *Arras*, and partly towards *Douay*. The Allies Encamp'd that Night in the Plain of *Lens*, and the next Morning march'd again very early to dislodge the *French*, who having Assembled their Troops near *Vitry*, behind the *Scarpe*, made a Shew of disputing the Passage of that River. For which Purpose the Chevalier *de Luxembourgh*, and the Horses from *Arras* and *Bethune*, had the Night before joined the Mareschal *de Montesquiou*; but tho' they were advantageously posted, yet being much inferior in Number, and the Soldiers not having yet recovered their Surprize and Consternation, they precipitately retired towards *Cambray* upon the Approach of the Confederate Troops, leaving behind them part of their Tents and Baggage. The Allies having laid their Bridges over the *Scarpe*, the Prince of *Hesse Cassel* was detached by his Grace with Twelve Squadrons to fall upon the Enemies Rear; but they broke down so many Bridges, and fled so fast, that his Highness only overtook some few of them, who were made Prisoners. That Night (*April* the 22d) the Army under the Duke of *Marlborough* pass'd the *Scarpe*, his Grace encamping with his Right near *Vitry*, on the same River, his Left at *Gony*, and fixing his Quarters at the Extremity of his Left at *Goulessin*, whilst the Army under Prince *Eugene* remained on the other Side of the *Scarpe*, between that River and the

the *Canal*, in order to invest *Douay*, the Siege of which Place had been resolved on.

Nor could the Allies at this Juncture have aimed at a more Important Conquest: For as it cover'd the Enemies Frontiers, and laid the *Spanish Netherlands* open to their Invasions, so ever since the Reign of *Henry* II. the *French* left no Means untried to get Possession of it; in which having at last succeeded in 1667, they immediately added new Works to the Fortifications, made it a Place of Arms, erected Magazines and a Foundery therein, and cut a Canal for uniting the *Deule* and the *Scarpe*, which gave them an easie Entrance (as has been before said) into the *Spanish* Provinces. On the other Hand it was wisely considered, that the *Chastelenie* of *Lisle*, which was still in Part possess'd by the Enemy, would, by the taking of *Douay*, be wholly reduced under one single Power; that *Lisle* itself, *Tournay*, and other Places along the *Scheld* and the *Lys*, as far as *Ghent*, would be more and more secured; and that a Passage for Transporting by Water, the Necessaries from that Province into *Artois*, would thereby be open'd, which would afford a Conveniency for maintaining numerous Garrisons in those Parts, and an Opportunity to make a further Progress into the Enemies Country.

Pursuant to this Resolution, General *Cadogan* was detach'd on the 23d of *April*, in the Morning, to take Post at *Pont a Rache*, and other Generals, with Troops likewise under their Commands, to open the Communication over the *Lower Scarpe*, with *Lisle* and *Tournay*; wherein they met with no Difficulty, the Allies being already Masters of *Mortaigne*, and the Enemies having quitted St. *Amand*, *Marchienne*, and the Abbey of *Hasnon*, below *Douay*. The same Day both Armies made a Motion to Invest *Douay*, that under Prince *Eugene* reaching from *Vitry* on the *Scarpe* to *Pont Oly*, and that under the Duke

...ke of *Marlborough* from the other Side of the ...pe, over-against *Vitry*, to *Pont a Rache*.

...he Line of Circumvallation was no sooner fi-...'d, and other Preparations made for carrying on ...Siege, but his Grace gave Orders that Lieute-...t-General *Cadogan* should view the Plains between ...s and *Esquerchien*, and to mark out a proper ...ce for ranging the Army on a Line of Battle, in ...e the Enemy should attempt to disturb the Lea-...r. But either for want of Forrage, or other Ne-...aries, the *French* were not yet in a Condition to ...e the Field; and the Mareschal *de Montesquiou* ...ing put most of his Troops into Garrisons, was ...ired to *Cambray* with the rest, tho' not without ...pes that the Town of *Douay* would hold out a ...icient Time, to give the *French* an Opportunity ...Assemble in order to relieve it. Nor were these ...pes ill grounded; for the Garrison consisted of ...teen Battallions, Six Companies of Invalids, and ...ne Squadrons of Dragoons, besides Three other ...tallions in *Fort Scarpe*. The whole under the ...mmand of Lieutenant-General *Albergotti*, an Of-...r of approv'd Valour, and consummate Experi-...e: But as the Enemy did not expect to be so soon ...ted; a great Number of Officers were absent ...m their respective Posts, some of which were ...en as they endeavour'd to get into the Place.

...On the Night, between the 4th and 5th of *May*, ...Trenches were open'd the Day before, which ...e Rector of the *English* Colledge of *Douay* having ...tain'd Leave of the Duke of *Marlborough* to retire ...Lisle during the Siege, was conducted thither, ...h his Students, to the Number of Sixty. The ...ge was carried on in the Ordinary Methods by the ...nces of *Anhalt*, *Dessau*, and *Friesland*, with For-...Battallions appointed for that Service, till the 7th, ...en about Ten at Night, the Besieged, to the Num-...r of 1000 Foot, most Grenadiers, and 200 Dra-...ons, made a Vigorous Sally, under the Command

mand of the Duke of *Mortemar*, a Brigadier, a[gainst] the Left Attack, Commanded by the Prince [of] *Nassau Friesland*, put the Workmen into great D[is]order, and levell'd some Paces of the Parallel. C[o]lonel *Sutton*'s Regiment, which was the first th[at] supported the Workmen, suffer'd very much; b[ut] Major-General *Makartney*, with the other Reg[i]ments in the Trenches, coming up to their Relie[f] the Enemy were repulsed with considerable Loss, an[d] pursued to their Counterscarp. The Action was ve[ry] hot, insomuch that the Allies had above 500 Me[n] either killed or wounded; and among the latte[r] Lieutenant Colonel *Gledhill* of *Sutton*'s Regiment who being taken Prisoner, and carried into th[e] Town, was very civilly used by the Governou[r]. The Dammage done in the Parallel was repaire[d] the same Night, and the Approaches carried o[n] with so great Application and Success, that on th[e] 12th the Besiegers advanced to the first Ditch th[e] Enemy had made since the taking of *Tournay*.

All this while the Enemies Troops began to Assem[]ble in separate Bodies near *Bethune*, *Bapaume*, A[r]ras, *Cambray*, *Landrecy*, and behind the River Somm[e] and the Mareschal *de Villars*, whom the Fren[ch] Court had appointed to Command in the Nethe[r]lands, being arrived at *Peronne* on the 14th, a R[e]port was spread that he designed to pass the Sche[ld] between *Bouchain* and *Denain*, in order to advan[ce] towards the Confederates by the Plain of *Osberan*[] between the *Scheld* and the *Lower Scarpe*. Here[]upon the Duke of *Marlborough* went on the 15th i[n] the Morning to view the Post of *Arleux*, as also t[o] survey the Ground between that Place and the Low[er] *Scarpe*, and give Directions for marking out a Fiel[d] of Battle on the Plains towards *Valenciennes*, i[n] case the Enemy should attempt to succour *Douay* o[n] that Side.

On the 17th the Enemy made another Salley, but with the same Success as the former, they meeting with such a warm Reception, as oblig'd them on the first Fire from the Retrenches to retire into the Town in great Confusion. On the 21st and 2d following they did the like, but were repuls'd with Loss, which made them more cautious as to their Way of Proceeding.

The Mareschal *de Villars* having held a Council of War at *Peronne*, at which assisted the Mareschals of *Berwick*, *Bezons*, and *Montesquion*, with the Bavarian General, the Count *de Arco*, in which it was resolved forthwith to Assemble the *French* Army, in order to attempt to raise the Siege, set out with the Chevalier St. *George*, for the Place of Encampment of his Troops, that were drawn together pursuant to his Orders, and pass the *Scheld* on the 22d, after which he took Post with his Right near *Bouchain*, and his Left at *Ribecour*. Upon Advice of this Motion the Confederate Generals thought fit to alter the Disposition of their Forces, except Thirty Battalions left at the Siege, and Twelve Squadrons at *Vitt a Rache*. Accordingly the 24th, in the Morning, all the Cavalry of my Lord Duke's Army march'd over the *Scarpe*, and took their former Camp near *Goulessin*, and on the next Day the Infantry moved the same Way, encamping with the Right over against *Vitry*, and the Left near *Arleux*. At the same time likewise the Prince of *Savoy* made a Motion, placing the Right of his Army at *Iseles Esquerchien*. By which Situation they were ready to repair immediately to either of the Fields of Battle already mark'd out, according to the next Motions of the Enemy, for which Purpose Roads were made for the Armies to march in Four Columns either Way. The 25th Bridges were lain in several Places over the *Scarpe*, which parted the Two Armies, for the more easy Communication of the Troops; and the same Day, upon Intelligence that the Enemy were in Motion, the Troops were order'd to be in a Readiness to March. On the 26th, upon Notice that the *French* extended their Line nearer to *Arras*, placing their Left within a League of that Place, and their Right at *Oisy*, the Confederate Generals rightly conjectur'd that they judg'd it not practicable to Attack the Allies on the Side of *Arleux*, but rather intended to march into the Plains of *Lens*, and try what they could do on that Side. Accordingly on the 28th the Enemy marched by *Blangis*, *Arras*, and *Mont St. Eloy*; whereupon Prince *Eugene* extended the Right of his Army to *Henin Lietard*, and the Duke of *Marlborough* repass'd the *Scarpe* with the Right of his, encamping very near the Left of the Prince of *Savoy*, and taking his Quarters at *Esquerchien*: Which Motion brought their Two Armies very near the strong Camp mark'd out from *Vitry* to *Montigne*, beyond *Henin Lettard*, having the Village of *Bois-Bernard* in Front, and that of *Beaumont* in the Rear, for the greater Security of which several Redoubts were Erected, and Cannon drawn from the Lines of Circumvallation, to be placed on the Batteries.

On the 29th of *May* the *French* pass'd the *Scarpe*, and Encamp'd with their Right at *Roquelincourt*, near *Arras*, and their Left at St. *Eloy*, having the Hills before them: Whereupon the *Dutch* Infantry left between *Vitry* and *Arleux*, on the other Side of the *Scarpe*, under the Command of Count *Tilly*, were by Order from his Grace appointed to join his Army, which by this Time was reinforced by the Arrival of the *Prussians*, *Palatines*, and *Hessians*, and the recalling of several Detachments. The Allies had great Reason to expect to be Attack'd, upon Advice, That the Mareschal *de Villars* having positive Orders from Court, had Harangued the several Brigades of his Army, and represented to his Men, that Things were come to that Pass that they must either vanquish or die; and that for their greater

Encou-

Encouragement he had ordered the Chaplains to give a General Absolution to the Troops.

The Expectation of a sudden Engagement encreased, when on the next Day (*May* 30) about Eight in the Morning the *French* decamp'd from *Rarelincourt*, and *Mont St. Eloy*, march'd in Order of Battle between *Fresne* and *Lens*, and one of their Columns advanc'd to *Bertricourt*, with all their Generals, to view the Scituation of the Allies: Whereupon all the Confederate Generals repair'd to their respective Posts; the Cannon were placed on the Batteries that defended the Avenues to their Camp; the Prince of *Nassau*, with Twenty Battallions from the Siege, and Eleven others from the Entrenchments between *Decby* and *Fierin*, joined the Grand Army; and all other necessary Dispositions were made to give the Enemy a warm Reception. But the Mareschal *de Villars* having for some Time continued at *Bertricourt*, within Musquet Shot of the Confederate Army, did not think his Superiority in Numbers (which were a Hundred and Ten Thousand Men, whereas the Allies could scarce muster One Hundred Thousand) sufficient to ballance the Advantage of the Ground which the Confederates had on their Side; and so march'd back, and joined the Centre of his Army between *Lens* and *Fresne*, his Right extending towards *Montauban*, and his Left towards *Noyelles*, within half a League of his Grace.

Soon after his Return he made a Motion towards his Left, and encamped between *Noyelles-Sous-Lens* and the Heights of St. *Laurens*, from whence the Two Princes of *Savoy* and *Marlborough*, judging that he had no other Design but to retard the Siege, thought fit to send back the Troops they had withdrawn from before *Douay*. Those under General *Fagel* return'd into the Lines on the other Side of the *Scarpe*; and to prevent any Surprize, Orders were given to join the several Redoubts made before the Front of the Camp, by an Entrenchment from

Montigny,

Montigny, at the Extremity of the Right of Prin[ce] *Eugene*'s Army to *Vitry* on the *Scarpe*. On the othe[r] Hand, Count *Vehlen*, General of the *Palatines*, wa[s] sent with a Detachment of Eight Battallions an[d] Ten Squadrons to secure the Post of *Pont a Ven*[*]*din*, that the Enemy might send no Parties into th[e] *Castelenie* of *Lisle*.

The Communication with that City and *Tournay* b[e]ing thus secured, the Siege of *Douay*, which by all the[se] Motions was very much obstructed, was carried o[n] with all possible Application and Vigour; and th[o'] the Garrison of the Town made several very fier[ce] Sallies, in one of which they burnt the Villages [of] *Derchy*, *Sains*, *Nazieres*, *Fierens*, and *Pont a Rach*[e] and took General *Fagel*'s Equipage, with a gre[at] Number of Cattle, was very considerably advanc'[d] The Duke of *Marlborough* suspecting that the En[e]my might attempt to seize the Post of *Bioche* on t[he] *Scarpe*, about half a League from *Vitry*, went thith[er] on the 2d of *June*, with Count *Tilly*, and reinfo[r]ced the Troops posted there with Eighty Men, givi[ng] positive Orders to the Commanding Officer to d[e]fend himself to the last Extremity, and assur'd hi[m] that he should be supported in due Time; but [he] surrendred the same that very Night upon the A[p]proach of the Enemy, and Two Captains, Two Lie[u]tenants, and as many Ensigns, with an Hundre[d] and Fifty Men, were made Prisoners; though t[he] *French* being sensible that they could not maintai[n] themselves in the Possession of it, quitted that Post t[he] next Day early in the Morning, after having ruin['d] in a great Measure the Sluice that is there and stopped the New Canal made from th[e] *Scarpe* to the River *Sanset*. Hereupon the Alli[es] ordered thither some Troops again, who immed[i]ately opened the New Canal, whereby the Wate[rs] of the *Scarpe* had their free Course towards t[he] *Sanset* and *Bouchain*, as they had since the Begi[n]ning of the Siege, and the Inundation did the Alli[es] no Dammage. Th[e]

Tho' the Duke of *Marlborough* was by this Time pretty secure that the *French* would not venture to attack him, yet he had Reason to conjecture that they designed to continue in their Camp between *Montauban* and *Noyelles Sons-Lens*, and thereby keep the Confederates in perpetual Alarm; the rather, because they had begun to cast up Entrenchments to cover their Left. But having suffered there very much for Want of Water, they made a Motion (on the 4th of *June*) about a League backwards, encamping with their Right at *Pampouz*, and their Left at *Mont Vimin*, where they consumed all the Forrage in the Neighbourhood of *Arras*.

In the mean Time, whilst the Garrison of *Douay* defended themselves with all possible Obstinacy, daily springing several Mines, throwing Abundance of Bombs, or making Sallies, his Grace, in Concert with his Colleague, Prince *Eugene*, whose Genius in a particular Manner lyes in Stratagem, considering that the Enemy, upon the first assembling of their Army, had strengthened it by Troops drawn out of the Frontier Towns, and thereby had left those Places very weak, form'd the Project of surprizing *Ipres*. A Detachment being for that Purpose sent from the Army under Pretence of reinforcing the Posts of *Warneton* and *Commines*, and strengthening the Garrisons of *Lisle* and *Menin*: The Troops appointed to put the Design in Execution march'd accordingly from those Places on *Monday* the 9th at Night, and about Two in the Morning the advanced Party that was to have secur'd the Gate had it opened to them, as was concerted: But finding the Enemy within prepared to receive them, they were obliged to retire, and the Whole Detachment return'd to their former Posts. When the Mareschal *de Villars*, upon Notice of the Besieged being in Distress, repass'd the *Scarpe* near *Arras* on the 17th of *June*, and being return'd to the Camp he was in on the 28th of *May*, with his Left toward

Arras,

Arras, and his Right to *Ossy*, near *Arleux*, th[e] Horse of the Army Commanded by the Duke [of] *Marlborough* decamped the same Evening, and h[a]ving pass'd the *Scarpe* at *Vitry*, possess'd themselv[es] of the same Camp they had before, between *Vit[ry]* and *Arleux*. The next Morning the Horse w[as] followed by the Foot, the Prince of *Savoy* remain[n]ing on the other Side of the *Scarpe* to guard th[e] Entrenchments, but in a Readiness to march and joi[n] the Duke upon the first Motion of the Enem[y] whose Generals still gave out that they were re[so]lved to attack them in Order to relieve *Doua[y]* However, this Report appeared very unlikely, no[t] only by reason of the sudden Departure of th[e] Mareschal *de Berwick* with Orders to repair with al[l] Diligence to *Dauphine*, but also because the Maresch[al] *de Villars* thought fit to detach several Battallion[s] from his Army to reinforce the Garrisons of suc[h] Places, as, upon the Reduction of *Douay*, would lye most expos'd to the Attempts of the Confe[de]derates.

To come to a Conclusion of this Memorable Siege; all Things being in a readiness to storm Two Ravelins at the Left Attack, the Troop[s] Commanded for that Service performed it with Wonderful Bravery, but met with so vigorous Resistance that a great many Men were kill'd on both Sides. At last the Besiegers took Post on the Ravelin of Earth, above the Breach on the Rampart; but at the other Ravelin of Stone-work they could not lodge themselves farther than the Top of the Breach; and the Sappers found it very difficult to work there, by reason that several Wooll-packs that were Burning, being set on Fire by the springing of Six Mines, by which many of the Confederates were blown up. The Besiegers continued enlarging their Lodgments, carrying on the Saps, and laying of Bridges, till the 24th about Three of the Clock in the Morning, when all the Dispositions for attacking

the

Two Ravelings at the Right Attack being made [the] Night before, the Prince of *Anhalt* caused the [same] to be storm'd. This Encounter prov'd more [suc]cessful and less Bloody than the former; for [aft]er a small Resistance the Allies made a Lodg[me]nt, and in the Night began to fill up the Capi[tal] Ditch, and to make Galleries over it.

Things being thus brought to the last Extremity, [the] Garrison of *Douay* thought fit to beat a Parley [on] the 25th of *June*, offering to Capitulate for the [to]wn only, without including Fort *Scarpe*; but this [bei]ng refused, they sent Hostages to both Attacks, [wh]o were conducted to the Duke of *Marlborough's* [Qua]rters, where they were again told, that no Ca[pitu]lation could be granted to the Town without in[clu]ding the Fort abovemention'd. Whereupon he [wro]te to Monsieur *Albergotti*, and in the mean Time [Or]ders were given to the Troops in the Trenches to [hol]d themselves in a Readiness to renew the Hostili[ties] upon the first Orders; but the 26th in the Morn[ing] Monsieur *Albergotti* signified to the Besiegers, [that] he was willing to surrender that Fort at the [sam]e Time with the Town, but that the same being [not] attack'd, he pretended to remove all the Provisions [and] Ammunition that were in it. This Pretension oc[casi]oned a Conference in Prince *Eugene's* Quarters, [and] at last the Capitulation for the Town and [For]t *Scarpe* were agreed upon the same Day, and [sign]ed on the 27th, by the Princes of *Marlborough* [and] *Savoy*, and the Field-Deputies of the State, on [the] one Part, and Monsieur *Albergotti*: The most [ma]terial Articles being, that the Garrison should [mar]ch out on the 29th with the usual Marks of Ho[nou]r, Six Cannon, and Two Mortars, to be con[duc]ted to *Cambray*, with Six Cover'd Waggons; [bu]t it was also condition'd for those in Fort *Scarpe* [tha]t they should likewise be allow'd Two Cannon, [and] Two Cover'd Waggons, provided they left their [Mus]quets in the Magazine.

According

According to the Tenour of this Agreement a Gate of the Town, called *Morel*, and the Outworks of Fort *Scarpe*, were deliver'd up to the Confederate Troops on the same Day the Capitulation was sign'd, and General *Albergotti*, who, besides his former Actions, had gain'd Immortal Honour by the Vigorous Defence of the Place, was entertain'd at Dinner by the Prince of *Nassau Friesland*, as he was, on the 28th, by the Duke of *Marlborough*, who, on this Occasion, wrote the following Letter to the States-General.

High and Mighty Lords,

'YOUR High Mightinesses will be pleased to
' allow me the Honour to congratulate you
' upon the Surrender of the Town of *Douay*, and also
' of Fort *Scarpe*, according to the Articles which
' your High Mightinesses will receive from your
' Deputies: 'Tis to be wish'd that this New Con-
' quest, with which it has pleas'd God to bless the
' Arms of the High Allies, may induce *France* to a
' Just and Reasonable Peace, for the Quiet and Re-
' pose of *Europe*. I am, with very great Respect,

High and Mighty Lords,
Your High Mightinesses most Humble
From the Camp   *and most Obedient Servant,*
before *Douay*,
June 27, 1710.   *The Prince and Duke of* Marlborough

On the 29th, about Ten in the Morning, Monsieur *Albergotti* marched out of *Douay* at the Head of his Garrison, which was reduced to 4527 Effective Men and having saluted the Princes of *Marlborough* and *Savoy*, and march'd to some distance, he came back, and continued with their Highnesses till all his Troops were marched off; and having Dined with the Duke of *Marlborough*, followed his Garrison, and was conducted to *Cambray* under a Guard of 250 *Dutch* Horse

As soon as the *French* were gone off, Five Battallions of *Dutch*, and one *Saxon* in the States Pay, marched into the Place, of which Lieutenant-General *Hompesch* took Possession as Governour, while Brigadier *Des Roques* did the same by Fort *Scarpe*. The Generals went afterwards to view the Town, in which they found 40 Pieces of Brass Cannon, 200 of Iron, 8 Mortars, with abundance of Ammunition and Small Arms, but a very small Store of Provisions.

The next Day the Two Princes, and the States-Deputies, being gone into the Town, in order to view it again, they were met and severally complimented by the University in a Body; but as these Memoirs chiefly relate to his Grace's Conduct, so I shall only insert the Speech that was made to him by Messieur *Adrian Delcourt*, Provost of St. *Peter*, and Chancellor of the said University, who address'd him in these very Words.

My Lord,

'WE come to assure your Highness of our most
' humble Respects, and of the inviolable
' Fidelity we shall have towards our New Sove-
' reign. 'Tis with much Joy and Justice that we
' pay you our Devoirs. We cannot sufficiently re-
' spect a Sovereign Prince of the Empire, a Duke,
' a Generalissimo of the Armies of *Great-Britain*,
' a Heroe, whose Victories and Conquests have
' amaz'd the World. *Germany* and the *Netherlands*
' are, *my Lord*, Eye-witnesses of your Heroic Acti-
' ons; you have beaten your Enemies at *Hochstet*, *Ra-*
' *millies*, *Oudenarde*, and *Blangies*, you have forc'd
' Lines in *Germany* which seem'd impenetrable, and
' in *Brabant* you have broken into others by a singular
' Conduct, in Sight of a Powerful Army, which
' you put into Confusion. You have conquer'd the
' Country of *Liege*, the *Spanish Gelderland*, *Brabant*,
' *Flanders*, and Part of *Hainault*. You go from
' Conquest to Conquest, and the least Step you
' advance further you subdue a whole Kingdom.

M m We

'We do not compare you, *my Lord*, with Heroes
'of Antiquity, whose great Actions were sullied
'with all Manner of Vices. You are a Heroe, Wise,
'Moderate, Just, Gracious, Generous, and equally
'averse to Cruelty and Debauchery. No Wonder
'then that the Emperor has made you a Prince of
'the Empire, that the Queen of *Great-Britain* has
'conferr'd the highest Honours, and multiplied Fa-
'vours upon you; that Her Parliaments have given
'you all possible Proofs of Esteem and Affection,
'and that the *French* themselves have, on a Thou-
'sand Occasions, proclaimed your Praises. *My
'Lord*, should we enter into a Particular Survey of
'all your Heroic Actions, and your Admirable
'Qualities, we should never have done; and we
'must consider that we ought not to detain a Prince
'too long, whose Moments are so Precious. Give
'us Leave only to desire the Protection of your High-
'ness for our University, which stands in great need of
'it. We might, in a Revolution, be exposed to some
'Storm, inconsistent with that Peace and Tranquility
'which are so necessary to make the Sciences flourish;
'but we shall have no Cause to entertain any Fear
'if you are pleased to grant us the Favour we most
'humbly ask. We shall be infinitely obliged to
'you, *my Lord*, for it, and shall offer up our Prayers
'to God for the Queen of *Great-Britain*, your
'Highness, and a Happy Success to all your Enter-
'prizes.

*To this the Duke replied with his wonted Modesty
and Humanity.*

Gentlemen,
'YOUR Obedience to your New Sovereign
'will render you assured of the Queen my
'Mistress's, and Her High Allies, Protection; and
'you have no Reason to doubt but all the good
'Offices that I can do for you, upon all Occasions,
'shall be employed in procuring you such Advantages

'tages as may be of Use to you, and conformable to
' your best Wishes; since it is to establish the
' Publick Tranquility that the Confederates have taken
' Arms, and the Sciences must flourish of Course,
' by the Restoration of Peace, which they so ardent-
' ly seek for.

The Allies paid certainly very Dear for this Important Conquest, but their Loss being very much magnified by the Enemy, he thought fit to ascertain the Number of the Killed and Wounded at both Attacks, which was 2142 Men of the first, and 5865 of the last, among these 570 *English* were killed, and 1339 wounded, tho' more Impartial Computations hold this Account to be too much moderated.

The Confederate Armies continued a few Days in their Respective Camps near *Douay*, both to give the Soldiers that had been employed in the Siege some Refreshment, and to see the Trenches, and other Works made before that Place, levell'd. This done, and all the detach'd Troops being come into the Line, they march'd on the 10th of *July* in the Morning; and the Army, Commanded by the Duke of *Marlborough*, encamp'd at *Vitry*, with the Left at *Montauban*, and the Right at *Telu*; and the Prince of *Savoy*'s Forces extended from the Left at *Telu*, to the Right at the opening of the Plain, between the *Scarpe* and the River of *Lens*: Here they were obliged to halt the next Day for the coming up of their Baggage and Bread Waggons, which had been retarded on their March by the Badness of the Roads, occasion'd by the Rains that fell for several Days successively. On the 12th they pursued their March from *Vitry* to the Camp at *Villers-Brulin*, extending from the Right upon the Source of the *Lave*, to the Left upon the River of *Lens*, having the *Scarpe* before them; by which Situation their Parties were at Liberty to make Excursions into the Enemy's Country from the *Boulonnois* to *Picardy*.

Had

Had the *French* been now as willing to Fight as they seem'd to be Six Weeks before, the Generals of the Allies would not have declined an Engagement but tho' the Mareschal *de Villars* was rejoined by the Detachments he had sent out under the Command of the Chevalier *de Luxembourgh*, and Monsieur *de Broglio*, and had likewise drawn out the Garrisons of *Conde, Quesnoy, Valenciennes,* and *Cambray*, yet instead of expecting the Confederates in his Camp between *Arras* and *Oisy*, he made a Motion, and retired behind his new Lines from *Arras* along the *Crinchon*, towards *Mirtamont*. The Enemy having by this Situation made it impracticable for his Grace either to attack them, or invest *Arras*, he, in Conjunction with Prince *Eugene* and the other Generals, resolved to turn his Victorious Arms against *Bethune*, which was accordingly invested on the 15th by 25 Battallions, and 18 Squadrons. The necessary Preparations being made for that Siege, the Trenches were open'd on the 23d, and Two Attacks carried on, under the Command of Monsieur *Schuylemburgh*, General of the *Saxon* Troops, and of Baron *Fagel*, General of the *Dutch* Infantry. On the 24th the Garrison made a vigorous Salley, which occasioned a sharp Dispute, and the Loss of some Hundreds on each Side, and a great many wounded.

The *French* had so positively given out that they would fight the Allies if they attempted another Siege, that on the 31st of the same Month (*July*) when their Army march'd out of their Intrenchments, it was believed the *Intrepid Villars*, for so that Mareschal was called in *France*, would attack the Allies, who lying in a Camp, without any Intrenchment, gave him a fair Opportunity for an Engagement. Hereupon the Two Princes of *Marlborough* and *Savoy* drew up their Army in Order of Battle, and recalled the Prince of *Hesse Cassel*, who, with a strong Detachment, was Posted between *Lens* and *la Bassee*, to secure the Convoys from *Lisle* and *Tournay*. But on on the First of *August*, when the Duke of *Marlborough* advanced with a select Party of Horse to observe the *French* Army, he found them, instead of preparing to fight, casting up a new Line and Entrenchments from the River *Ugy*, that falls into the *Scarpe* near *Arras*, to the Source of the River *Cunche*, having their Right at *Aguy*, on the *Ugy*, their Centre at *Avesne le Comte*, and their Left behind *le Comte*, at *Bertancourt*. By which it appeared that they did not design to disturb the Siege of *Bethune*.

On the 24th of *August*, in the Morning, the Right Wing of Prince *Eugene*'s Army Forrag'd in the Front towards St. *Pol*, near the Enemies Camp, under a Guard of 500 Horse, and 1000 *Danish* and *Hessian* Foot; but the Mareschal *de Villars* having Notice of it the Night before, detach'd 30 Squadrons under the Count *de Broglio*, to attack the Forragers, and follow'd in Person to be an Eye-witness of that Action. That General being arriv'd at the Mount of St. *Pol*, order'd the Forragers to be attack'd on that Side by Four Squadrons of Carabiniers, while some other Squadrons were advancing to fall upon them another Way. They accordingly broke in upon the Squadrons of the Allies which gave Way; but the Forragers joining with their Guard, beat them back with great Slaughter. However, the Enemy growing too numerous, they retired in very good Order to the Village of *Ligni St. Flochel*, and sent an Account of it to the Camp. Monsieur *de Villars* advanced in Person, and having in a manner surrounded that Post, summon'd the Infantry to Surrender, and upon their Refusal order'd Part of his Horse to dismount to force them; but they were so warmly received by the *Hessian* Foot posted there, that they fell back in great Disorder, and in the mean time the Piquet Guard of the Army advancing, and the Prince of *Savoy* marching with Part of his Cavalry, Monsieur *Villars* thought fit to Retreat with great Precipitation;

cipitation, lest this Skirmish should draw on a Ge[ne]ral Engagement, after having in this fruitless [at]tempt lost a great many Men, besides a Colon[el and] 20 other Officers, with 300 private Soldiers t[hat] were made Prisoners. The Allies likewise lost [on] their Side the Major of *Mercy*'s Regiment, T[wo] Captains of *Hussars*, and a good Number of co[m]mon Centinels.

In the mean Time the Siege of *Bethune* was ca[r]ried on with all possible Assiduity and Diligence, b[ut] the Place being strong, both by Art and Nature, a[nd] the Garrison numerous, Monsieur *de Puy Vauba[n]* Nephew to the late Famous Engineer of that Nam[e] who Commanded there, made a very Brave Defen[ce] till the 28th of *August*, when the Counterscarp b[e]ing taken Sword in Hand, he desired to Capitulat[e] and the next Day surrender'd the Town on Honoura[b]le Terms. On the 31st of *August* the Garriso[n] march'd out with Two Pieces of Cannon, and all th[e] other usual Marks of Honour, in Order to be Co[n]ducted to St. *Omer*, to the Number of about 170[0] Men, having lost near 2000 in the Defence of th[e] Place, when the Allies put into *Bethune* Three Ba[t]tallions, under the Command of Major-Genera[l] *Keppel*, Brother to the Earl of *Albemarle*.

The *French* Army still declining an Engagement[,] Prince *Eugene* and the Duke of *Marlborough* cam[e] to the Resolution of improving the remainin[g] Part of the fair Season, by laying Siege to *Aire* and *St. Venant* at the same Time. In order to that, on th[e] 2d of *September* both Armies marched from thei[r] respective Camps of *Villers-Brulin* and *Rebreuvre*[,] and the Prince of *Savoy* extended his Right to *Etree-Blanche*, and *Lingbem*, on the little River *Laquette*[,] and the Left of the Duke of *Marlborough*'s to *Drvion*, on the *Lave*, his Grace taking his Quarters in the Castle of *Liere*. On the 3d a Detachment was made to secure several Posts about *Aire*, which took in the Castle of *Liberque*, a Captain, a Lieutenant, and 70 private

...te Men, Prisoners, besides a Captain, and 30 ...adiers in the Village of Lambre. On the 4th ...etachment of 2000 Horse, and Six Battallions, ...ch'd from the Camp, to make Bridges over the ... at St. Quinting, pass'd that River, and block'd ...Aire on that Side; and the Armies march'd nearer ... Place, encamping the Right of the Imperialists ... Terrouanne, and the Left of my Lord Duke to ...llers.

...Aire, and St. Venant were both invested on the ...th of September, N. S. Forty Battallions being ...pointed for the Siege of the former, under the ...mmand of the Prince of Anhalt, and Twenty Bat...lions for the Attack of the latter, at which Com...ded the Prince of Nassau Friesland. On the 8th ... Quarter-Masters mark'd out a Field of Battle for ...Confederate Armies, in Case the French should ...e any Motion to disturb either of the Two Sieges, ...Right at Estree-Blanche, and the Left to the ...ghts near Liller; and the next Day they mark'd ...her on the Side of St. Omer for the same Pur...

...t the Allies being obliged to get their Provisions ...Ammunition from Lisle, Tournay, and Ghent, ...French form'd a Design of surprizing a Convoy ...veral Boats coming up the Lys from the last of ...e Places, under a Guard of 1200 Men, who were ...e reinforced by another Detachment; but Mon... de Ravignan, with 4000 Men from Ipres, At...'d them with great Fury on the 19th of September ...St. Eloy-Vive, not far from Courtray, beat the ...ard, killed about 200 Men, took Six Hundred ...oners, blew up some Boats laden with Ammuni...n, sunk some others Laden with Cannon-ball and ...mb-shells, to interrupt the Navigation of the Lys, ...d then retired with so much Diligence and Precau...n, that a Detachment sent out on the Part of the ...lies could not effect it. The French extolled ... Action with their usual Method of Multi-
plication;

plication; nor was it of little Consequence towards retarding the Sieges, for tho' no Time was lost in repairing the Dammage occasioned by this Misfortune, yet it had that Effect as to keep employed a Body of Men that would have been of Service elsewhere, and to stop the Execution of Designs that might have been otherwise put in Practice.

The Approaches of St. *Venant* being very difficult, the Besiegers could not break Ground before it till the 16th of *September*, but then the Attack was carried on with such Vigour, that on the 29th the Garrison beat a Parley, and the next Day delivered up a Gate, having obtain'd to march out, after a very indifferent Defence, with all Marks of Honour, Cannon only excepted, and to be conducted to *Arras*. The Sieur *Bruyn*, one of the Engineers of the States, who had the Direction of the Siege, was made Governour of the Place.

But tho' the Trenches were opened Four Days sooner (*viz. September* 12.) before *Aire*, yet that Place being very Strong, chiefly by its Situation among Morasses and Inundations, and defended by a very Numerous Garrison, under the Command of Lieutenant-General *de Goesbriant*, that Siege prov'd extremely difficult and tedious, and occasioned the Loss of a great many Men.

On *Sunday* the 21st of *September*, at Night, the Besieged sallied out with Four Hundred Fuziliers, and Two Hundred Workmen, but were repulsed with the Loss of Forty of their Men, without doing any Dammage to the Works of the Besiegers. The next Day there happened a Bloody Skirmish near the Village of *Rebek*, on the other Side of the *Lys*, after this Manner: The *French* advanc'd with a Thousand Horse to beat up the Quarters of the Confederate General Officers, on the Right of the said Village, but were so warmly receiv'd by the Guard, that the Piquet having had Time to come up to the Assistance of the latter, about 450 of the E-
nemy

nemy were kill'd upon the Spot, Twelve Officers, with 220 Troopers, all Mounted, made Prisoners, and 300 Horses taken, without any other Loss on the Side of the Allies than 40 or 50 Men kill'd or wounded. On the 23d the Besiegers attack'd a Redoubt on the Right, and made themselves Masters of it with little Resistance and inconsiderable Loss. Upon Notice of this Attack Monsieur *de Goesbriant* sent out a Body of Troops to sustain the Men in the Redoubt, and a great many Officers who were then with him at Dinner came out with them as Volunteers; but as they pass'd under the Fire of the Batteries, and Parallel of the Allies, most of them were either kill'd or wounded, and a Colonel of Dragoons taken Prisoner.

On the 26th of *September* the Chevalier *de Luxembourgh* laid a Design to surprize Fort *Scarpe*, and in order thereto march'd from *Bouchain* with a strong Detachment to *Pont a Rache*, sent a Hundred Men in the Night into the Wood of *Bellefonties*, near the Fort, and had Two Waggons laden with Hay, in which were hid some Grenadiers These Waggons were driven by some other Soldiers disguised like Boors, who were to seize the Barrier, and upon a Signal to be supported by the others, and then by the Chevalier himself. But Major-General *Amatama* coming at the same Time to visit General *Hompesch*, who having some Suspicion of the Design of the Enemy, was gone into the Fort to give the necessary Orders for its Security, left his Guard without the Barrier, who walking their Horses, and following the Waggons by meer Chance, the Enemy believed they were discovered, and so run away, leaving the Captain and One of their Men Prisoners. The Day before the Marshal *d' Harcourt* arriv'd in the *French* Army, of which the Marshal *de Villars* resign'd the Command to him, and the same Day set out for *France*. It was then given out, and generally believed, that this Change happened upon Monsieur de Villars's having desired Leave to go to the Waters of Bourbon upon Account of his Health; but [I] have been informed from very good Hands, that the true Reason of his Removal from that Command was owing to some Words that dropt from him the Day he attack'd Prince Eugene's Forragers, which reflecting on the Dutchess of Burgundy, some Officious Intermeddler reported the same to that Princess, who complaining to the King of France, the Marshal de Villars was suddenly recalled.

On the 5th of October the Allies before Air[e] having carried on their Approaches towards a Redoubt that cover'd the Causey of Bethune, took the same Sword in Hand, and on the 8th began to batte[r] the Bastion of Arras. However the great Rain and bad Weather were no small Hindrance to the Carrying on of the Saps and other Works; and o[n] the other Hand, through the Fault of the Enginee[r] the Place being attack'd on the Strongest Side, and [at] the same Time very couragiously defended by t[he] Garrison, it was the 8th of November, between [5] and 6 in the Evening before the latter thought [fit] to beat the Chamade, and to give Notice of the[ir] Desires to capitulate. Hostages were thereupo[n] exchanged about 10, the Besiegers sending out [a] Brigadier, a Colonel, a Lieutenant-Colonel, and [a] Major, and the Assailants sending into the Town [the] Officers of the same Quality. The former bein[g] come the next Morning to the Duke of Marlborough['s] Quarters, the Conditions of Surrender were sign'[d] in the Evening by that Prince and his Highness [of] Savoy, with the Field-Deputies. Those Articles co[n]tain'd in Substance, ' That the Gate of Arras shoul[d] ' be immediately delivered, all Acts of Hostilit[y] ' cease, and Care taken to prevent any Disorde[r] ' from the Officers and Soldiers; that the Garriso[n] ' should march out on the 11th following with all th[e] ' usua[l]

' usual Marks of Honour, Four Pieces of Cannon,
' and Two Mortars, and be conducted to St *Omer*.
' That whereas so many as desired it had Three
' Months Time allowed them to remain in the City,
' and dispose of their Effects; such of the Inhabitants
' of *Aire*, as had lodg'd any of their Effects at St.
' *Omer*, or elsewhere, for their better Security,
' should, if they thought fit, have the same Space
' of Three Months allow'd them to claim and reco-
' ver them; that the Sick and Wounded should re-
' main in the Town till their Recovery; that the
' Garrison should be allowed Six Cover'd Waggons,
' Deserters be delivered up on both Sides, and Priso-
' ners exchanged, that Hostages should be left for
' the Payment of the Debts of the Garrison, a Faith-
' ful Discovery made of all the Mines, and the Keys
' of the Magazines deliver'd up to the Allies.

But the Garrison of *Aire* having, upon the Solici-
tation of the Governour, who, upon his Brave Defence, was allow'd Two Pieces of Cannon more than
those agreed for in the Capitulation, been allow'd
one Day more to provide Carriages, and other Necessaries, did not march out till the 12th of *Novem*-
ber in the Morning, when it evacuated the Place, with
Monsieur *de Goesbriant* at their Head, who was told
by his Grace at their taking Leave of one another,
*that so Brave an Officer deserved a better Fate, and
that he did not doubt but the King, his Master's Sentiments were conformable to his, by holding him in
Esteem for his Gallant Defence.*

The whole Body, which consisted at first of Fifteen
Battallions of Foot, and Three Squadrons of Dragoons, amounted at their going out of the Place to
no more than 3628 Men, their Numbers being much
diminish'd by the Losses they sustain'd during the
Siege, and besides those that were killed, there were
above 1500 wounded left in the Town. As soon
as the Enemy had quitted it, the Count *de Nassau*

Woudenburgh, Son to the late Velt-Mareschal *d'Auverquerque*, and a Major-General, took Possession of that Important Fortress with Eight Battallions appointed for the Winter Garrison, and Men were immediately set at work to level the Trenches, clear the Breaches, and put the Town in a Posture of Defence; which done, the Confederate Army broke up from before *Aire* on the 5th of *November*, march'd that Day to *Bethune*, the next to *Pont a Vendin*, and so to the Plains of *Lisle*, whence the Troops design'd to Quarter in that Place, *Tournay*, and *Douay*, went to their Respective Garrisons, and the rest towards the several Places assigned them for their Winter Quarters, the *French* having gone to theirs some Time before.

Thus ended the Campaign in the *Netherlands*, which, tho' not so Glorious as those wherein the Memorable Victories of *Ramillies*, *Oudenarde*, and *Blaregnies*, were gained, was however of great Advantage to the Allies, who in it made themselves Masters of Three Towns of mighty Importance, viz. *Douay*, *Bethune*, and *Aire*, and another of less Consideration, *St. Venant*, tho' perhaps they paid a little too Dear for one of these Conquests, I mean that of *Aire*, which not being so well attacked at first as it might have been, cost the Confederates much the same Number of Men as *Douay*. But as no one can describe the Great Actions done this Year better than those that reap the Benefits of them, so it may be of use to refresh the Reader's Memory by recapitulating them, as they are set down in the *Preamble to the Petition of the Council of State for the Year* 1711, call'd, *The State of the War, presented to the States-General on the* 17th *of* November, 1710.

According

'According to this Project, *says that Excellent Piece*, a Contract was made on the Part of Her Majesty, the Queen of *Great Britain*, and your High Mightinesses, for the Delivery of a great Quantity of Forrage for subsisting the great Army, which was to be formed early in the Spring, till the Country afforded Forrage, and sufficient Precautions were taken for the Transportation of that Forrage, and other Things requisite for the Operations of War, to *Lisle* and *Tournay*. In order thereunto, *Werwick*, *Commines*, and *Warneton*, along the *Lys*, were secured, in Sight of the Garrison of *Ipres*, and other Places; as were also the Town and Castle of *Mortaigne* on the *Scheld*, whereby the Navigation and Passage of the *Scarpe*, and the *Deule*, being secured with all imaginable Dispatch and Success, it was thought necessary about the middle of *April* last to assemble the Army about *Tournay*, for the executing of the Designs aforesaid, which was done accordingly; and all Things being in a Readiness, as it was concerted, they were in a Condition few Days after to pass with almost Incredible Diligence the *Canal* between *Douay* and the *Deule* in several Places, and so got into the Lines of the Enemy.

'The Town of *Douay* was soon after attacked, and notwithstanding the same was cover'd by good Fortifications, and an Inundation, and defended by a Numerous Garrison, yet such was the Bravery, and invincible Courage and Resolution of the Besiegers, that the Place was oblig'd to surrender in Sight of a great Army of the Enemy. *France* has all along esteem'd that Town so Important for covering their Frontiers, and laying the *Spanish Netherlands* open to their Invasion, that since the Reign of King *Henry* II. they have used open Force and Artifices to get the Possession thereof, in which they succeeded at last in the Year 1667.

'As

'As they knew its Importance, they were hardly
'Masters of it, but they began to form Magazines
'therein, made it a Place of Arms, and went im-
'mediately to work for uniting the *Deule* and the
'*Scarpe* by a Canal; and by these Means facilitated
'the Invasion of the other *Spanish* Provinces, as it
'has since too often evidently appear'd.

'Through the Conquest of the City of *Douay*,
'the *Castelenie* of *Lisle*, which was still partly pos-
'sess'd by the Enemy, is wholly reduc'd under one
'single Power; and the Capital City thereof, with
'*Tournay*, and other Places, along the *Scheld* and
'the *Lys* to *Ghent*, are more and more secured. A
'Passage for Transporting by Water the Necessaries
'from that Province into *Artois* is likewise opened
'thereby, which will afford a Conveniency for
'maintaining Numerous Garrisons in those Parts this
'Winter, in order to disturb the Enemy perpetually,
'and when the Opportunity is favourable, to obtain
'further Advantages over them. This will likewise
'enable the Allies early to take the Field the next
'Spring, and subsist their Armies in the Territories
'of the Enemy.

'The Reduction of *Douay* was soon after follow'd
'by the taking of *Bethune*, which it was thought
'necessary for us to be Masters of, for covering
'more and more the *Castelenie* of *Lisle*, and en-
'larging the Opening to penetrate farther into *Ar-
'tois*. St *Venant* was taken afterwards, and lastly,
'the Town and Fortress of *Aire*, whereby a Way
'will be opened for extending the Contributions
'into the Government of *Calais*, and the Countries
'on this Side the *Somme*, and in the Dukedom of
'*Guize*, as far as the River *Oize*, which will be a
'sort of Compensation for the Dammages sustained
'in other Parts.

'Thus has ended this Glorious and Advantagious
'Campaign in the *Netherlands*, which has given
'the Allies so firm a Footing in *Artois*, that all the

'Places,

'Places, which the Enemy are still possess'd of
'in that Province, are now exposed; and there is
'Reason to hope that the Forces of the Allies will
'penetrate to the *Somme*, and into *Picardy*; and
'that their Progress will be attended with the like
'Advantage, as were in former Times obtained
'over *France*, by the Conquerors in the Battles
'fought in those Parts, as at *Crecy*, *Agincourt*,
'and *St. Quintin*, which had this Effect, that each
'of those Victories brought the Affairs of *France*
'into so much Confusion and Disorder, that for
'securing their Kingdom they were obliged to buy
'Peace of their Enemies at a very Dear Rate, and
'upon very Hard Conditions, of which the Treaty
'of *Chateau* in *Cambresis*, not to speak of several
'others, is a Memorable Instance.

So much for the Sentiments of Foreigners on the foregoing Campaign, but to come Home to ourselves, those of the prevailing Party at this Time in *Great-Britain* were quite different. For the Duke, who, at his leaving the Kingdom the last Year during Dr *Sacheverell*'s Trial, was in great Esteem with those at the *Helm*, where he had the Lord Treasurer, and one of the Secretary's of State, for his nearest Allies by the Marriages of Two of his Daughters, and in the highest Reputation of both Houses of Parliament, was now grown out of that implicite Credit he was before possess'd of; and whether justly, or not, (that is left to the Reader's Determination,) publickly accus'd in Print for being design'd to be a *General for Life*, and of employing our Men and Money upon reducing Towns of no Manner of Import to any other of the Allies but those who were to be put in Possession of them.

This Treatment the Duke was sensible of long before the End of the Campaign, and the superseding some Commissions, was an evident
Prognostick

Prognostick enough, that he was not to be so much in the good Graces of some Gentlemen, as he had been in those of others: However, after he had tarried some Time at *Brussels*, where he adjusted several Difficulties about raising 1500000 Gilders to supply the *Imperial* and *Palatine* Troops, and continued about a Month at the *Hague* for dispatching Affairs there, he arriv'd in *London* on the 28th of *December*.

Upon his Entrance into the City about Five a Clock in the Evening his Coach was attended by Multitudes of People with Links and Flambeaux, who by their Acclamations express'd their Joy at his Grace's happy Return. Tho' the Duke well knew the Instability and Emptiness of the Applause, yet he could not but be well pleas'd to see himself welcome to a Mobility, which some Months before was Tumultuous in Favour of Opinions, those of his greatest Friends ran counter to, and were the main Occasions of the late Alterations. However, his Grace, who never courted nor affected Popularity, thought it Prudence to avoid the least Shew of it, and therefore instead of going directly to St. *James's* Palace, bid his Coach drive to *Mountague-House*, where having rested an Hour or Two, he went out by a private Door, leaving those that would have been his Attendants behind. Immediately upon his Arrival at St. *James's* he waited upon the Queen, who gave him a Gracious Reception, and discoursed with him about half an Hour; after which his Grace went to his Apartment.

The next Morning the Duke was summon'd to, and assisted at, a Committee of the Privy-Council, and that Day and the following receiv'd the Visits of the Earl of *Rochester*, President of the Council, the Earl *Poulet*, first Lord Commissioner of the Treasury, the Two Secretaries of State, and other Persons in the Ministry. However, it was for many Days a Question among those that discours'd of such Affairs, whether the Person who had the greatest Share, both in the late Alterations, and in the Queen's Confidence, had an Interview with him: But those who had a near Insight into the Intrigues of the Court, were persuaded that Her Majesty had resolved to remove any Strangeness and Coldness that might be between them, and the Event justified their Conjectures.

In the mean time the Uncertainty, whether the Duke of *Marlborough* should be continued in his Command in *Flanders*, cast a fresh damp upon the Publick Credit, which had suffer'd very much before upon the new Scheme. Wherefore it was the general Wish and Expectation of the most Wealthy and Substantial Citizens, that in order to remove that fatal Doubt his Grace should receive the Thanks, if not of both, at least of one of the Two Houses of Parliament. But his Grace's Friends in the House of Lords having been already disappointed in the Motion that was made for it by the Earl of *Scarborough*, upon some Objections rais'd against it by the Duke of *Argyle*, were shy of attempting it a Second Time, the rather, because they found the Majority of that House inclined to pass that Compliment on the Earl of *Peterborough*: And those his Grace had in the House of Commons, thinking themselves too few to dare to attempt it at all, declin'd moving it till a better Opportunity.

This, together with some dubious Expressions that dropp'd from his Grace in the subsequent Debates about the Affairs of *Spain*, encreas'd the Apprehension of many, that the Duke would gratifie his private Disgust, and lay down his Commission; it being, they thought, natural for his Resentment to suggest, ' That he had acquired a sufficient Stock of ' Honour and Wealth to despise the Frowns of For-
'tune

'tune; that it would be derogatory to his Character
' to stoop to the Authors of the Disgrace of his Re-
' lations, who, whatever their Pretences might be,
' would never heartily embrace his Interest, and con-
' tribute to the Support of the Glory he had already
' gained: That the Fate of War being uncertain, the
' least Diminution of the Property that had hitherto
' attended the Arms of the Allies might be charged
' to him as a Crime; whereas, if any Misfortune
' should befal them under another General, the
' Court would have Reason to regret the Loss of so
' prosperous a Commander, and to solicite him to
' serve again, which would add a fresh Lustre to his
' Reputation. But his Grace, who upon his Departure from *Holland* had promis'd the States-General, and Prince *Eugene*, not to abandon the Common Cause, resolved to act the Part of a true Heroe, and good Patriot, and indeed of a consummate Politician, and to sacrifice his private Disgusts to the publick Welfare, by concerting Measures with the New Ministry, with the same Confidence, and hearty Zeal, as he did with the Old; wisely considering, that the preserving his Command in *Flanders* was the most effectual Means to maintain his Credit Abroad, and retrieve his Interest at Home. Pursuant to this prudent Resolution, his Grace, on the 19th of *January*, 17$\frac{10}{11}$, made a free Resignation of his Dutchess's Places at Court, by delivering into Her Majesty's Hands the Golden Key of Groom of the Stole. This voluntary Sacrifice of a Person so Dear to him, but who had had the Misfortune to incur the Queen's Displeasure, was so acceptable to Her Majesty, that she was pleas'd not only to renew his Commission, but likewise to make a Disposition of the other Generals entirely to his Grace's Satisfaction, in particular by employing the Duke of *Argyle* in *Spain*, who had not made the Campaigns with him

in

in *Flanders*, especially the last, with that Harmony that was between his Grace and some other Generals that serv'd under him.

Some will indeed have it, and those must be his Enemies, that the Duke of *Marlborough*'s Predominant Passion, the Love of acquiring Wealth, kept him in his Command; and that he chose rather to make a Surrender of what belonged to his Dutchess, than to part with his own, out of Consideration that the Profits arising from thence were of small Consequence, if compared to the Advantages that were to be had from the Command in *Flanders*; but as these are nothing but empty Surmises, and wholly inconsistent with a Person that is possess'd of such vast Riches and Demesnes as must needs subdue all farther Desire of getting more, so I shall convey this Illustrious Person to the Duties of his High Trust, after I have told the Reader, that the most Material Transaction relating to him during his Stay in *England*, was his being a strenuous Advocate in the Debates of the House of Lords concerning the Affairs of *Spain* for the Earl of *Galloway*, tho' without his wonted Success.

Matters being settled for the ensuing Campaign, his Grace set out from St. *James's* on *Sunday* the 18th of *February*, 17$\frac{1}{2}$, and arriv'd at the *Hague* on the 6th Day of *March*, N. S. with an entire Satisfaction that the Payment of the Troops under his Command would be effectually taken Care of by the *New* Administration as it had been by the *Old*. Here he continued some Time in Expectation of Prince *Eugene*, when after several Conferences with the Ministers of the States-General, and the other Allies, about the War in the *North*, and the Neutrality for the Territories of the Princes concern'd in it lying in *Germany*, as well as the Payment of the Arrears due to the *Prussians* and *Hessians*, all which were happily concluded, the Duke of *Marlborough* set out from the *Hague* the 23d of *April*, and embark'd the same Day at *Streynsas*, on Board a Yacht of the States, which conducted him to *Ghent*, which Place he arrived at on the 25th, and the next Day to *Tournay*, near which Fortress the Troops were encamped in several Bodies. His Grace having held a Council of War with the Deputies of the States and the Generals, it was resolved that those several Bodies should join and form the Army, which was done accordingly on the 30th, and the Army encamped with the Right on the *Marque*, and the Left on the *Scarpe*, the Town of *Orchies* being in the Centre, where the Duke took his Quarters. Upon these Motions the *French* Troops drew likewise together, and encamped behind the *Senset*, the Right to *Oisy*, and the Left to *Mouchy le Procuse*, having diverted the Course of the *Scarpe* at *Broche*, whereby that River fell into the *Senset*, and rendered the *French* Camp almost unaccessible on the Left and in the Front, and then their Flank was covered by the *Scheld*.

His Grace thereupon decamped on the 1st of *May*, 1711, and his Army having passed the *Scarpe*, partly at *Pont a Rache*, and partly at *Marchienne*, took Post all along the Road from *Douay* to *Valenciennes*, the Left to *Sommain*, and the Right to *Goulezin*, *Warde* being almost in the Centre, where the Duke took his Quarters. But nothing Material happened, except on the 9th of the same Month 3000 *French*, detach'd from *Valenciennes* and *Conde*, attack'd at *Tuns*, between St. *Amand* and *Mortagne*, a Convoy of 45 Boats laden with Hay and Oats for the Confederate Army, which was set out from *Tournay* under a Guard of Two Battallions Commanded by Brigadier *Chamebrier*. The Action was very Hot, and notwithstanding the vigorous Resistance of the

Guard,

Guard, the Enemy burn'd 12 Boats; but the Garrison of St. *Amand* coming to the Assistance of the Guard, the *French* retired, having had about 100 Men killed and wounded, the Loss on the Side of the Allies being near the same. All the other Boats escaped, so that the Dammage the Allies sustained on this Occasion was very inconsiderable.

The Death of the Emperor *Joseph* having disconcerted some Measures which the Allies had taken in the *Netherlands*, and made it necessary for a Detachment to be sent from thence for the Security of the Empire, which was very much threatned by *France* during the *Interregnum*, soon after the Arrival of the Prince of *Savoy*, who came to the Army on the 12th of *June*, the Confederates who had continued in their Camp at *Warde*, near *Douay*, ever since the opening of the Campaign, decamped the 14th, and that under the Command of the Duke of *Marlborough* having passed in Six Columns the Canal of *Arleux* and the *Scarpe*, in Sight of the Enemy, encamp'd in the Plain of *Lens*, the Right to *Lewen*, and the Left near *Henin-Liztard*; whereupon the Mareschal *de Villars* march'd from his Camp behind the *Sanset*, and encamped his Right at *Mouchy le Preux*, and the Left at the Rivulet of *Ugy*, their Front being everywhere covered by the *Scarpe*, and *Arras* in the Centre. The Army of Prince *Eugene* having passed the *Scarpe* below *Douay*, marched to *Orchies*, from whence the *Danes*, *Saxons*, and *Hessians*, rejoined the Army of the Duke of *Marlborough*, and the *Imperialists* and *Palatines* consisting of Fifty Squadrons and Twelve Battallions, march'd towards *Brussels*, in order to proceed to the Upper *Rhine*, to reinforce the *Imperial* Army, and put it into a Condition to oppose the *French*, who had reinforc'd their Troops on that Side with

Two

Two Detachments from the Army of Monsieur *de Villars*, and some other Troops.

The Duke's Army continued in this Camp of *Lens* to the 19th without any Thing worth Notice, as did the Enemy in theirs, when on the Day beforementioned the latter made a Detachment of Grenadiers, sustained by Four Hundred *Hussars*, with a Design to surprize the Post the Allies had taken at the Convent of *Winy*, to cover the Grand Guards on the Hills of *Arras*; but Colonel *Cholmley* of the *British* Guards, who Commanded Three Hundred Men posted therein, gave them so warm a Reception, that tho' they advanced with a great Shew of Bravery, they retired upon his first Fire, leaving a Captain of Grenadiers and several other Men kill'd on the Spot, only one Man being wounded on the Colonel's Side. On the 22d a Major belonging to the Army of the Allies, with a Hundred Dragoons, and as many *Hussars*, advanc'd to the Banks of the *Scarpe*, over-against the Enemies Camp, where they had laid some Bridges for the Passage of their Patroles, and having left the greatest Part of his Detachment at some Distance from the River, made towards the Enemy to shew himself with the rest; upon which the *French* taking the Alarm, sent Three Hundred *Hussars* to pursue him. The Major retreated towards the Place where he had left his main Body, and then charged the Enemy with such Fury, that he kill'd Forty of them, took Two Captains, a Cornet, and 17 others, Prisoners; and had not the Night coming on favoured the rest, it was believed few would have escaped.

Such Skirmishes as these was the Result of the Operations of War in both Armies till the 6th of *July*, at which Time the Duke of *Marlborough* having view'd the Lines made Three Years ago by the Enemy, to cover the Country on that Side of the Upper *Deule*, and finding them to be of no Use to

his

his Troops, order'd them to be levell'd. After which the Enemy having repaired their Dykes near *Arleux*, upon the March of his Army from the Neighbourhood of *Douay* to the Camp at *Lens*, to prevent the Water of the *Sanset* falling into the *Scarpe*, whereby the Mills of *Douay* were rendred of no Use, and fortified the Castle of *Chanterin*, made a Redoubt at the Mill of *Arleux* to cover it; a Disposition was made for attacking those Posts, and cutting those Dykes, which was put in Execution that Morning by Seven Hundred Men of the Garrison of *Douay*, with Four Pieces of Cannon, and the Piquet of the whole Army, who were order'd to sustain them, and took Post the Night before against *Sailly* and *l' Ecluse*, on the other Side of the *Scarpe*, to prevent the Enemy from passing at either of those Villages, or at *Binche*, to relieve their Men. The Confederates advanced to attack the said Posts with great Resolution, and notwithstanding the Fire of the Enemy, passed the Ditch, which was very deep and broad, upon which the *French* flung down their Arms, and were made Prisoners of War, to the Number of 90, with a Captain of Grenadiers and Three Subalterns in the Castle, and 25 Men with a Subaltern in the Redoubt of the Mill. As these Posts were but a League from the Right of the Enemy's Camp, and Five from the nearest Part of the Confederate, a Disposition was made for the March of the whole Army in Case they had offer'd to oppose them: But tho' all their Right was in Motion, and came down as far as the Village of *Sailly*, there they remained without giving the Allies the least Disturbance, and when the Posts were taken, retired to their Camp.

The maintaining of the Post of *Arleux*, which was thus possess'd by his Order, being thought by his Grace to be of great Consequence, Mr. *des Rocques*, an Engineer, was detach'd thither with 600 Workmen,

men, to put it in a better Posture of Defence, and Ten Battallions, and Twelve Squadrons, under the Command of the Baron *de Hompesch*, encamp'd at *Fierin*, between *Arleux* and *Douay*, to sustain them till the Works were finished: But on the 12th following Thirty *French* Squadrons passed the *Scheld* at *Bouchain* about One in the Morning, with a Design to surprize those Troops, and by Favour of the Night went by their Out-guards without being perceiv'd, and sent Eight Hundred Dragoons, and Two Hundred *Hussars*, which fell in with Four Squadrons of the Allies, posted on the Right, and put them into some Disorder, but the other Squadrons drawing up behind their Tents, repuls'd them with Vigour. The Battallions of Colonel *Selvin*, and Colonel St. *Maurice*, advancing at the same Time to charge them, they retired with great Precipitation, being pursued by General *Hompesch* with his Cavalry, which by that Time were mounted on Horseback, as far as the Village of *Fierin*, where the rest of their Troops were drawn up to favour their Retreat. The Baron had Fifty Men killed, and about Sixty wounded, with Mr. *Robinson*, of Lieutenant-General *Palmes*'s Regiment, and a Cornet of *Westerlo*'s, taken Prisoners, who were sent back the next Day upon their Parole; and the Enemy left Sixty dead on the Spot, among whom Eight or Nine Officers, and had a great many wounded. One of their Colonels of Dragoons died of his Wounds as they were carrying him off; and Major-General *Selwyn* was dangerously wounded on the Part of the Allies.

The Duke of *Marlborough* having visited the Works of *Arleux* on the 12th, which he found in great Forwardness, and to prevent any further Attempt from the Enemy, chang'd the Situation of the Camp which cover'd the Workmen, and which he caus'd to be reinforced by Three Battallions from *Douay*, made a March with his Army to *Villers-Brulin*

Brulin on the 20th, by which Time the Fortifications of that Post were compleated: Hereupon the Mareschal *de Villars* detached the Count *de Estain* with Twelve Battallions and Eight Squadrons to go to *Quievrain*, near *Mons*, but sent him Orders to halt at *Cambray*, in order to be at Hand for the Attack of *Arleux*. The Mareschal *de Montesquiou* would take upon him the Care of this Expedition, and the Artillery was conducted, the Bridges on the *Sanset* made, and the Troops under the Command of the Count *de Estain*, the Marquiss *de Coigny*, and the Prince *de Isenguien*, march'd with that Diligence and Secrecy, that the Post was invested the 23d, and the Besieged, after a very Brave Resistance, made Prisoners of War, to the Number of Six Hundred Men, with Colonel *Savary*, who Commanded them. But to make himself Amends for this Loss, his Grace, who was indefatigable in Contrivances to get into the Enemies Lines, which the Mareschal, his Opponent, called the Duke's *Ne plus ultra*, his Grace march'd from his Camp by break of Day, on the 4th of *August*, with a Detachment of Two Thousand Horse, and the greatest Part of the Grenadiers, to the Mill of *Grvency le Noble*, to take a View of those Lines, and the Situation of their Camp. The first appeared very Strong, well Fortified, guarded by all the Troops that were capable of being brought together upon the Motion of the Confederates that Way. My Lord Duke being return'd to *Viller-Brulin* about Noon, made the necessary Dispositions to march back towards the *Sanset*, in order to get into those Lines, (which had been all along his Design,) and the Reason which had induc'd him to march to *Villers-Brulin*, that the Enemy drawing their Forces that Way, he might have an Opportunity to put his Project in Execution. In order thereunto, General *Hompesch* was sent in the Morning to *Douay*, and was follow'd in the Afternoon by the Lieutenant-Generals

P p

rals *Cadogan*, and *Murray*, with Orders to draw out the Troops of that Garrison, and assemble some others, which, upon Pretences, had been detach'd from *Lisle*, and other Parts, making in all Thirteen Battallions and Seventeen Squadrons, with which the said Generals were order'd to march to *Arleux*, and *Baca Bacheul*, and to post themselves on the other Side of the *Sanset*, and continue there till the Army came up to sustain them. This, and other Preparations, being made, Brigadier *Sutton* march'd with the Artillery, and Pontons, and Four Battallions, and Three Hundred and Fifty Horse, with Orders to lay Bridges on the *Scarpe* near *Vitry*, as also in the Canal of *Arleux* about *Goulezin*, and at 9 the whole Army march'd in Eight Columns. The Duke of *Marlborough*, with the Horse of the Left Wing, marched before with all possible Diligence, being followed by the rest of the Army with great Alacrity. At Five in the Morning, on the 5th of the same Month, his Grace passed the *Scarpe* at *Vitry*, where he received Advice that the Detachment under General *Hompesch* had found Means to repair the Bridges the Enemy had broken down about *Arleux*, and so to pass the *Sanset* without Opposition, and take Post about *Oisy*; whereupon my Lord Duke sent Orders to the Army to continue their March with all Expedition, and march'd with his Cavalry to *Arleux*, to support the Detachment aforesaid, and drew up his Troops in Order of Battle near the *Sanset*, as fast as they pass'd that River. The Mareschal de *Villars*, who had been inform'd of that March, advanced with the Head of his Line of Horse, consisting of the Troops of the Houshold, in hopes to hinder the Confederates from passing the *Sanset*, appear'd in Sight of them at Eleven of the Clock, and passed the Defile of *Marquion* with Twenty Squadrons. But the Duke of *Marlborough* marching to attack

him

him with the Cavalry that he had drawn up; the *French* retired thro' the Defile, and encamped behind the same, where they were joined by the rest of their Forces. In the mean Time that Mareschal detach'd the Chevalier *de Luxembourgh* with Two Regiments of Dragoons to throw himself into *Valenciennes*, and sent a Brigade of Foot to *Cambray*. He likewise left a Hundred Dragoons and 8 Officers in the Castle of *Oisy*, who surrendred Prisoners of War. While this was transacting the Whole Army of the Allies came up, and notwithstanding the Fatigues of a March of Ten Leagues without halting, were drawn up in Order of Battle as they came, because the Enemy gave out that they would attack them next Morning, in Possession of the Ground from *Oisy* and *Vergier* to *Esrun* near the *Scheld*. On *Thursday* the 6th it was expected the *French* would have fallen upon them, as they had given out; but they had posted themselves behind the Morass of *Inchi*, where it was impossible for the Confederates to come at them, being fearful of being attack'd themselves, so that his Grace's Army continued in the same Post, extending their Right somewhat towards *Thun St. Martin* on the *Scheld*, while Six Battallions were detach'd to secure the Bridges which the Enemy had abandoned. The same Day about Noon Advice came, that the Enemy were in Motion to pass the *Scheld* at *Crevecoeur*, and post themselves between *Cambray* and *Bouchain*, to prevent the Siege of the last Place, whereupon General *Ross*, the Earl of *Athlone*, and the Major Generals *Grovenstein* and St. *Laurent*, were Commanded with Forty Squadrons to endeavour to fall upon their Rear; but being advanced about half a League they discovered the main Body of the Enemies Army from which they were separated by a sort of a Morass. The Duke of *Marlborough*, upon this their Situation, on, held a Council of War with the States Deputies and the other Generals, wherein it was proposed whether they should attack the Enemy, or immediately pass the *Scheld*. and the latter was resolved upon, lest the Enemy having pass'd that River, should hinder them from passing the same between *Cambray* and *Bouchain*, and consequently prevent the Siege of the last, which seem'd their only Design. Whatever it was, the Army pass'd the *Scheld* at *Estruen*, and General *Ross*, with the Detachment aforesaid, was left to bring up the Rear of the Army, and secure the Artillery and Light Baggage.

On the 7th about Eight in the Morning all the Troops were got over the *Scheld*, without any Disturbance from the Enemy, and encamped with the Right at *Juvis*, about half Way between *Bouchain* and *Cambray* and the Left to *Neufuille*, on that River below *Bouchain*, making a sort of a Semicircle about that Place. The Duke of *Marlborough* took his Quarters at *Avesne le secq*, and the Count *de Tilly* at *Haspre*, near the River *Selle*. The same Day the Enemy made a Motion, encamping with their Right near *Thun St. Martin* on the *Scheld*, and their Left to *Oisy*, where the Confederates Right was posted the Day before. The Mareschal *de Villars* caus'd a Battery to be erected on the Hills near St. *Martin*, from whence they fired upon the Village where the Generals of the Right Wing had their Quarters, but without any Effect: That Day their Right Wing continued in Sight of the Allies, being parted by the *Scheld*. The same Day his Grace gave Orders for Bridges to be laid below *Bouchain* at *Neufuille*, to open a Communication with *Douay* and other Places on the *Scarpe*, from whence his Army was to receive their Provisions and Ammunition, and also for the Passage of the Troops to be employed in the Siege

of

of *Bouchain*, which was to be attack'd on the other Side of the River: On the 8th Brigadier *Voorst*, with a Thousand Horse, was sent to meet the Bread Waggons from *Douay*, and upon Advice that the Enemy had sent over the *Sanset* a great Detachment to intercept the said Waggons, and the Artillery from *Pont a Rache*, my Lord Duke passed the *Scheld* with the Left Wing of the Horse, and took Post at the Hill of *Vignonette*, where his Highness continued till the Convoy was safely arrived at *Neufville*, when he returned to the Camp.

On the 9th in the Morning Lieutenant-General *Wood* was detach'd with Two Thousand Horse to *Marchienne*, to convoy the heavy Baggage, which he brought safe to the Camp, and on the same Day the Siege of *Bouchain* being resolved on, Thirty Battallions, (*viz*) Seventeen from the Right, and Thirteen from the Left, and Twelve Squadrons were appointed for that Service, under the Command of General *Fagel*, with the Lieutenant-Generals *Colyer*, and *North* and *Grey*, the Majors-General *Govin*, *Siburgh*, *Ivoy*, and *Huffel*, and the Brigadiers *la Roche*, *Lebec*, *Schmeling*, and *Schavonne*. On the 10th his Grace went in Person with the Troops design'd to Invest the Place, to view the Approaches, and order'd the Lines of Circumvallation to be made; but upon Advice that the *French* Army had pass'd the *Scheld*, as if they would attack the Forces under his Command, his Highness return'd to his Army, which he drew up in Order of Battle, and made to advance towards the Enemy: So that the Two Armies, came very near, but could not come to any Action, by reason of the difficult hollow Ways and Defiles, whereby they were parted. To prevent any further Alarm, my Lord Duke order'd several Lunettes and Redoubts to be made in the Front of his Camp, which might be joined in case of Need by Lines, and were so far perfected, that they were

all

all mounted with Cannon on the Eleventh, and joined together by Lines, for the better Security of the Camp.

On the 12th, at Two in the Morning, the Duke, with Fifty Battalions, and Fifty-two Squadrons, passed the *Scheld*, and having view'd *Bouchain* again, and the Entrenchments made by the Enemy from *Bacau Vasne* to *Waverechin*, gave Orders for the beginning the Lines of Circumvallation from the *Scheld* over-against *Neufville* to the *Sanset*. The Mareschal *de Villars*, with about One Hundred Hussars, came out of his Lines to observe their Motions, and like Number of Confederate Hussars were order'd to attack them, upon which Four Squadrons of the *French* Carabineers, who were near at Hand, advanced to his Relief, apprehending the Mareschal to be in Danger; but Four of the Duke's advancing likewise, charged them with so much Resolution, that they immediately broke them, killed several, and took a Brigadier-General, a Major, and Two Captains, Prisoners, Monsieur *de Villars* himself having narrowly escaped.

On the 13th the Enemy having begun in the Evening Three Redoubts between *Bouchain* and *Waverechin*, as well for preserving their Communication with the Town, which they still held, on Account of the Allies being unable to invest it everywhere, by reason of an Entrenchment from the Hill *Marquette* to the Inundation, which was furnished with Cannon, and Thirty Battallions behind it, as for preventing the carrying on the Line of Circumvallation to the *Sanset*, the Disposition was made for attacking them on the 14th with the Troops on the other Side, with which the Duke of *Marlborough* himself marched at Three in the Morning, having taken Twenty Pieces of Cannon with him; and coming before the Redoubts at Break of Day, the Enemy immediately quitted them, and retired to their Entrenchment:

trenchment: Upon which his Grace gave Orders for the Workmen to continue their Line with all Diligence, which was compleated Two or Three Days afterwards, and the Town wholly invested.

To be as brief as possible, the Trenches were open'd in spight of the Enemies Opposition on the 23d of *August* at Three several Attacks, Two against the Upper Town, and One against the Lower, which were carried on with so much Success, that tho' the *French* made several Attempts to intercept the Besiegers Convoys, and form'd a Design against *Douay*, by Way of Surprize, that the Confederates might raise the Siege, both which miscarried, thro' the Vigilance of his Grace the Duke of *Marlborough*. They had made a mighty Progress in it by the Eleventh of *September*, when, notwithstanding all Endeavour had been used towards its Relief by the Mareschal *de Villars*, who by the Neighbourhood of the Two Armies had repeated Skirmishes with the Allies, and had taken the Count *d' Erbach*, and several other General Officers, Prisoners, the Bastion on the Right of the Lower Town was storm'd and taken, with little or no Loss, only in making the Lodgment, by that of a Lieutenant-Colonel, and Ten private Men killed, and about Thirty wounded. The Besieged quitted at the same time the Bastion on the Left, where the Allies likewise lodged themselves; upon which the Garrison seeing that the Breaches at the Two Attacks against the Upper Town were very wide, and that all Things were preparing for a General Assault, had the Prudence to prevent it by a Capitulation. They beat the Chamade about Twelve at Noon, and the Hostages being exchanged, and those on the Part of the Enemy being conducted to General *Fagel*'s Quarters, where his Grace, with the Deputies of the States-General, repaired, and consulted together about the Conditions which were to be allowed them. The Result of which was, that

those

those Hostages were called in, but when they offer'd to deliver their Articles, my Lord Duke told them, That he would not have them read; but seeing they had waited to the last Extremity, they had no other Terms to expect than to be made Prisoners of War, bidding them to acquaint their Commander with it, and send back the Hostages if he would not accept this Condition. The Hostages being returned into the Town, the Governour refus'd to comply, and so the Hostilities began again with greater Fury than ever, and the Besiegers made such a terrible Fire from their Cannon, Mortars, and Small-shot, that the *French* hung out a White Flag at all the Attacks, and beat a Parley a Second Time.

New Hostages were accordingly exchanged, and the Enemy proposed to Surrender Prisoners of War, upon Condition that they should march out with all the Marks of Honour, and be conducted into *France*, where they should do no manner of Service till they were exchanged; pretending they desired this Favour because of the Misery the Prisoners were reduced to in *Holland*, where they seem'd abandon'd by their Court, which took no Care for their Subsistance. This Demand being likewise rejected, the Governour agreed at last to surrender upon the Terms proposed by my Lord Duke; but this Debate taking up much Time, one of the Gates of the Town was not surrendred till the 13th in the Morning. On the 14th, the Garrison having delivered 24 Colours, and all their Arms, marched out, to the Number of above Two Thousand Men, Messieurs *de Ravignan* and St. *Luc* at the Head of them, and the Soldiers were conducted to *Marchienne*, in order to be sent to *Holland*, but the Officers continued in *Bouchain* till further Orders; Major-General *Grovestein* being appointed Governour in the Place, took Possession thereof with a Detachment of the Troops that form'd the Siege. The

Garrison

Garrison, which at first consisted of Eight compleat Battallions, and a Detachment of 600 *Switzers*, besides another of Dragoons, lost a great many Men in the Defence of the Place, being reduced to the Number of Two Major-Generals, Two Brigadiers, Eight Colonels, Four Lieutenant-Colonels, Three Majors, 76 Captains, 83 Lieutenants, 51 Under Lieutenants, and 2717 Private Men. Such amongst them, both Officers and Soldiers, who by reason of their Wounds and Sickness were not able to march out with the rest, were sent to *Cambray*, to be accounted for as Prisoners. The Governour pretended, That he was in a Condition to have defended himself some Days longer, but that the Soldiers perceiving the Mareschal *de Villars* did not attempt their Relief, as he had promised them, forced him to Capitulate. 'Twas surprizing indeed, that that General having a superior Army to the Allies, suffer'd this Important Place to be taken under his Nose, without making any real Efforts to raise the Siege: But he may excuse himself upon the Precautions of the Duke of *Marlbrough*, who had taken such Measures to put this Glorious Enterprize in Execution, that Monsieur *de Villars* foresaw that if he offer'd to attack his Grace's Camp, he should lose most of his Army, as well as the Town.

After the Surrender of this Place, which he gave out was only a *Dove-House*, and several *English* Authors made very light of, tho' the Stratagem in passing the Lines without the Loss of a Man, the cutting off the Communication of the Enemy with *Bouchain*, the manner of the Dukes investing the Town with an Inferior Army, his casting up Lines, making Regular Forts, raising Batteries, laying Bridges over a River, making passable a Morass, and providing for the Security of his Convoys against a Superior Army on the one Side, and the numerous Garrisons of *Conde* and *Valenciennes* on the other. But tho' his Grace was so unhappy as to fall under the Censure fure of infolent Scriblers of his own Nation, he had the Satisfaction to see this Enterprize recorded for the Use of Posterity by the States Deputies in the following Letter to their Principals.

High and Mighty Lords,

'THE Enemy having beaten a Parley Yesterday,
' the Capitulation was agreed to this Morn-
' ing, by which the Garrison are made Prisoners of
' War. It is with the utmost Satisfaction that we
' give ourselves the Honour to Congratulate your
' High-Mightinesses on the Conquest with which
' God Almighty has been pleas'd to bless the Arms of
' the State, and your High-Allies. This Place is of
' such high *Importance*, in respect to its Situation,
' which opens a Way to penetrate farther into the
' Territories of the Enemy, and even into the Heart
' of their Country, that in order to prevent it they
' have thought necessary to consume by Fire in their
' own Country. If the Circumstances that have attend-
' ed this Conquest are duly considered, as the Passing
' of the Lines, which the Enemy, and all the World,
' thought impossible, and the Siege itself carried on
' with so much Speed, and in so glorious a Manner,
' in Sight, and within the Reach, of an Army, which
' if not superior, was at least of an equal Strength,
' if all these Things, we say, are rightly considered,
' it will appear, that the *Conduct*, *Firmness*, and
' *Valour*, which the Duke of *Marlborough* and the
' Count *de Tilly* have express'd in the Prosecution of
' this Glorious Enterprize, cannot be sufficiently
' praised. We find ourselves obliged, that we may
' do Justice to General *Figel*, who commanded the
' Siege, to say, that his Courage and Indefatigable
' Care has very much contributed to the speedy Con-
' quest of this Important Place: But above all, we
' return Thanks to Almighty God, who has made
' Use of these Generals as happy Instruments for the
' accomplishing of his Will and Mercies —We pray
' God

'God that he will continue his Blessings on the
'Arms of your High-Mightinesses, that this Bloody
'and Expensive War may be changed into a happy
'and lasting Peace. We take the Liberty to propose
'Major-General *Grovenstein* for Commander, and
'Captain *Keppel* for Major, of the Place, who are to
'take Possession thereof, and hope that your High-
'Mightinesses will be pleased to approve the same,
'and remain with the utmost Respect,

Your Humble

and Obedient Servants.

From the Camp be-   A. Van Capelle. W. Hooft.
fore Bouchain,   S. Van Goslinga.
Sept. 13. 1711.   P. F. Vegelin Van Claerbergen.

To return to the other Operations of the Campaign after the Evacuation of the foregoing Town; the Duke of *Marlborough*, who foresaw that the Enemy might be troublesome in the Winter to the Conquer'd Places that lye near them, without the Reduction of *Quesnoy*, dispatch'd the Earl of *Albemarle*, a Person of great Note and Interest, for the States-General's Concurrence for that Siege, because that as their Troops were to be put in Garrison in such Places as should be taken by the Confederates, so it was allotted to them by certain Articles agreed to between them and the High Allies to find Cannon for Battery, Ammunition, and other Things necessary for bringing them under their Obedience. But that Nobleman having communicated to their High-Mightinesses the Condition of the Army, which had suffer'd considerably by Death and Desertion, and the Duke's Opinion of what further Measures were to be taken, return'd with this Answer, That their High-Mightinesses could in no wise approve of undertaking another

her Siege, because the Enemy had destroyed the Country about *Quesnoy*, *Valenciennes*, and other Places, insomuch that the Army could not be capable of subsisting. To this it was thought fit to add, that the Season of the Year was so far spent, that People ought not to expect a long Continuance of fair Weather; from which it was concluded, that so brave an Army ought not to be expos'd to the Hardships of a new Siege that Campaign; but the States consented that all the Troops should be Quartered in the Frontier Places, to hinder the Enemy from making any New Lines the ensuing Winter, and be ready in the Beginning of the Spring to Besiege *Arras*, or to go upon any further Enterprize without Loss of Time. Because this would prevent a great Inconveniency the Generals lay under at the Opening of this very Campaign, for the *Prussians*, *Palatines*, *Hessians*, and other Troops, being Quarter'd at a great Distance, the Army could not be suddenly drawn together before the Enemy had Time to Assemble their Forces. Besides, this would oblige the *French* likewise to Quarter their Troops on their Frontiers, and how they would be able to subsist them, if the Winter should prove bad, was very difficult to imagine, and therefore they would have very great Reason at *Paris* to take this Resolution of the Allies as a fatal Stroke, which would Ruin, or at least very much Embarras, their Affairs.

The Duke, who had been acquainted with the Negotiations that were then carrying on in *England* by Monsieur *Mesnager* from the *French* Court, and the Proposals he had given in to the Ministry from his Master, could not but perceive that the States had this also for an Inducement to make no more Sieges during the Residue of the Campaign, tho' their High Mightinesses did not think fit to insert it among the other Arguments they made Use of for putting an End to it. He therefore, without making any Remonstrance against lying still so considerable a
while,

while set the Forces at Work to level the Approaches, fill up the Breaches, and put the Town of *Bouchain* into a Posture of Defence, which was not compleatly done till about Three Weeks after its Surrender, thro' the Badness of the Weather, which very much incommoded both the *French* and the Allies, who continued encamp'd to see each other drawn off to their Winter Quarters.

The Count *de Ravignan*, late Governour of *Bouchain*, and the other Principal Officers of that Garrison, having represented to the *French* Court, that the Conditions promis'd them during the Parley were not made good to them, and insisting they were only to be deem'd Prisoners, to be conducted Home, and to be accounted for in future Exchanges; and the said Representation having been transmitted to the Duke of *Marlborough* by the Mareschal *de Villars*, his Grace, in Answer to it, return'd him Attestations signed by General *Fagel*, and Colonel *Pagnies*, one of his Hostages, who they pretended made them that Offer in the Name of Monsieur *Fagel*, by which it plainly appears that their Complaint was altogether groundless, and that they had never the least Encouragement given them to hope for any other Conditions than to be made Prisoners of War. The Original Pieces that relate to this Military Controversie being very Curious, were as follow.

A Letter from the Prince and Duke of Marlborough *to their High-Mightinesses the States-General of the United Provinces.*

High and Mighty Lords,

'I Do my self the Honour to send to your High-
' Mightinesses a Copy of a Letter and Memorial

'I have just now received from the Mareschal *de Villars*, wherein he complains of the Infraction of the Capitulation of *Bouchain*, and pretends we have violated the good Faith towards the Garrison. I would not miss imparting them to you immediately, together with my Answer, and the Declarations of General *Fagel* and Colonel *Pagnies* upon the Facts the Enemy complain of, that your High-Mightinesses may see how little Grounds there are for their Allegations, and that we have acted on that Occasion with Honour, and according to the Rules of War. Your High-Mightinesses will also be pleased to observe, that all has been transacted in Concert with your Deputies and Generals, and I flatter myself, you will likewise approve the last Article of my Letter to the Mareschal, and give Instruction to your Deputies accordingly: I am, &c.

From the Camp at Bouchain, Sept. 29. 1711.

The Prince and Duke of Marlborough.

The Letter from the Mareschal Duke of Villars *to the Prince and Duke of* Marlborough.

SIR,

'I Have been throughly informed by Count *Ravignan*, and the other Chief Officers of the Garrison of *Bouchain*, of their Just Complaints of the Word and Faith infringed in the Capitulation granted them by Colonel *de Pagnies*, Commander of the *Dutch* Guards, by Monsieur *de Fagel*'s Order. You will perceive, Sir, by the inclosed Copy of all that passed thereupon, and of which these Brave Men send the Original to the King, to vindicate themselves for not having preferr'd all Dangers, and even Death itself, to the Shame of surrendring Prisoners of

'of War, that the Word given them has been formally
'broken. The Place was not in a Condition to be
'stormed, since you were not Masters of the Half-
'moons, and the Passage of the Ditch was not yet
'begun. Give me Leave to tell you, that the Want of
'your Consent does not hinder the good Faith from
'being violated, when the General who Commands
'the Siege sends his Word by a Colonel, that upon
'that Word, the Firing, which had been begun anew,
'is discontinued, Hostages given again, and even a
'Gate delivered up.

'I don't question, Sir, but your own Glory will,
'after serious Consideration, engage you to send
'back the Garrison upon the Conditions that were
'offer'd them to surrender.

'What can be more Authentick thereupon than
'the Publick Protestation Monsieur *de Pagnies* has
'made, as a Man of Honour and Probity, in the
'Presence of all your Army, and the Garrison itself,
'to which he declared, That he knew not the Max-
'ims upon which they broke the Word he had Or-
'der and Power to engage.

'I expect from you, Sir, an Answer conformable
'to Equity: The King Commands me to make Com-
'plaints to you upon a Fact without Example in
'War.

'The Count *de Bork* may be exchanged for Mon-
'sieur *de Ravignan*, provided this last be set at
'Liberty upon the Faith of the last Capitulation.
'I am, &c.

From the Camp at Pallien-   *The Duke of* Villars,
  court, *Sept.* 28. 1711.   *Mareschal of* France.

The Duke of *Marlborough* having enquired and examined into this Affair, and found that the Complaints of the Garrison were altogether frivolous and groundless, returned the Mareschal *Villars* an Answer as follows.

SIR,

'SIR,

'I Have received the Letter you did me the Honour to write to me Yesterday by the King's Order, to accompany the Account of M. de Ravignan, and the Chief Officers of the Garrison of Bouchain, concerning the Capitulation; and tho' it appears by that very Account that those Gentlemen own, that all they pretend was told them by M. de Pagnies was without my Consent, or that of the Deputies of their High-Mightinesses; I am however equally surprized and sorry that it should be believed, that I should have permitted any Infraction of Things promised, or the least Violation of the Publick Faith. The Manner in which I have acted on so many Occasions of this Nature, and with many of the General Officers, ought to be to the King and the Whole World so many Pledges of my Uprightness: And I flatter myself that they will do me the Justice to believe, that nothing was done in the Treatment that Garrison has received contrary to the Capitulation that was granted them: You will find by the inclosed Accounts of the Baron de Fagel and M. de Pagnies, that Things were transacted so differently from what is represented in that Memorial, 'that there is not the least Ground for the Complaints mentioned in it; and that General Fagel far from taking upon him to grant the Capitulation mentioned by those Gentlemen, sent them Word by the Hostages he sent them back into the Town, That *he hoped that they would not accept what I had offer'd them in Concert with the States Deputies, viz. To be Prisoners of War, that he might have the Honour to carry the Place Sword in Hand*, which those Gentlemen will agree would not have fail'd of being executed in less than Four and Twenty Hours; the Breaches in in the Body of the Place, as well as in the Ravelin,
'being

' being then ready, and our Men lodged on the Brink
' of the Ditch, so as to be able to storm the next Day.
' And it was some Hours after that Message had been
' sent to them, and the Hostilities were renewed, be-
' fore those Gentlemen thought fit to hang out White
' Colours for the Second Time, and to deliver up a
' Gate to us. As for what they alledge, that in the
' mean Time we carried on our Works, I shall have
' the Honour to tell you, Sir, that when the Che-
' valier *d' Artagnan* went out with the Hostages, it
' was declared to them before the States Deputies
' that we would not be amused, but that they should
' expect that the Works should be continued during
' the Treaty. This is a Circumstance which those
' Gentlemen agree to, and I am much persuaded of
' your Equity, that when you have seriously consider-
' ed these Facts, you will do me the Justice that is due
' to my Proceedings, and, if necessary, inform the King
' that the Complaints of those Gentlemen are ground-
' less; and that all that was promis'd them has been
' performed according to the Letter. You will give
' me Leave, Sir, to add, that the Refusal of letting
' the Count *d' Erbach*, Major-General *Burck*, Count
' *Denhoff*, Colonel *Savery*, and Major *Waſſanaer*, re-
' turn to our Camp upon their Parole, is so contrary
' to the Way we always us'd towards your Officers,
' that the Generals of this Army complain of it pub-
' lickly, and that except this Grievance is redressed, I
' shall be obliged in Justice, and by Order of the Queen,
' and the States-General, to recal all the Prisoners
' that have been suffered to continue in *France* so
' long upon their Parole. I should be sorry if Things
' came to that Extremity, the preventing of which
' will only depend on the ready Compliance that
' shall be given on your Part. I am, &c.

From the Camp at Bouchain,
    Sept. 29. 1711.

The Prince and Duke
of Marlborough.

So soon as the Court of *France* had seen the Duke's Letter, they were readily convinced, and without dropping any further Remonstrances about the Officers or Garrison, gave immediate Orders for returning the Persons demanded by his Grace the Duke of *Marlborough* to the Confederate Camp, and providing for such an Exchange, in Lieu of those taken by their Enemies, as had been practiced before by the Two Armies upon the like Occasions.

The Campaign, as has been said before, being at an End in the *Netherlands*, the Fortifications of *Bouchain* repaired, and all the Troops on their March to their respective Garrisons, except a Flying Camp under Major-General *Ivoy*, who was to continue at *Maude* on the *Scarpe*, between St. *Amand* and *Tournay*, to secure the Navigation to *Douay*, and the Workmen employed in fortifying several Posts along that River and the *Scheld*, the Duke of *Marlborough* quitted the Army on the 27th of *October*, and came the very same Day to *Tournay*, where he was nobly received and entertain'd by the Earl of *Albemarle*, Governour of that Fortress. On the 3d of *November* his Grace arrived at *Antwerp*, attended by several General Officers, under a Triple Discharge of all the Artillery. There he supp'd with the Cardinal *de Bouillon*, and din'd the next Day with the Marquiss *de Terracena*, Governour of the Citadel, who had invited all the Persons of Quality in that City, upon Account of the Feast of the Name of his Imperial Majesty *Charles* the VIth, who had been some Time before Elected to that High Dignity in the room of his Brother lately deceas'd. On the 5th he set out from thence for the *Hague*, where he was received on the 6th with all possible Marks of Distinction; and in several Conferences with the States General, entered upon Consultations as well relating to Peace, which was then upon the Anvil, as War.

Having

Having hinted at Propositions of Peace made in *England*, and inserted in the foregoing Sheets the Proceedings upon the same Subject in *Holland*, where his Grace as First Plenipotentiary of Great-Britain was One of the Principal Actors, it will be of Significancy likewise to set down the Steps that have lately been made towards that Desirable End for which the War was at first begun. In Order to this I shall begin with the Preliminary Articles which are said in all the *Dutch Gazettes* to be Sign'd by the *French* Minister abovementioned, and are as follows.

The King being willing to contribute all that lyes in his Power to the Re-establishment of the General Peace, his Majesty declares,

I. *That he will acknowledge the Queen of Great-Britain in that Quality, as also the Succession of that Crown, according to the Present Settlement.*

II. *That he will freely, and* bona Fide, *consent to the taking of all Just and Reasonable Measures for hindering the Crowns of France and Spain from ever being united on the Head of the same Prince, his Majesty being perswaded that this Excess of Power would be contrary to the Good and Quiet of Europe.*

III. *The King's Intention is, that all the Parties engaged in the Present War may find their Reasonable Satisfaction in the Treaty of Peace that shall be made: That Commerce may be re-established and maintained for the future, to the Advantage of Great-Britain, of Holland, and of the other Nations who have been accustomed to exercise Commerce.*

IV. *As the King will likewise maintain exactly the Observation of the Peace when it shall be concluded, and the Object the King proposes to himself being to secure the Frontiers of his Kingdom, without disturbing, in any Manner whatever, the Neighbouring States, he promises to agree by the Treaty which shall be made: That*

K r 2   *the*

the Dutch shall be put into the Possession of the Fortified Places which shall be mentioned in the Netherlands, to serve hereafter for a Barrier, which may secure the Quiet of the Republick of Holland against any Enterprize on the Part of France.

V. The King consents likewise that a Secure and Convenient Barrier should be formed for the Empire, and for the House of Austria.

VI. Notwithstanding Dunkirk cost the King very great Sums, as well to acquire, as to fortifie, it, and that it is further necessary to be at very considerable Expences for razing the Works, his Majesty is willing however to engage to cause them to be demolished immediately after the Conclusion of the Peace, on Condition that for the Fortifications of that Place a proper Equivalent, that may content him, may be given him, and as England cannot furnish that Equivalent, the Discussion of it shall be referr'd to the Conferences to be held for the Negotiation of Peace.

VII. When the Conferences for the Negotiation of the Peace shall be formed, all the Pretensions of the Princes and States engaged in the present War shall be therein discuss'd bona Fide, and amicably: And nothing shall be omitted to regulate and terminate them to the Satisfaction of all Parties.

By Virtue of a full Power from the King, We the underwritten Knight of the Order of St. Michael, Deputy of the Council of Commerce, have concluded in the Name of his Majesty the Present Preliminary Articles. In Witness whereof We have Sign'd. DONE AT LONDON, the 27th of *September*, Old Stile, and the 8th of *October*, New Stile, 1711.

MESNAGER.

As the Contents of the preceding Articles were neither agreeable to the Emperor, nor some other Potentates engaged in the Grand Alliance, so would the Purport of these Memoirs permit, I might here insert Memorials from that Prince, and his Electoral Highness of *Hannover*, presented to Her Majesty on that Subject; but since the King of *Prussia*, who has declared to his Imperial Majesty, *that he will act in Concert with the Queen of* Great-Britain, and the States General have approved of the Measures taken in *England* to put an End to this Burthensom and Expensive War, I shall omit entring into the Detail of what has been done by Way of Remonstrance against the ensuing Treaty of Peace, and leave further discoursing on that Head, till I bring the Duke of *Marlborough* over to his Native Country.

The Duke having transacted such Affairs in *Holland*, towards the forwarding of which his Presence was altogether necessary, set out for the *Brill* on the 23d of the same Month, and came to his House at St. *James*'s on that Day which is with us, according to the *Julian* Account, the 18th of *November*, about Nine in the Morning, which quite defeated the Intent of a Story raised by his Enemies, that his Grace was to have made his Publick Entry into *London* on the Night before, when in Commemoration of Queen *Elizabeth*'s Inauguration Publick Rejoicings were to have been made in the Burning the Pope, the Devil, and the Pretender, and the Mob raised. What the Design of those was that were Masters of these Ceremonies I shall not venture to explain, but the Duke came early through the City for Privacy Sake, to give no Handle for Detraction, and had no sooner shifted himself, and taken a short Repast, but took Coach again immediately for *Hampton-Court*, where he waited upon Her Majesty, and was very graciously received by that Incomparable Queen, after which he assisted in Council the same Night.

For

For some Days following he paid Visits to the Great Officers of the Crown, amongst whom to show that he had no Personal Dissatisfaction at his Lordship's Prudent Management, he, in Particular, paid his Compliments to the Lord High Treasurer, tho' he did not think fit to give his Attendance at the Committees of the Cabinet, to which he was summon'd as a Member. Peace at this Time was the Subject of every one's Conversation, and it was no longer a Secret, there was none but did suppose that a Treaty would be set on Foot, since Her Majesty had been pleas'd to name Her Plenipotentiaries, and had given Commissions to the Bishop of *Bristol*, Lord Privy Seal, and the Earl of *Strafford*, for that Purpose, for whom Instructions were actually drawing up. The *French* King had likewise named those on his Part, which being to the Number of Three, People did not stick to affirm that his Grace was to be at the Head of those from *Great-Britain*, having been invested with that Character ever since the first Commencement of the War: But as these were only Surmises, and still continue so, I shall keep close to Matter of Fact, and acquaint my Reader, that both Houses of Parliament met on the 7th of *December*, when the Queen gave them to understand, that both Place and Time (one of which was *Utrecht*, and the other the 12th of *January*, N. S.) was appointed for opening a Treaty of a General Peace, in concert with Her Allies, the States General, whose Interest She look'd upon as inseparable from Her own, notwithstanding the *Arts of those that delight in War*, which was back'd with very Indulgent Assurances of Her Majesty's utmost Endeavours to enlarge Trade and Commerce for the Advantage of Her Subjects, and procuring such Conditions as should be highly beneficial to the Princes and States engaged in Alliance with Her, as also with very Gracious Resolutions to unite with them in the strictest Engagements for continuing the Alliance, in order to render the General Peace Secure

and

and Lasting. But the Seven Preliminary Articles, which are expresly mention'd before, having got into the Publick Prints, and receiv'd as Authentick by the Generality of the People, the House of Lords, after voting an Address of Thanks to Her Majesty for Her most Gracious Speech, were pleas'd to put it to the Question, whether a Peace could be Safe or Honourable, if *Spain*, or any Part of the *West-Indies*, were to be allotted to any Branch of the House of *Bourbon*? Which was carried in the Negative by a very small Majority, his Grace's Vote being one of those for the Question; and the Speech he made on this Occasion applied to that Part of Her Majesties Speech, which took Notice *of those who delight in War*, to this Purpose. ' That he referr'd himself to the Queen, (*making a Bow to the Place where Her Majesty was incognito,*) whether he had not
' constantly, whilst he was Plenipotentiary, given
' Her Majesty, and Her Council, an account of all
' the Propositions that had been made, and had not
' desired Instructions for his Conduct on that Sub-
' ject, &c. That he could declare with a good Con-
' science, in the Presence of Her Majesty, and that
' Illustrious Assembly, and of God himself, who
' was infinitely above all the Powers of the Earth,
' and before whom, by the ordinary Course of Na-
' ture, he must soon appear, to render an Account
' of his Actions. that he ever was desirous of a safe,
' honourable, and lasting Peace, and that he was
' always very far from any Design of prolonging the
' War for his own private Advantage, as several
' Libels had most falsly insinuated, &c. That his
' great Age, and the many Fatigues of War, made
' him ardently wish for the Power to enjoy a quiet
' Repose, in order for him to think of Eternity. As
' for other Matters, he had not the least Motive on
' any Account whatsoever to desire the Continuance
' of the War for his particular Interest, since his
' Services had been so generously rewarded, both by
' Her

'Her Majesty, and the Parliament, but that he
' thought himself obliged to such an Acknowledg-
' ment to Her Majesty, and his Country, that he
' was always ready to serve them, (whenever his
' Duty should require,) to obtain an Honourable and
' a Lasting Peace; yet, that he could by no Means
' give into the Measures that have been taken to
' enter into a Negotiation of Peace with *France*,
' upon the Foot of the Seven Preliminaries, since his
' Opinion was the same with the rest of the Allies,
' that the leaving *Spain* and the *West-Indies* to the
' House of *Bourbon*, would be the entire Ruin of
' Europe; which he had with all Fidelity and Humi-
' lity declared to Her Majesty, when he had the
' Honour to wait on Her, a little after his Return.
Hereupon their Lordships Address'd Her Majesty, pursuant to the foregoing Resolution, who return'd for Answer. ' *My Lords*, I should be sorry any
' One should think I would not do my utmost to
' recover *Spain* and the *West-Indies* from the House
' of *Bourbon*.

The Commons likewise had a Motion of the same Nature made in their House, but rejected it by a great Majority, and left it in their Address entirely in the Queen's Breast to do what She in Her Great Wisdom should be pleas'd to think fit, out of *a Just Confidence in Her Honour and Justice to Her Allies, and in Her particular Care of her own Subjects*. To which Her Majesty was graciously pleas'd to reply after this Manner, *This very Dutiful Address is what I expected from the Zeal and Loyalty of such an House of Commons. I return you my Hearty Thanks for the Confidence you have in me. I entirely rely upon your Assurances, and you may depend upon my Affection and Care for your Interests.* The Duke likewise, in concert with the Lord Nottingham, appear'd strenuously in Favour of *a Bill for Preserving the Church of England*, which was brought into the House of Lords, and read the first
Time

Time on the 14th of *December*, and had the Royal Assent on the 22d, which I presume will leave it beyond a Question that he is a true Son of the Church, as what has been before submitted to the Reader's Judgment, has prov'd him to be a True Friend, and Faithful Servant, to his Queen and Country.

But as the Commons had on the said Twenty Second Day of *December*, fall'n into very warm Debates, concerning a Report made from the Commissioners for Taking, Examining, and Stating the Publick Accounts, wherein were several Depositions of Sir *Solomon Medina*, said to be proving great Sums of Money taken by his Grace, and *Adam de Cardonel*, Esq; his Secretary, and others, on Account of the Contracts for supplying Bread, and Bread-Waggons, to Her Majesty's Forces in the *Low Countries*. So I should fall short in my Pretensions to Impartiality, should not I set both the Accusation and Defence in as true a Light as I can, that neither the one may be injur'd by what is alledg'd against him nor the other traduced for not making good their Allegations.

The Duke had receiv'd Intimations of these intended Proceedings against him upon his Arrival at the *Hague*, and to clear himself from all Imputations of either embezeling or misemploying the Publick, wrote the following Letter to the Commissioners, which having been Printed by itself, I shall take the Liberty to insert in this Place.

Hague, November 10th, 1711.

Gentlemen,

HAving been informed, on my Arrival here, that Sir *Solomon de Medina* has acquainted you with

' with my having received several Sums of Money
' from him, that it might make the less Impression
' on you, I would lose no Time in letting you know
' that this is no more than what has always been
' allow'd as a Perquisite to the General or Comman-
' der in Chief of the Army in the Low Countries,
' even before the Revolution, and since, and I do
' assure you at the same Time, that whatever Sums
' I have received on that Account, have been con-
' stantly imploy'd for the Service of the Publick, in
' keeping Secret Correspondence, and in getting In-
' telligence of the Enemies Motions and Designs;
' and it has fallen so far short, that I take Leave to
' acquaint you with another Article that has been
' applied to the same Use, and which arises from
' Her Majesties Warrant, whereof the inclosed is a
' Copy. Though this does not properly relate to the
' Publick Accounts, being a Free Gift of the Foreign
' Troops. You will have observed by the several
' Establishments, that before the late King's Death,
' when the Parliament voted Forty Thousand Men
' for the Quota of *England* in the Low Countries,
' Twenty-one Thousand Six Hundred and Twelve
' were to be Foreigners, and the rest *English*, for
' these last they gave Ten Thousand Pounds a Year
' for Intelligence, and other Contingencies, without
' Account. But his Majesty being sensible, by the
' Experience of the last War, that this Sum would
' not any ways answer that Service, and being unwil-
' ling to apply for more to the Parliament, he was
' pleased to order that the Foreign Troops should
' contribute Two and a Half *per Cent.* towards it,
' and being then his Ambassador, and Commander
' in Chief, Abroad, he directed me to propose it to
' them, with an Assurance that they should have no
' other Stoppage made from their Pay; this they
' readily agreed to, and Her Majesty was afterwards
' pleased to confirm it by Her Warrant, upon my
' acquainting her with the Uses it was intended for;
' and

'and it has been accordingly applied from Time to
'Time for Intelligence, and Secret Service, with
'such Success, that next to the Blessing of God, and
'the Bravery of the Troops, we may in a great
'Measure, attribute most of the Advantages of the
'War in this Country to the timely and good Ad-
'vices procured with the Help of this Money; and
'now, Gentlemen, as I have laid the whole Matter
'fairly before you, and that I hope you will allow
'I have served my Queen and Country with that
'Faithfulness and Zeal which becomes an Honest
'Man, the Favour that I intreat of you is, that
'when you make your Report to the Parliament,
'you will lay this Part before them in its true Light,
'so that they may see this Necessary and Important
'Part of the War has been provided for, and carried
'on, without any other Expence to the Publick than
'the Ten Thousand Pound a Year; and I flatter my
'self, that when the Accounts of the Army in *Flan-
'ders* come under your Consideration, you will be
'sensible the Service on this Side has been carried
'on with all the Oeconomy and good Husbandry to
'the Publick that was possible. I am,

Gentlemen,

Your Most Obedient,

Humble Servant,

MARLBOROUGH.

ANNE

ANNE R.

'Right Trusty, and Right Well-beloved Cozen
'and Councellor, We Greet you well.
'Whereas, pursuant to the Direction you have re-
'ceived in that Behalf, you have agreed with the
'Persons Authorized to Treat with you for the ta-
'king into Our Service a certain Number of Foreign
'Troops, to Act in Conjunction with the Forces of
'Our Allies, that there be reserved Two and a Half
'*per Cent.* out of all Moneys payable to and for the
'said Troops, as well for their Pay and Entertain-
'ment, as on any other Account, towards defraying
'such Extraordinary Contingent Expences rela-
'ting to them, as cannot otherwise be provided for.
'Now, We do hereby Approve and Confirm all such
'Agreements as you have, or may hereafter, make,
'for reserving the said Two and a Half *per Cent.* ac-
'cordingly; and do likewise hereby Authorize and
'Direct the Pay-Master General of our Forces for the
'Time Being, or his Deputy, to make the said De-
'duction of Two and a Half *per Cent.* pursuant
'thereunto, out of all Moneys he shall be directed
'to Issue, for the Use of the Foreign Troops in Our
'Pay, and thereupon to pay over the same from
'Time to Time according to such Warrants, and in
'such Proportions as you shall direct, for which this
'shall be to you, and to all others whom it may
'concern, a sufficient Warrant and Direction.

Given at Our Court at St. James's, this 6th *Day of*
 July, 1702, *and in the First Year of Our Reign.*

By Her Majesties Command,

C. HEDGES

To Our Right Trusty, and Right Well-
beloved Cozen and Councellor, John,
Earl of Marlborough, our Ambassador
Extraordinary and Plenipotentiary to the
States General of the United Provin-
ces, and Captain General of Our Land
Forces.

Sir

Sir Solomon de Medina's *Depositions* against his Grace ran thus:

'SIR *Solomon de Medina* Kt. being Sworn on
' the *Pentateuch*, deposeth, that from the Year
' 1707 to this Present Year 1711, both inclusive, he
' has been solely, or in Partnership concerned in the
' Contracts for Bread, or Bread-Waggons, for sup-
' plying the Forces in the *Low-Countries* in the Queen
' of *Great-Britain*'s Pay; and that he gave the D.
' of *M*——, for his own Use, the several Sums fol-
' lowing, *viz.* For the Year 1707, Sixty-six Thou-
' sand Eight Hundred Gilders. For the Year 1708,
' Sixty-two Thousand Six Hundred Twenty-five
' Gilders. For the Year 1709, Sixty-nine Thousand
' Five Hundred Seventy-eight Gilders, and Fifteen
' Stivers. For the Year 1710, Sixty-six Thousand
' Eight Hunnred and Ten Gilders, Nineteen Stivers,
' and Eight Penings, also Twenty-one Thousand
' Gilders for the Present Year, in Part of a like
' Sum with those abovementioned, all which Sums
' he gave his G. because the former Contractors
' had given the like Annual Sums.
' He further deposeth, that he allowed yearly
' Twenty-two Waggons *gratis*, to the General Offi-
' cers, Twelve or Fourteen of which were for the
' D. of *M*——'s own Uses, and the former
' Contractors did the same.
' This Deponent further saith, that from the said
' Year 1707 to the Year 1711, both inclusive, he gave
' Yearly, on Sealing the said Contract, a Gratuity of
' Five Hundred Gold Ducats to Mr. *C*——*l*, Secre-
' tary to the D. of *M*——, for his Trouble and
' Pains in transacting the *Dutch* Contracts, and put-
' ting the *English* Contracts into Form: And he
' further saith, that for all the Money he received

in

'in *Holland* from Mr. *Sweet*, Deputy-Paymaster, at
' *Amsterdam*, on Account of the said Contracts, he
' was obliged to pay him One *per Cent.* for Prompt
' Payment, and that the former Contractors did the
' same; but he found him notwithstanding so back-
' ward in his Payments, that he complained to the
' D. of M———, and at the same Time acquainted
' him with the Allowance he made to Mr. *Sweet*
' of One *per Cent* as aforesaid, and that his G———
' reproved him, the said Mr. *Sweet*, for not paying
' this Deponent more punctually.

' And this Deponent further saith, that it appear-
' ed by the Accounts of *Antonio Alvares Machado*,
' who had supplied the Bread, and Bread-Wagons
' for the Forces in the *English* Pay, as aforesaid,
' from the Years 1702, 1703, 1704, 1705, and
' 1706, that he gave as large Yearly Sums to the
' D. of M——— as this Deponent hath done
' since.

Jurat. 6 Decem.
1711.
S. *de Medina.*

The Commissioners Observ'd upon the foregoing Letter and Warrant, after calculating the
Sums mentioned in the Depositions, and making
them to amount to Sixty-three Thousand Three
Hundred Nineteen Pounds, Three Shillings and Nine
Pence, *English* Money, ' That they could not find,
' by the strictest Enquiry they could make, that any
' other General in the *Low Countries* or elsewhere,
' ever claim'd or reserv'd such Perquisites; but if any
' Instance should be produced, they apprehended it
' would be no Justification of it, because the Public
' or the Troops must necessarily suffer in Proportion
' to every such Perquisite, and how agreeable this
' was to that *Oeconomy* and good Husbandry, with
' which the Service in *Flanders* was carried on, re-
' main'd as then to be explain'd; and that by the
' Assurance his Grace was pleas'd to give, that this
Money

'Money was constantly employed for the Service
' of the Publick, it must be either allowed that he
' relinquish'd his Right to that Perquisite, or that
' he had been wanting to himself in concealing so great
' an Instance of his own Generosity to the Publick.

' That the great Caution and Secrecy with which
' this Money was constantly received, gave Reason
' to suspect that it was not thought a Justifiable Per-
' quisite; for Mr. C———l, the Duke's Secretary,
' and Auditor of the Bread Account, declared on
' Oath, that he had never heard of any such Per-
' quisite till the late Rumour of Sir *Solomon de Me-
' dina's* Evidence before the Commissioners. That
' if the General was allowed to take this Money for
' a Perquisite, he might with equal Reason claim a
' Perquisite for every other Contract relating to the
' Army, as for those of the Bread and Bread-Wag-
' gons; which Point his Grace was silent to.

' That as to what his Grace was pleas'd to say,
' concerning the Deduction of Two and a half *per
' Cent.* from the Foreign Troops, in Her Maje-
' sty's Pay, they could only offer such Remarks as
' occurr'd to them upon comparing what was urg'd
' in the Duke's Letter with the Tenour of the War-
' rant, and with the Method of Accounting for other
' Payments to the Army: And that they took leave
' in the first Place to observe that the Warrant had been
' kept Dormant for Nine Years, and the Deduction
' concealed so long from the Knowledge of the Par-
' liament; for which, in their Apprehension his
' Grace has not assign'd Sufficient Reasons.

' That he was pleased to say, that the Two and
' a half *per Cent.* was a *Free Gift* from the Foreign
' Troops, and that it did not belong to the Publick
' Accounts. But the First of those Assertions seem'd
' inconsistent, not only with the Words of the
' Warrant, which supposes and expresses an Agree-
' ment, but with that Part of his Grace's Letter,
' which took Notice, that he being Ambassador and

General

'General, stipulated for this very Purpose by the
'late King's Order, wherefore they were of Opinion,
'that a Deduction so made was Publick Money,
'and ought to be accounted for as other Publick
'Money was

'They likewise observ'd, that the Ten Thousand
'Pounds granted yearly for the Contingencies of
'the Army, was first intended by the Parliament for
'the Service of the Forty Thousand Men without
'Distinction and not for the Use of the *British*
'Forces only, and that they found that Sum so far
'from having been always thought exempt from
'Account, that a Privy-Seal, Dated the 5th of
'*March*, 1706, for passing Mr *Fox's* Accompts had
'a Clause in it to release the D—— of M——,
'his Heirs, Executors, and Administrators from a
'Sum of Seven Thousand Four Hundred Ninety-
'nine Pound, Nineteen Shillings, and Ten Pence,
'Part of that Money, which supposed his Grace
'would have been otherwise Accountable for it

'That the Commissioners submitted it to the
'*House* to consider, whether the Warrant produc'd
'to justifie the Deduction of Two and a half *per
Cent.* was Legal, and duly Countersigned, or whe-
'ther, admitting it to be so, either the Stoppage or
'the Payment of it had been regularly made; be-
'cause the Warrant directed it should be stopt in
'the Hands of the Paymaster, or his Deputy, and
'it did not appear by the Paymasters Account to
'have been at all pursued, so far otherwise, that the
'Payments to the Foreign Troops were always made
'and their Receipts always taken in full, without
'any Notice of this Deduction

'That when any Part of the abovementioned
'Ten Thousand Pounds, Contingent Money, was
'drawn out of the Paymasters Hands for any *Secret
'Service*, the General's Warrant, and the Secretary's
'Receipts are the Paymaster's Vouchers. But
'Mr. *Cardonnel*, as he declared on Oath, never gave
'any

' any Receipt for any Part of the Two and a half
' *per Cent.* nor did Mr. *Bridges*, as he also declared
' on Oath, ever see any Warrant for that Purpose,
' or knew any Thing, *as Paymaster-General*, of this
' Deduction.

' That if Mr. *Sweet* had taken upon himself to
' transact the Disposition of the Two and a half *per*
' *Cent.* with the D. of *M———*, they are of Opini-
' on, that he ought to have transmitted constant
' Accounts of it to Mr. *Bridges*, whose Agent he
' only is, and not to have Negotiated such Large
' Sums of Money in so Clandestine a Manner.

' That by the Warrant this Deduction was reserv'd
' for the defraying Extraordinary Contingent Ex-
' pences of the Troops from whom it was stopp'd:
' And if the Whole has been employed in Secret
' Correspondence and Intelligence, there must have
' been some Neglect of the other Services for which
' it was originally designed; and such Disposition
' being in no sort Authoriz'd by the Warrant was a
' Misapplication of it,

' That besides the Commissioners apprehended,
' that the Article for Secret Service, to which that
' Deduction was pretended to have been applied,
' was always included in the Ten Thousand Pounds
' abovementioned for the Contingencies of the Army
' and if so, the Whole remain'd to be accounted for,
' which on a Computation made on the Whole
' Sum of Eleven Millions Two Hundred Ninety-
' four Thousand Six Hundred and Fifty nine Pound,
' Four Shillings, and a Peny Halfpeny paid *per*
' *Britain* to, and for, all the Forces since the 13th
' of *December*, 1701. (according to the Return of
' th. Auditor and Paymaster) amounted to Two
' Hundred Eighty-two Thousand, Three Hundred
' Sixty six Pounds, Nine Shillings, and Seven
' Pence.

' That in a Computation, made from the Sum of
' Seven Millions One Hundred Seven Thousand Eight
' Hundred

'Hundred Seventy-three Pounds, Eighteen Shillings,
'and Eleven Pence Halfpeny, paid to, and for, the
'Foreign Forces since the Time aforesaid, (exclusive
'of *Italy, Spain,* and *Portugal,*) amounted to One
'Hundred Seventy-seven Thousand Six Hundred
'Ninety-five Pounds, Seventeen Shillings, and Three
'Farthings, &c.

The Result of this Report being not yet known on Account of the *House's* Adjournment from the 22d of *December* to the 14th of *January*, we shall not either enter into the Merits of the Commissioners Representation, or the Duke's Defence, being sensible, that the Latter will have all the Justice done him at the next meeting, that is consistent with their Countries Good, and the Services he has done it: But since the Queen has thought fit to remove him from all his Employments during the Adjournment, and all his further Scenes of Action seem to be determined, in his Dismission from Court, I shall without entring into Her Majesties Reasons for so doing, which none ought to enquire into, exclude the Reader from any other Passages of so Important a Life, since his Disgrace may be naturally said to be his *Political Decease*, and henceforward he is only taken Notice of in a Private Capacity, who has acted with so much Splendor in a Publick.

What remains for me to do is to clear his Memory, that may be otherwise as ill treated by Posterity as his Person is by the Present Age from that Aspersion, which seems to carry most Weight with it, of his unnecessary prolonging the War for his Private Interest: a Calumny which every one that is Impartial will, I dare say, conclude to be very groundless from what I have already said. But because this is the Capital Accusation, and It is Natural for People when they grow weary of a War, to give into any Surmizes of this Kind, be they never so ill grounded, I shall convince those for whose Use this is written, that the most implacable Malice
could

could have invented nothing more stupidly Ridiculous than to accuse him of prolonging the War, who has more Reason than any one to wish a good End to it, and has done more towards than his best Friends could ever hope for.

Now if there were any Truth in this Accusation, and the Duke of *Marlborough* had unnecessarily prolong'd the War, it would appear against him, either in his Negotiations as Plenipotentiary, or his Proceedings as General. If he has transgress'd in the first Capacity, it was in his Consent to admit of the Conferences held between the *French* Ministers, and those Commission'd by the Allies, and insisting upon the 37th Article of the Preliminaries, wherein it was agreed to evacuate *Spain* and the *Indies* in Right of King *Charles*. But the Majority of the House of Lords having absolv'd him as to his Management in this Particular, by their late Vote, mention'd in their above-written Address, so I shall leave it to enquire how he has been Tardy as *General*.

If he has offended in this Quality, he has the Happiness to offend with Good Company, with Prince *Eugene*, and with the Deputies of the States, whose Consent is necessary in all the Operations of the War. If therefore there be any Blame in the Management of that, it must not all lye upon the Duke of *Marlborough*, unless it appears he has hindered the good Measures they would have taken, or forced upon them his own ill ones. But neither of these is so much as pretended, nor, I suppose, will be. I can't hear there have ever been any Differences between the Duke and the Prince, not so much as in their Opinions in any one Enterprize: Nobody has observ'd any Coldness or Reservedness between them, or any other the least Sign of Misunderstanding. But on the contrary, 'tis Notorious to all the World, that they act with the most perfect Harmony, and with the greatest Esteem of each other, without any Marks of Jealousie, without the least Suspicion of Envy,

T t 2

or having any separate Ends or Aims to eclipse the Glory of one another, or advance their own. The Friendship is so great, the Agreement between them is so entire, the Intimacy and Secrecy they concert with is so Wonderful, that the Armies under them enjoy all the Advantages they can have, from the Commands of Two Generals, without any of the Inconveniences that one would think Advantages must unavoidably be attended with. They are to all Purposes (when together, as in several Campaigns before the last) but One Army, and under One General, there is no Sign of more than One, the Unity between the Two is so perfect If therefore there be any Fault in the Conduct of the Duke for the Three Years before this last, and the last will not surely be charg'd with Blunders after what has been before said in Defence of it is attentively read) the Prince must come in for his Share, they must both be absolved or both condemned, or else the Duke's Accusers have some strange Rules of Judgment which I am yet to learn But let us see whether it will mend their Cause to consider the Parts the Deputies of the States have in these Matters. If they agreed with his Grace in the Measures that have been taken, can he be in Fault, and not they? Or have we heard they have ever differ'd from him, in opposing any Thing that would tend to prolong the War? Have they desired the Army might take the Field sooner than he would have them, or continue in it longer? Have they press'd any Brave and Bold Undertaking that he has declined has he been against Fighting when they were for it? If any Thing of this Kind could be made appear that would be a Discovery indeed But we may depend upon it, they have never proposed any one Thing that would push on the War, which he has been against. But on the contrary his Hands have been tyed, as these Memoirs have already told you, when he was impatient to be doing something Brave and Enterprizing. But I had

rather

rather leave his Grace without Defence than pretend to do him Justice, by entring into Things he thinks fit to make a Secret of; the End of the War, which in some Peoples Opinion is near approaching, will be Time enough for that. In the mean while one may be sure, that Deputies are something like *Socrates* his Genius, which never put him in Mind of doing any Thing; its whole Business was to check him, when he seemed to be too forward. If therefore one would do the Duke Justice, the Vigour that has been used in pushing the War should be imputed to him, and that there has not been more done, to the Restraints he has been always under, always but one Campaign, that of *Blenheim*, in which he has shewn what he would do were he left to himself. Had he a Mind to a lingring War, he needed only to have lost that Battle, and the War might have lasted there long enough, which that Day ended at a Blow.

In one Sense indeed his best Freinds are willing to allow he has prolonged the War, that without him must have ended long ago in an ill Peace, Which he hindred our coming so soon to as some seem to wish we had: And this may sometime or other be made his Crime. In Truth his Conduct during the whole War has been one constant Endeavour to hinder its ending ill, so soon as it might, and must have otherwise done. This made him so earnest to Fight the *French*, as we all know he was, the first Campaign, when he thought he had them at a great Advantage. This made him take so much Pains to bring them to an Engagemet the Second Campaign, when he stole a March, and pass'd a River, and got between their Lines: This made him march to *Bavaria* the Third; and to the *Moselle* the Fourth: This made him endeavour to go to *Italy* the Fifth, to prevent the Ruin of the Duke of *Savoy*, and the Loss of all on that Side: This made him the Sixth so importunate with the States, for near Two Months together, to march from

from the Camp at *Meldert*, and after that to try to fall upon the *French* Army at *Seneffe* This made him the Seventh pass the *Scheld*, and Fight the Battle of *Audenard*, without which all *Flanders* must have been lost; and afterwards make the Siege of *Lisle*, which was the most sensible Part *France* could have been wounded in, and begin in *December* the Siege of *Ghent* which, had it been left in *French* Hands, the Allies, instead of doing any Thing themselves next Campaign, must have seen *Lisle* and *Menin* taken from them, without a Possibility of relieving them: This made him the next Year, when he could not Fight the *French*, surprize them with the Siege of *Tournay*, when they expected nothing less, and take so much Care that the rest of the Campaign might not be lost. With this View he endeavoured to surprize St *Gislain*, and that failing, by the Time the Garrison of *Tournay* march'd out, he had passed the Lines of *Mons*. After which he fought the Great Battle of *Tanters*, in which the Enemy were so defeated, that they who had hazarded a Battle to prevent the Siege did not dare to venture any Thing for the Relief of it, towards which they did not make the least Step, tho' the Allies had neither River nor Entrenchment to cover them. 'Twas this made him begin the Campaign in 1710 Six Weeks sooner than the Enemy were able to take the Field, which gave him Possession of their Lines, and soon after of *Douay*; and had that Siege been ended in the Time proposed, *Arras* had met with the same Fate, which however was in great Measure compensated by the Reduction of *Bethune*, St. *Vinant* and *Aire*, the last of which Places, though some may think it a slight Conquest, the *French*, who best knew the Importance of their own Places, thought so great an Enterprize, that they could not believe the Allies would venture on it, and when 'twas taken they own'd it opened to them a Passage to the *Seame*; and without much Skill in Military Affairs, a Man can't look upon a Map and not see that besides the Command of all the *Lys*, which was a vast Advantage for erecting Magazines, and giving the Allies a large

Front

Front against this present Year, wherein his Grace has again by an unparallell'd Stratagem got within the Lines that were thought Impregnable, and by taking *Bouchain* is entred into the very Bowels of *Old France*.

These have been the Endeavours and Steps the Duke of *Marlborough* has made this War, which have all contributed to prolong in it one Sense, as they have kept the Allies in Heart, and set them above the mean Conditions of an Ill Peace, which they must have long since submitted to, had either the Emperor or the Duke of *Savoy* been ruined; or had the Enemy gain'd any considerable Advantage in *Flanders*, or if our Inaction there had left them at Liberty to act offensively in other Parts; all which has been prevented by the Conduct of the Duke of *Marlborough*, as can't but be seen in what I have already said; except that which respects the Duke of *Savoy*; in the saving of whom some People may be apt to think his Grace to have no Part. But not to affirm that he made all the Use he could of the Queen's Interest to support Prince *Eugene* at the Imperial Court, where at that Time he had his Enemies, nor to mention the Supplies he procured him from *England*: If we look back Six or Seven Years we shall find that the Duke made in the Depth of Winter a long Journey to *Berlin*, which obtained from the King of *Prussia* Succours of 8000 Men for *Italy*, which had been often and peremptorily refused to the Imperial Court, and the Applications of the Ministers of *England* and *Holland* had been made to as little Effect. These were the Troops that, as we all know, enabled Prince *Eugene* to make a Stand; and Two Years after, the same Zeal for the Common Cause procured for *Italy* Two more Reinforcements, a lesser of *Palatines*, and another of 10000 *Hessians*, which last is in a particular Manner owing to the Duke, that after they had not only been agreed for, but had actually begun their March, they had been diverted from this Service and employed on the *Rhine*, had not he persisted for their being sent to *Italy*, where some were inclined to think they would not be wanted upon the Turn the Battle of *Ramelies* would probably give to Affairs. But the Event shewed how right the Duke judged. Nothing could have saved *Turin* but a Battle, and without those Troops a Battle had been impossible, which was difficult enough with them. And now, I believe my Reader will allow

Now I have Reason to put the Methods that were taken to prevent the Ruin of the Duke of Savoy; among the Ways the Duke of Marlborough has taken to prevent an ill Peace: To which I ought to add another which was as strange an Action in him as any of the rest; and that was his Journey to Saxony, to persuade the King of Sweden not to disturb the Allies by the Jealousie his Stay in Saxony gave the Emperor. What a very ill Influence his Stay there had on the Common Cause we all know: How far that Journey contributed to remove it I am not enough in the Secret to know; but 'tis certain, that King from that very Time gave no fresh Jealousies by making any New Demands, but on the contrary, receded from several Points, and set himself in earnest, to make the necessary Dispositions for quieting Saxony; which he did at the End of the Summer, as soon as ever the Treaty between him and the Emperor was signed; which put an End to the Fears the Allies had been so long under, and enabled both King Augustus and the Emperor to send Troops to the Support of the Common Cause, instead of drawing any from it; which had the King of Sweden not removed, they must have done. Now what Part the Duke of Marlborough had in this I shall not take upon me to affirm; but I believe I may venture to say, that had some others done what he did, it would have made no Difficulty to give these Men all the Merit, who are so unwilling to allow any Thing to him.

I hold with them that this has been no more than his Duty, and that were he actually at the Gates of Paris, the Rewards he has received from the Queen and Parliament, and the Rich Presents that have been conferr'd on him by Foreign Princes would have made him ample Amends for that Service; but to charge him with Prolonging the War, is what a Mind which has any Sence of Common Gratitude is abhorrent of. For all this he has done, we are sure, and more, besides a great deal of Management and Negotiation which is yet a Secret to us: Tho' thus much is open and aboveboard, and if his Accusers don't mean an *Ill Peace*, and *Prolonging* the War to hinder it, I cann't imagine what they would pretend. I always thought to take all Opportunities of acting offensively in an Offensive War had been the Right Management, and the most Natural Way to put a

good

good End to it, since I never could have suspected, that Great Armies, Long Campaigns, Surprizing Marches, Glorious Battles, and Important Sieges had been the Way to prolong the War, if some late Writers had not told me so.

But 'tis Time to draw towards a Conclusion, I shall therefore only say, that nothing can be more ridiculous and absurd, than to charge with a Design to perpetuate the War, a Man who has in every Respect out-done our Wishes, and has done more towards a *Good Peace*, by his own Address and Ability both in War and Peace, by his Conduct in the Field, by his Interest with the Allies, by his Happy Temper to prevent or make up Differences, by his Dexterity and Wisdom, by his great Humanity and Sweetness of Behaviour which is peculiar to him, by his Zeal for the Honour of the Queen, whom he has served with more Affection than most Men ever did a Mistress, and by his true Concern for the Good of his Country, and the Liberty of *Europe*, in which he has few Equals. By these Admirable Qualities, which so eminently shine in him, he has struck such a Terror into the Enemy, and preserved so perfect a Harmony among our Allies, that nothing, humanly speaking, could have destroyed our Hopes of a *Good Peace*, but the Endeavours that have been used to destroy him: And if Quiet, Unity, Credit, Vigour, Harmony, can be made use of as the Means to perpetuate the War, then he has bid fair by the Practice of those Virtues, towards being a *General for Life*.

FINIS.

Lightning Source UK Ltd.
Milton Keynes UK
UKOW07f1825130415

249572UK00010B/379/P